INSPIRE / PLAN / DISCOVER / EXPERIENCE

MILAN

AND THE LAKES

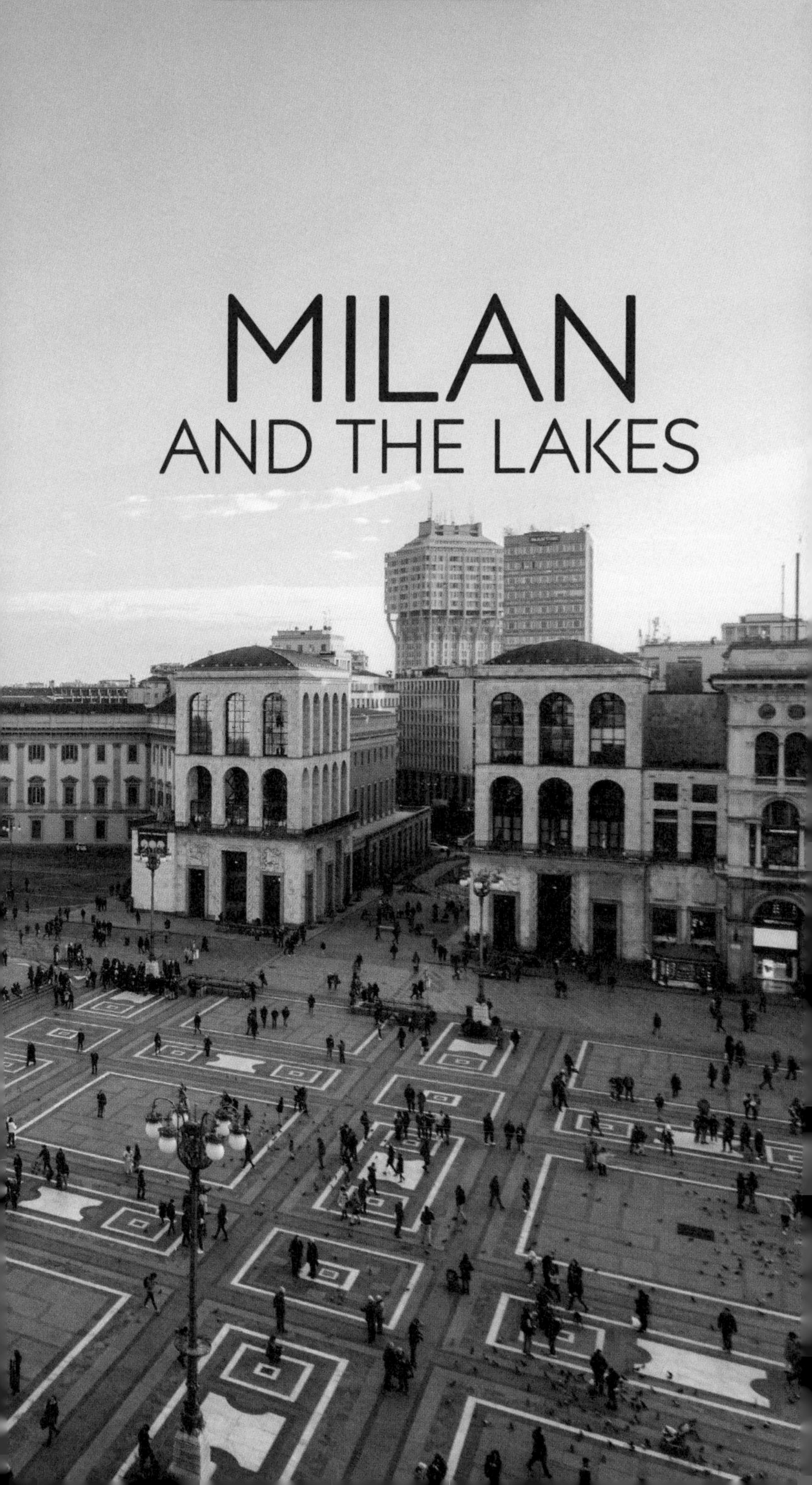

CONTENTS

DISCOVER 6

EXPERIENCE 50

NEED TO KNOW 188

Left: Marble carvings in the Arco della Pace

Previous page: Piazza del Duomo, Milan's main square

Front cover: Careno's bell tower by Lake Como

DISCOVER

The Duomo illuminated at night

WELCOME TO MILAN AND THE LAKES

A city that breathes fashion and art. A region with spectacular lake panoramas. Milan has history behind every corner while the Lakes are an area of endless romance. Whatever your dream trip to Milan and the Lakes includes, this DK Eyewitness travel guide is the perfect companion.

1

2

3

4

1 Shopping in Galleria Vittorio Emanuele II.

2 The blooming gardens of Villa Taranto.

3 A hearty portion of *risotto alla Milanese*.

4 Lake Como's colourful *comune* of Varenna.

Located in the heart of Lombardy, Milan is the country's economic powerhouse and its most cosmopolitan metropolis, with a pulsating, dynamic energy like no other Italian city. Just north of Milan lies glamorous Lake Como, only a few kilometres from the Swiss border. The surrounding area is home to several equally stunning destinations – Orta, Maggiore, Iseo and Garda – where charming lakefront villages are squeezed onto rugged shorelines, and elegant boats glide along cobalt blue waters.

Shopping, fashion and a wealth of museums and art galleries draw the crowds to Milan. This is foodie territory too, where award-winning restaurants serve delicate Italian fare and rustic bars deliver beautifully crafted cocktails, many of which were invented in the city.

Meanwhile, it's natural beauty that mostly attracts visitors to the Lakes. Many flock to marvel at elegant villas flanked by lush, manicured gardens, while others go to enjoy the variety of water sports available or the scenic lake views from trails that snake along the surrounding mountainsides.

With such a wealth of sights and experiences, it can be hard to know where to begin. We've broken the area down into easily navigable chapters, with detailed itineraries, expert local knowledge and comprehensive maps to help plan the perfect trip. Whether you're staying for the weekend or longer, this DK Eyewitness travel guide will ensure that you see the very best of the region. Enjoy the book, and enjoy Milan and the Lakes.

REASONS TO LOVE MILAN AND THE LAKES

Fabulous shopping, delicious food and dramatic lake scenery. There are endless reasons to love Milan and the Lakes. Here are some of our favourites.

1 APERITIVO

Join Milanesi at aperitivo hour for this much-loved ritual featuring beautifully executed drinks and light bites designed to stimulate the appetite before dinner.

BUZZING NIGHTLIFE 2

Milan is home to some of the coolest bars and clubs in the country, with the Navigli district the beating heart of the city's nightlife *(p113)*.

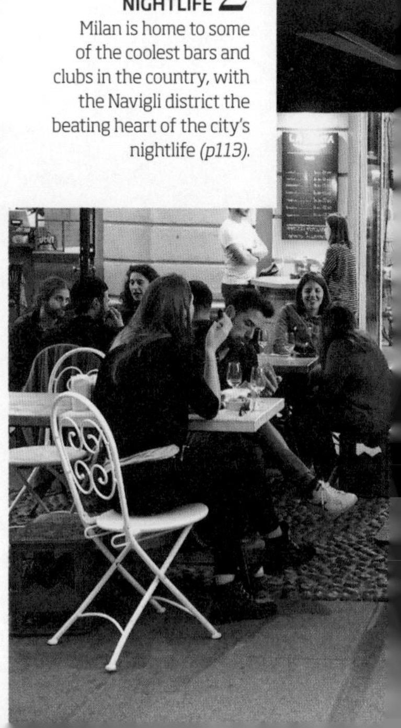

3 LEONARDO'S LAST SUPPER

You can't leave the city without seeing Leonardo da Vinci's most famous mural painting *(p82)*, housed in the Church of Santa Maria delle Grazie, a UNESCO site.

DAZZLING DUOMO 4

Milan's iconic Gothic cathedral *(p56)* took six centuries to complete - head up to its rooftop to walk amid spires and pinnacles as you take in glorious city views.

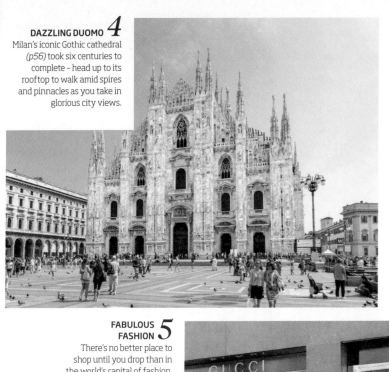

FABULOUS FASHION 5

There's no better place to shop until you drop than in the world's capital of fashion. Don't miss the city's Fashion District *(p154)*, lined with high-end brands and boutiques.

CYCLING AND HIKING 6

Strap on your favourite hiking boots or hop on a trusty mountain bike to explore the Lakes' many scenic trails, taking in stunning panoramas along the way.

MILAN'S MUSEUMS 7

The city has a wealth of museums and galleries. Admire Renaissance art at the Pinacoteca di Brera *(p138)* and contemporary masterpieces at the Museo del Novecento *(p67)*.

A NIGHT AT THE OPERA 8

Watch a breathtaking performance at the world's most famous opera house, La Scala, where composer Giuseppe Verdi premiered his opera *Nabucco (p60)*.

9 LOMBARD CUISINE

Meals are rich and hearty, with saffron-infused *risotto alla Milanese* the city's star dish. Fish takes centre stage by the Lakes with *pesce persico* (perch) and *missoltini* (shad).

10 LAKESIDE TOWNS

The shores of the Italian Lakes are bordered with elegant villas and charming little villages featuring cobbled streets and pastel-hued buildings.

AMAZING ARCHITECTURE *11*

Featuring sustainable designs and green open spaces, plus three stunning skyscrapers, the CityLife neighbourhood is one of Milan's most ambitious urban projects *(p85)*.

ON THE WATER *12*

The northern shore of Lake Garda is an open-air adventure playground – glide across deep, blue waters while trying your hand at windsurfing, sailing, kitesurfing or SUPing.

EXPLORE MILAN AND THE LAKES

This guide divides Milan into five colour-coded sightseeing areas, as shown on the map above. Find out more about each area on the following pages. For the Lakes, see page 158.

CASORETTO
Monument to the Shoah
Stazione Centrale
Bosco Verticale
Pirelli Building
Cascina Pozzobonelli
ISOLA
S. Camillo
CITTÀ STUDI
S. Gregorio
Ospedale Fatebenefratelli
Piscina Cozzi
Palazzo della Permanente
S. Carlo al Lazzaretto
Giardini Pubblici
LOCATOR MAP
SWITZ.
Museo di Storia Naturale
Archi di Porta Nuova
Milan
CROATIA
FRANCE
Palazzo Morando
BOSNIA AND HERZEGOVINA
Palazzo Isimbardi
Basilica di San Babila
ITALY
MONT.
HISTORIC CENTRE
p52
Palazzo Archinto
ALBANIA
Duomo
San Pietro in Gessate
San Gottardo in Corte
Palazzo di Giustizia
Ca' Granda
Rotonda della Besana
SOUTHEAST MILAN
p118
Piscina Caimi
CALVAIRATE
Parco Ravizza
MORIVIONE
Fondazione Prada
0 metres
800
0 yards
800
N

GETTING TO KNOW MILAN AND THE LAKES

Milan, the capital of Lombardy, lies in the middle of the Po river valley and is home to historic canals, state-of-the art museums and impressive architecture. A sprawling city like no other, it's the perfect stop before exploring the pristine Italian Lakes, which are a stone's throw away.

PAGE 52

HISTORIC CENTRE

Home to the city's iconic Duomo, the Historic Centre buzzes with sightseers, Milanese professionals and shoppers hunting for locally designed fashion. It's here that you'll find some of Milan's most famous sights, including the acclaimed Teatro alla Scala opera house and the Pinacoteca Ambrosiana, home to the largest collection of drawings in the world by Leonardo da Vinci. The majestic Vittorio Emanuele II shopping arcade is another highlight, its galleries lined with boutiques and elegant cafés ideal for morning cappuccinos or evening cocktails.

Best for
Shopping, iconic city views

Home to
Duomo, Teatro alla Scala, Pinacoteca Ambrosiana

Experience
A performance at La Scala

PAGE 74

NORTHWEST MILAN

One of Milan's most leafy areas, Northwest Milan is dominated by the Castello Sforzesco and Parco Sempione. The park is a welcome green oasis in the busy city, frequented by a mixture of sightseers, locals going about their daily business and residents walking their four-legged friends or enjoying a morning run. Tourists inevitably gravitate to the Church of Santa Maria delle Grazie, home to Leonardo da Vinci's *Last Supper*; walk further northwest from the church and you'll find a largely residential area, with the avant-garde CityLife district.

Best for
Green spaces, artistic masterpieces

Home to
Castello Sforzesco, the Last Supper

Experience
A stroll through verdant Parco Sempione

PAGE 98

SOUTHWEST MILAN

Southwest Milan is a lively district with scores of great restaurants and a dynamic nightlife scene centred around the historic Navigli canals. This vibrant waterfront neighbourhood is home to independent stores and vintage boutiques tucked away along narrow streets, and antique stalls that line the canal at the weekend. Quieter activities are also catered for here – you'll find two of the city's most delightful churches in Southwest Milan, as well as newly converted exhibition spaces around Via Tortona.

Best for
Nightlife, vintage shopping, historic churches

Home to
San Lorenzo alle Colonne, Sant'Ambrogio

Experience
An aperitivo by the Naviglio Grande

PAGE 134

SOUTHEAST MILAN

The area to the southeast of the centre remains largely off the tourist trail. It's mostly a residential and business area, with the streets around the old city hospital Ca' Granda (now the university) buzzing with students. Head here for a feel of local life or make your way further out of town to visit San Bernardino alle Ossa, one of Milan's most unusual churches complete with a spooky chapel. This is also where you'll find one of the city's most genteel green spaces, the Giardini della Guastalla, home to a delightful Baroque fish pond.

Best for
A feel for local life, escaping the crowds

Home to
Abbazia di Chiaravalle

Experience
A picnic in the Giardino della Guastalla, Milan's oldest garden

PAGE 118

NORTHEAST MILAN

Northeast Milan is home to several districts, each with its own character. Brera is arguably one of the city's most charming neighbourhoods, its cobbled streets studded with artisans' workshops, lively cafés and independent boutiques. The elegant Fashion District, lined with high-end fashion boutiques, is also well worth a visit, even if only for a little window-shopping. The area around Porta Garibaldi, meanwhile, is Milan's financial hub, with professionals making their way to and from Piazza Gae Aulenti. Locals head here too, to take advantage of the area's many bars and restaurants.

Best for
Shopping in Milan's elegant Fashion District

Home to
Pinacoteca di Brera

Experience
A stroll through Brera's characteristic winding streets

PAGE 158

THE LAKES

Como, Garda, Maggiore: the names of Italy's lakes are world-famous, and for good reason. Here, the picture-postcard images are true. Quaint fishing villages cling to shorelines, boats glide across azure waters and hiking trails trace mountains. Lake Como is often considered the most glamorous, while Lake Garda, the largest lake in Italy, is a magnet for water sports, and Lake Maggiore is home to glorious gardens. The smaller lakes, including Orta and Iseo, are less travelled by tourists and the perfect escape for foodies.

Best for
Strolling lakefront gardens and admiring historic villas

Home to
Lake Como, Lake Garda, Lake Maggiore

Experience
A boat trip on Lake Como, taking in the sights from the water

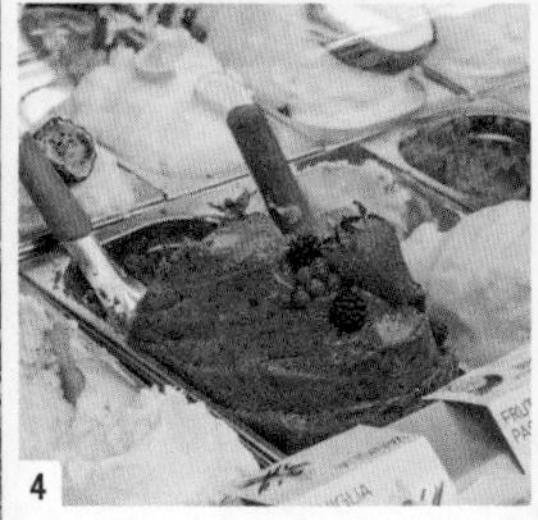

1 The Sforzesco Castle.

2 Majestic Galleria Vittorio Emanuele II.

3 A restaurant in the artistic Brera district.

4 Deep trays filled with Italian gelato.

A glorious blend of historic city and rural escape, Milan and the Lakes brim with travel possibilities. Wherever you choose to go, our handpicked itineraries will help you plan the perfect trip.

24 HOURS

in Milan

Morning

Start the morning with a flaky pastry and a cappuccino at the historic Pasticceria Marchesi *(pasticceriamarchesi.com)* before heading to your first stop, the Castello Sforzesco *(p78)*. Milan's imposing red-brick castle, which has served as a fortress, ducal residence and later military barracks, was originally constructed under the Visconti, a noble Milanese family. It was subsequently rebuilt several times including by the Sforza, a ruling family of Renaissance Italy based in Milan. Today, the castle houses several state museums but the grounds, which are free to access, are just as stunning. From the castle, make your way to the nearby Chiesa di Santa Maria delle Grazie to admire Leonardo da Vinci's most famous mural, the *Last Supper (p82)*, which adorns the refectory walls. This masterpiece dates back to the 15th century.

Afternoon

Have a panini lunch on the top floor of the Rinascente shopping centre *(rinascente.it)*. It's more exciting than it sounds: from here you can enjoy panoramic views of historic Milan and its most iconic landmark, the Duomo. After you've finished admiring from afar, enter the Duomo itself and ascend to the cathedral roof to enjoy glorious views of the skyline.

Once you're back on terra firma, savour an Italian gelato as you continue to steal glances at the spectacular Duomo. Then, continue on to the 19th-century Galleria Vittorio Emanuele II *(p64)*, a shopping mall like you've never imagined, lined with luxury boutiques and elegant cafés. Don't miss the floor mosaic near the central dome – visitors spin their heels three times on the bull's testicles, a tradition believed to bring good luck.

Evening

In the late afternoon, make for Brera *(p156)*, Milan's artistic quarter with charming cobbled streets dotted with artisans' workshops, independent boutiques and lively cafés. As the working day comes to a close, you'll spot Milanesi flocking to the area's bars to unwind with friends over an aperitivo. Join them at La Tartina *(Via San Carpoforo 4)* and sip Campari Spritz accompanied by a selection of tartines topped with delicious meats and cheeses. Then, enjoy dinner at one of the restaurants in the area, such as the historic La Libera *(lalibera.it)*, which has been going strong since the 1900s. Try the traditional *cotoletta alla Milanese* (breaded veal cutlet), washed down with a glass of local wine, and finish with generous helpings of the *gelato al forno* (baked ice cream).

→

1 The Duomo at dusk.

2 Basilica di Sant'Ambrogio.

3 The Fashion District.

4 Artwork by Padovanino in the Pinacoteca di Brera.

3 DAYS

in Milan

Day 1

Morning Start your day with a visit to the Duomo *(p56)*, the city's striking Gothic cathedral with stunning stained-glass windows and memorable sculptures – look out for the statue of flayed Saint Bartholomew. You could spend the whole day here but the Museo del Novecento *(p67)* is well worth a visit. A stone's throw away from the Piazza Duomo, the museum displays 20th-century art with masterpieces by Modigliani and Boccioni.

Afternoon After a busy morning, grab lunch at Luini *(luini.it)*, which has been serving *panzerotti* (deep-fried savoury turnovers) for over 150 years. Belly full, head to the Pinacoteca Ambrosiana *(p62)*, which houses the *Codex Atlanticus*, the largest collection of drawings and writings by Leonardo da Vinci in the world.

Evening End the day with a delicious aperitivo at Camparino *(www.camparino.com)*, an iconic bar based in the 19th-century Galleria Vittorio Emanuele II. Sip on a negroni as the sun sets.

Day 2

Morning Start the day at Teatro alla Scala *(p60)* visiting the on-site museum that houses the colourful costumes and props. If no performances are taking place, enjoy a guided tour of the magnificent auditorium. Make sure to look up – the dazzling crystal chandelier holds 383 bulbs.

Afternoon It's a short walk north to Giardino Indro Montanelli, the ideal spot for people-watching and a picnic lunch. Afterwards, head west and enjoy a leisurely stroll around Milan's famous Fashion District *(p154)*, a cluster of charming streets lined with designer brands. Continue west to the Pinacoteca di Brera *(p138)*, one of Italy's best art galleries, with masterpieces by Titian and Caravaggio.

Evening Come evening, hop on the metro to bustling Porta Genova for dinner at Langosteria *(Via Savona 10; langosteria.com)*, one of the city's best fish restaurants. Afterwards, amble over to the Navigli district *(p113)* for post-dinner cocktails overlooking the canals.

Day 3

Morning Begin your final day at San Lorenzo alle Colonne *(p102)* in southwest Milan. This 4th-century church is home to Cappella di Sant'Aquilino, a chapel with beautiful mosaics, and is fronted by 16 Roman columns. It's not far from here to the Basilica di Sant'Ambrogio *(p104)*, dedicated to the patron saint of the city, Ambrose, who remains buried in the crypt today.

Afternoon Enjoy a relaxed lunch at La Brisa *(ristorantelabrisa.it)*, then meander over to Santa Maria delle Grazie *(p84)*, which houses Leonardo da Vinci's *Last Supper*. Spend the rest of the afternoon strolling around the Castello Sforzesco *(p78)* grounds – the adjacent Parco Sempione *(p86)* is perfect for a stroll too.

Evening Tuck in to a traditional Milanese dinner of *ossobuco* (veal shanks) at the rustic Al Matarel restaurant *(almatarel.it)* and raise a large glass of chilled local wine to a successful city break.

1

2

7 DAYS
at the Lakes

3

Day 1

Begin your week in beautiful Stresa *(p165)* on Lake Maggiore. Beat the crowds by taking the first boat out to the Borromean Islands (check seasonal timetables, *p194*). Isola Bella *(p166)* should be your first stop, its extravagant villa, terraced gardens and six mosiaced grottoes a sight to behold. Next, it's time for a relaxing terrace lunch at Il Fornello *(338 794 5408)* before heading over to Isola Madre, home to explore the gorgeous gardens. As evening descends, return to Stresa and enjoy a light Mediterranean meal at Lo Stornello *(ristorantelostornello-stresa.it).*

Day 2

Ease yourself into the day with a boat ride from Stresa to Pallanza *(p167)*, a peaceful town offering wonderful lake views. Come lunchtime, dine at La Casera *(formaggidieros.it)*, a cosy deli serving charcuterie boards laden with cold meats and alpine cheeses. Spend the afternoon exploring the nearby gardens of Villa Taranto *(p167)*, with its stunning water features and parterres. At dusk, make for Il Portale in Pallanza *(ristoranteilportale.it)* to try the vibrant *risotto alla Milanese* before returning to Stresa.

Day 3

After a restful sleep, drive to Lake Orta *(p186)* and wander around the medieval streets of Orta San Giulio. Then, take a short boat ride over to Isola San Giulio and stroll the island's one and only little street. Return to Orta San Giulio to eat fresh fish from the lake at La Motta *(lamottarestaurant.it)*, before walking up to Sacro Monte, a UNESCO site with 21 frescoed chapels. For dinner, enjoy a Michelin-starred meal at Villa Crespi *(villacrespi.it)* and return to Stresa.

Day 4

Spend the morning on the northwestern shore of Lake Maggiore, stopping off at Cannobio *(p167)* to try some water sports. Towel off and take a short detour inland for a slow lunch at Grotto Sant'Anna *(032 370 682)* – saving room for a scoop of the mojito sorbet. Next, return to Stresa and

1 Palazzo Borromeo on Isola Bella. ↑
2 Water features at Villa Carlotta.
3 Relaxing by Lake Orta.
4 Swimming in Lake Maggiore.
5 Golden hour in Varenna.

catch a boat to Santa Caterina del Sasso *(p168)*. Visible only from the water, this striking rock-hewn hermitage is well worth exploring. End the day in Stresa by dining at La Rampolina *(larampolina.com)*, with a glass of crisp Piedmont wine.

Day 5

Grab some pastries from Café Savoy *(Corso Italia 8)* and drive 88 km (56 miles) east to Como *(p172)*. Catch the 19th-century funicular up to Brunate, taking in the incredible views of the city and lake. For lunch, enjoy a light bite at Visini *(visini.it)*, a popular deli, and then hop back in the car to visit Villa del Balbianello in Lenno *(p174)*. Spend the afternoon exploring the villa and its spectacular gardens before checking into your hotel. Finish the day with a plate of roast rabbit at La Fagurida *(lafagurida.it)*, a 10-minute drive away.

Day 6

Spend the morning at Villa Carlotta in Tremezzo *(p175)*, a 19th-century villa flanked by some of the most beautiful gardens on Lake Como. After, head to nearby La Darsena *(ladarsena.it)* for deliciously fresh pasta, then take the ferry from Caddenabia to Bellagio *(p177)*, dubbed "the pearl of the lake". After checking in to your hotel, order a gelato to go and walk south to reach the lakefront gardens of Villa Melzi. Bellagio has no shortage of restaurants – try Dispensa 63 *(dispensa63bellagio.com)* for a plate of hearty steak and polenta.

Day 7

Begin with a short boat journey to romantic Varenna *(p177)*. Explore the centre before making for Villa Cipressi and its botanical gardens. Stock up on picnic goods at Macelleria Salumeria Lillia *(Via 4 Novembre)* before walking 30 minutes uphill from opposite Villa Monastero to the Castello di Vezio. Tuck into lunch at the top while taking in the fabulous vistas, and explore the castle ruins before descending. Back in Varenna, enjoy a gourmet meal at Albergo Milano *(albergomilanovarenna.com)* – the perfect spot for your last evening at the Lakes.

Contemporary Art

Milan's art scene caters for all tastes and age groups. The city's most prominent venue, Padiglione d'Arte Contemporanea (PAC; *p153*), displays contemporary art sculptures, photography and multimedia installations, while the Fondazione Prada *(p131)* showcases modern exhibits in buildings designed by Rem Koolhaas.

The bright exterior of the Fondazione Prada Museum

MILAN AND THE LAKES FOR ART LOVERS

Milan has a thriving art scene with exhibitions and installations hosted in all corners of the city. The Lakes, meanwhile, offer a spectacular backdrop for artistic expression, with creativity flourishing here since Roman times.

HIDDEN GEM

Follow the Trail

The Lake Como Poetry Way is a pleasant 16-km (10-mile) walk from Cernobbio to hilltop Brunate. Browse the small community libraries and read the plaques inscribed with poetry en route.

Inspirational Lakes

The breathtaking panoramas of the Lakes have long inspired writers, artists and musicians. German poet Goethe (1749–1832) was struck by the flora around Lake Garda; Ernest Hemingway (1899–1961) stayed by Lake Maggiore; and Verdi (1813–1901) composed *La Traviata* while on Lake Como. Feeling creative? The Lakes could be the perfect spot to soothe a stubborn writer's block or give rise to a new masterpiece.

↑ Lake Como and its evocative panoramic views

↑ Admiring 18th century art at the Pinacoteca di Brera

Museums and Galleries

Milan has no shortage of museums and art galleries showcasing a diverse range of works, from classical paintings to contemporary design pieces. The city is home to one of Italy's premier art galleries, the Pinacoteca di Brera *(p138)*, whose highlights include Andrea Mantegna's *The Dead Christ*. For design enthusiasts, the Triennale Design Museum *(p88)* is a must, with regular exhibitions and a collection ranging from industrial design to fashion.

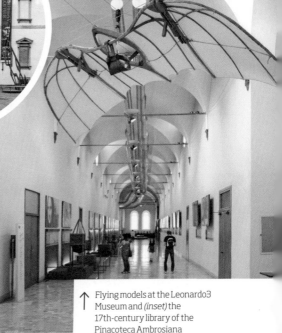

Did You Know?

When Leonardo da Vinci was working on the *Last Supper*, the Duke of Milan gifted him a vineyard.

Leonardo da Vinci

Leonardo (1452–1519) spent over 20 years in Milan, and it was here that he worked on one of his greatest paintings. The *Last Supper* adorns the refectory walls of the church of Santa Maria delle Grazie, while his largest collection of drawings – *Codex Atlanticus* – is on display at the Biblioteca Pinacoteca Ambrosiana *(p62)*. Head to the Leonardo3 Museum *(p64)* to view 3D reconstructions of his works and to uncover more about this Renaissance polymath.

↑ Flying models at the Leonardo3 Museum and *(inset)* the 17th-century library of the Pinacoteca Ambrosiana

Lake Splendour

The architecture in the Italian Lakes is often grand and elaborate in style, from the Baroque palazzi and intricate Italian-style gardens of Lake Maggiore to the grand Neo-Classical villas and Liberty-style mansions of Lake Como. This design shifted during the mid-1920s to align with Italian rationalism, most notably in Como. Visit the city's Casa del Fascio (also known as Palazzo Terragni) - it's a masterpiece of Italian rationalism, characterized by clean, linear shapes.

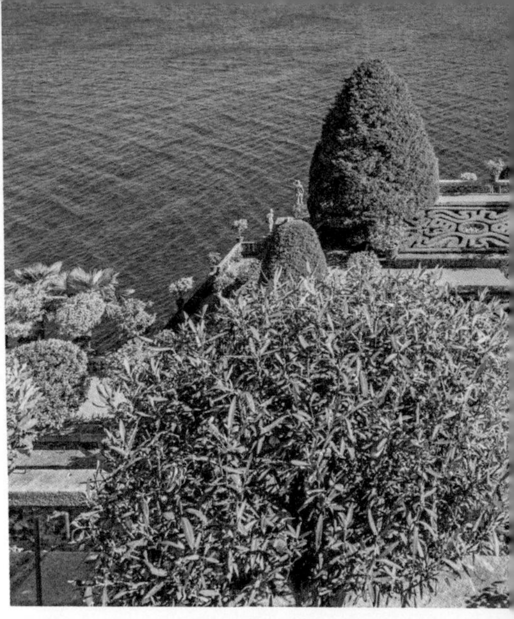

→ Manicured gardens of Isola Bella overlooking Lake Maggiore

MILAN AND THE LAKES FOR ARCHITECTURE

Milan and the Lakes serve an enticing hotchpotch of architectural styles to explore. Roman ruins and striking skyscrapers pepper the city, while historic villas and manicured gardens reveal the Lakes' beautiful designs.

Colourful 15th-century frescoes adorning the Cappella Portinari ↑

Renaissance Architecture

Milan was an important hub of artistic development during the 1400 and 1500s, and the Basilica Santa Maria delle Grazie *(p84)* is a telling example, its dome supported by a Renaissance cube. The Basilica di Sant'Eustorgio's Cappella Portinari *(p114)* is another lovely chapel with 15th-century frescoes.

Did You Know?

Heavy Allied bombing in August 1943 caused significant damage to the refectory of Santa Maria delle Grazie.

LAKESIDE VILLAS

Villa del Balbianello, Lake Como
This villa featured in *Casino Royale* and *Star Wars Episode II - Attack of the Clones (p174)*.

Villa Taranto, Lake Maggiore
A 19th-century, Taranto villa *(p167)* has fine botanical gardens.

Borromeo (Isola Bella), Lake Maggiore
A grand Baroque villa with shell-encrusted grottoes *(p166)*.

Baroque Influence

Milan's architecture displays Baroque influences, with the early 18th-century Palazzo Cusani *(p143)* on Via Brera one of the most beautiful examples. Another impressive example is the Rotonda della Besana *(p128)*, which has a church at its centre. Once the site of a cemetery, this unusual construction in the late Baroque style is lined with porticoes. Today, it houses a vibrant café and children's museum.

←

Relaxing on the grass outside the Rotonda della Besana

Modern Masterpieces

In recent years, Milan's skyline has greatly transformed, with the opening of new commercial and business districts. Lying northwest of the historical centre is CityLife *(p85)*, characterized by its Tre Torri (Three Towers) designed by Arata Isozaki, Zaha Hadid and Daniel Libeskind. In the bustling Porta Nuova district you'll find the famous Bosco Verticale *(p147)*, two residential skyscrapers carpeted in over 17,000 plants enhancing the city's urban biodiversity.

→

Green foliage growing on the Bosco Verticale residential buildings

Magnificent Malls

It's easy to do a spot of retail therapy in Milan, and the city's glorious malls are the place to do so, especially on a rainy day. The Galleria Vittorio Emanuele II *(p64)* is an iconic landmark, its elegant, light-filled arcades lined with luxury boutiques and historic cafés. On nearby Piazza del Duomo is the Rinascente department store, offering a vast array of goods from cosmetics to homeware, while the CityLife mall *(p85)* houses mainstream brands and food halls where you can refuel after hours of shopping.

→ The stunning interior of Galleria Vittorio Emanuele II

MILAN AND THE LAKES FOR SHOPPERS

Whether you're looking for a high-end brand in the world's foremost fashion capitals, or simply scouting for handmade local crafts and antiques in the local market, Milan and the Lakes has something to suit all budgets and needs. They don't call it a shopper's paradise for nothing.

Lakeside Shopping

The Lakes area provides a leisurely shopping experience, allowing you to sample regional specialities and browse locally crafted products, from wooden crafts to textiles. Boutiques selling Italian fashion and artisanal jewellery dot the cobbled streets of lakefront towns such as Como *(p172)*, Bellagio *(p177)* and Stresa *(p165)*, while farmers' markets offer an array of regional culinary specialities, including olive oil, cheeses and wines.

Shopping along colourful Salita Serbelloni in Bellagio ↓

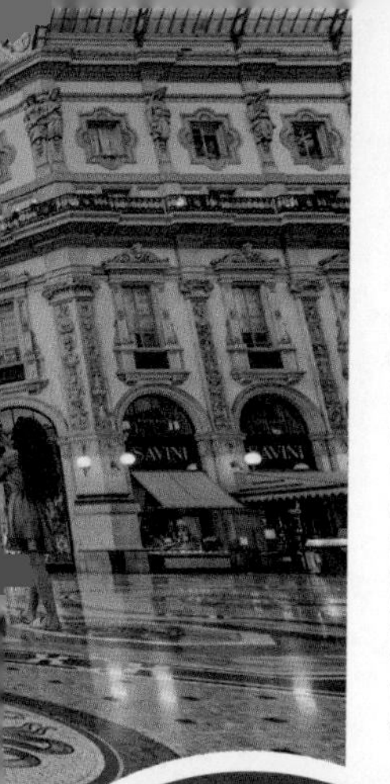

Designer Labels

No visit to Milan would be complete without a wander in the city's famous Quadrilatero della Moda, or Fashion District. This sophisticated little cluster of cobbled streets is lined with high-end fashion houses and luxury boutiques by top-tier designers offering everything and anything from stylish footwear and clothing to bespoke hats and intricate jewellery. For a slightly more affordable shopping experience that won't break the bank, make for Brera *(p156)*, the city's artistic quarter, home to independent boutiques, concept stores and artists' workshops.

← Designer outfits on display at the Gucci store

MILAN IN FASHION

Milan is at the forefront of the luxury fashion industry, giving life to some of the world's most famous brands and designers. Its bi-annual Milan Fashion Week is a hotly anticipated event attracting fashion aficionados and designers from across the globe and setting the trends for the seasons ahead. Milan's close connection with fashion is exemplified in the 2021 film *House of Gucci*. Partly filmed in Milan, it explores the rise and fall of the Gucci empire while providing a glimpse into the world of high fashion.

INSIDER TIP
Fashion Week Streaming

Getting hold of tickets for Fashion Week is a privilege reserved for a lucky few – fortunately for everyone else, the runway shows are screened live on a big screen in Piazza Duomo. It's free, too.

Meander the Markets

Milan offers an endless selection of markets, ensuring there's something for everyone, whether you're an antique collector or a casual shopper looking for a souvenir. The antiques market on the Naviglio Grande *(p113)*, held on the last Sunday of the month, features furniture, collectibles and art, while the Fiera di Sinigaglia, held every Saturday, displays a mix of vintage clothing, crafts and second-hand items. Foodies won't want to miss the Mercato Centrale for its artisanal produce and fresh ingredients, or December's Fiera Oh Bej! Oh Bej!, ideal for festive edible gifts.

↑ Antiques on sale at the Naviglio Grande market

Fantastic Festivals

Milan hosts festivals of all musical flavours, from JazzMi *(jazzmi.it)*, to Piano City *(pianocitymilano.it)*. In autumn, the city comes alive with concerts, workshops and DJ sets for Milano Music Week and the Festival Internazionale della Musica. The Lakes also has an exceptional array of live music on offer, with classical music festival LacMus by Lake Como, or the lively Stresa Festival by Lake Maggiore *(stresafestival.eu)*.

→ Crowds listening to a performance at Piano City festival

MILAN AND THE LAKES FOR ENTERTAINMENT

Milan has a calendar packed full of events year-round, from magnificent opera and ballet performances to lively sporting events. Beyond the city, in the Italian Lakes, the bulk of events unfold in the summer months, with energetic regattas and lakeside music festivals attracting quite a crowd.

Costumed actors lining up for curtain call at Teatro alla Scala ↑

Night of Culture

The world-famous La Scala *(p60)* is Milan's premier opera venue and the ultimate spot to immerse yourself in the grandeur of Italian opera. Performances occasionally take place at the Teatro degli Arcimboldi, which also hosts ballet productions, while the internationally acclaimed Balletto di Milano presents shows at various locations throughout the city.

INSIDER TIP

Behind the Scenes

Take a tour of La Scala's Ansaldo Workshops in Porta Genova to see the costumes and props worn on stage *(teatroallascala.org)*.

Classical Music

Milan is home to several classical music venues, most notably the Conservatorio Giuseppe Verdi di Milano *(p129)*, one of the country's most prestigious music institutions. Named after renowned Italian composer Verdi, the theatre showcases the talents of aspiring musicians as well as established performers. The Società del Quartetto di Milano, Le Serate Musicali, the Auditorium di Milano Fondazione Cariplo and the Orchestra Sinfonica di Milano all have close ties to the Conservatorio, with regular performances throughout the year. The orchestra I Pomeriggi Musicali, meanwhile, holds concerts at the Teatro Dal Verme, while the Associazione Culturale La Cappella Musicale conducts organ recitals in the Renaissance-style Basilica di Santa Maria della Passione *(p130)*.

← I Pomeriggi Musicali Orchestra performing at Teatro Dal Verme

↑ AC Milan (in black) in action against Spezia Calcio at San Siro stadium

pectacular Sport

oth Milan and the wider Lakes area have busy sporting calendars with live fixtures n throughout the year. Milan is home to one of the largest football stadiums in Italy, leazza (San Siro; *p89*), the home of AC Milan and Inter Milan. Cycling, meanwhile, is ugely popular in the Italian Lakes – the Giro d'Italia often passes through the area, with ros greeted by enthusiastic crowds lining the streets. Sailing regattas take place on both ake Garda and Lake Como, while Arco, on Lake Garda's northern basin, is a magnet for imbers, with international competitions held here annually.

LGBTQ+-Friendly

Milan is Italy's most LGBTQ+ friendly city, with a host of venues welcoming the community. The bulk of the LGBTQ+ nightlife centres around Porta Venezia, with popular venues including MonoBar, Red Cafè and Leccomilano. Further north, Loreto is a growing LGBTQ+ hub - head to the retro NoLoSo at aperitivo hour.

Dancing in the park near Porta Venezia during Pride Week

MILAN AND THE LAKES AFTER DARK

From evenings spent sipping Campari-based cocktails to all-nighters dancing in industrial chic warehouses, Milan showcases some of Italy's best nightlife. Meanwhile, the Italian Lakes are ideal for a sophisticated evening of relaxed wine tasting.

TOP 3 DRINKS INVENTED IN MILAN

Milano Torino (Mi-To)
This drink is named after the origins of its ingredients: Campari (Milan) and sweet vermouth (Turin).

Negroni Sbagliato
A "mistaken" negroni made with Campari, vermouth and prosecco.

Americano
Invented in the 1860s, this drink comprises equal parts Campari and sweet vermouth, topped with soda.

Cocktails by the Canal

Milan's canals, or Navigli *(p113)*, are the beating heart of the city's nightlife, lined with bustling bars that attract custom until the early hours. Come evening, Milanesi flock here at aperitivo hour to loosen their ties and catch up with friends over a drink and some light bites at one of the tables that spill out onto the canal-side promenade. Mag Cafè *(farmilygroup.com)* is something of an institution these days, as is Rita & Cocktails *(ritacocktails.com)*, which serves top-notch drinks.

→
Enjoying aperitivo hour in Milan's Navigli district

Feel the Beat

From sleek fashion-related dancing dens to mega clubs attracting nocturnal revellers in the thousands, Milan has it all. Among the city's top venues are Alcatraz *(alcatrazmilano.it)*, which hosts DJ sets including reggaeton and house, and Amnesia *(amnesiamilano.com)*, sister-venue to Ibiza's famous nightclub, set in an industrial chic warehouse to the east of the city centre. Old Fashion *(oldfashion.it)*, meanwhile, is the city's most historic venue - it's been going strong since 1933, attracting celebrities such as Jimi Hendrix and Madonna.

↑ Lively musicians performing at Alcatraz

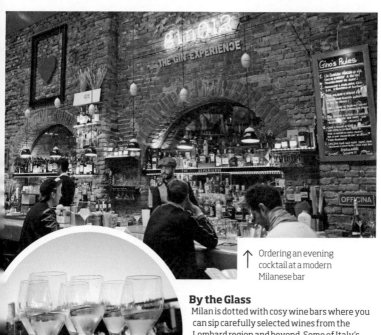

↑ Ordering an evening cocktail at a modern Milanese bar

By the Glass

Milan is dotted with cosy wine bars where you can sip carefully selected wines from the Lombard region and beyond. Some of Italy's best sparkling wine is produced in nearby Franciacorta, south of Lake Iseo - you'll be able to sample a glass at Bicerìn *(bicerinmilano.com)*, a delightful wine bar in the Porta Venezia area. This being Milan, there's no shortage of fashion-related bars, such as the glitzy DG Martini *(world.dolcegabbana.com/martini)*, and modish cocktail bars, many of which can be found in branded designer hotels.

MILAN AND THE LAKES FOR FOODIES

While classic cocktails and local wine tend to steal the limelight, the dynamic dining scene in Milan and the Lakes is more than worthy of a mention. Tuck into gourmet cuisine at Michelin-starred restaurants or enjoy locally sourced ingredients at laidback trattorias.

Sweet Treats

Milan's most famous dessert is the Christmas favourite panettone, a fluffy cake made with vanilla, citrus and candied fruit. Other Lombard hits include *torta paesana*, prepared with stale bread, milk and cocoa, and *pan de mej*, a corn-based speciality traditionally prepared for St George's Day in April. Lombardy is also the birthplace of amaretti, bitter-sweet macarons that hail from Saronno, northwest of Milan.

→ A generous serving of panettone, dusted with icing sugar

Evening Traditions

Come evening, Milan's bars become a hive of activity, with locals unwinding after a hard day's work. Aperitivo hour comes in many forms, with some venues serving a few nibbles to enjoy with your drink, others offering a veritable buffet of delights to indulge in. The latter, better known as an *apericena*, is coined from a combination of "aperitivo" and "cena" (dinner). From cold cuts and cheeses to *pizzette* (miniature pizzas) and focaccia, these buffet spreads feature a wide range of culinary treats.

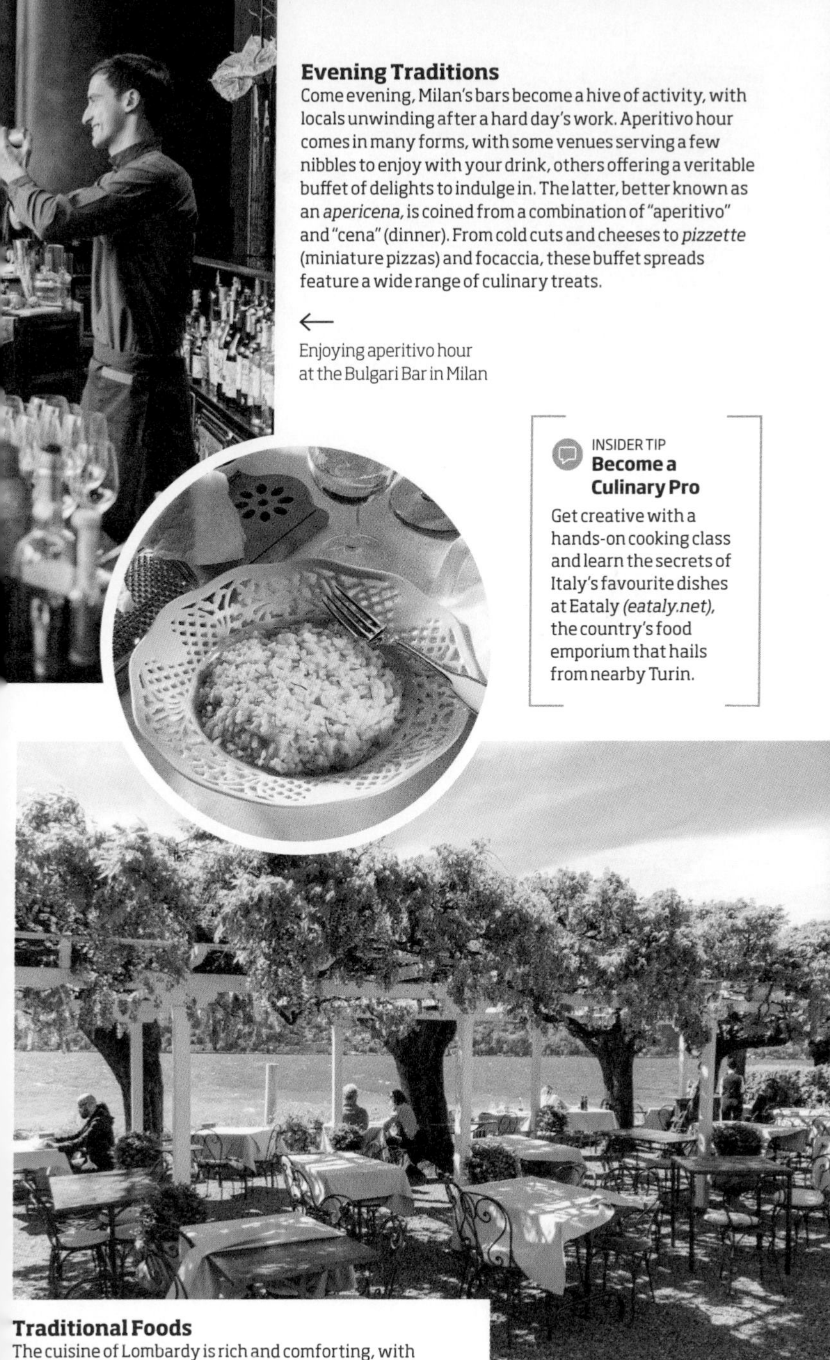

← Enjoying aperitivo hour at the Bulgari Bar in Milan

INSIDER TIP
Become a Culinary Pro

Get creative with a hands-on cooking class and learn the secrets of Italy's favourite dishes at Eataly *(eataly.net)*, the country's food emporium that hails from nearby Turin.

Traditional Foods

The cuisine of Lombardy is rich and comforting, with *risotto alla milanese* Milan's star dish, prepared with rice from the Po Valley and a pinch of saffron that gives it a vibrant yellow hue. By the Lakes, you'll find seasonal dishes prepared with ingredients sourced from both the lakes and the pre-alpine foothills, such as risotto with pan-fried perch, and *missoltini* (preserved shad) served with creamy polenta.

↑ Dining under the wisteria in Bellagio; *(inset)* a serving of *risotto alla milanese*

↑ Ordering a quick bite from a street vendor

Dine for Less

For coffee, head to a bar and join the locals at the counter – you'll be charged more if you take a seat at one of the tables. At lunchtime, satisfy your hunger with a picnic in Parco Sempione or buy tasty street food to go. In the evening, make the most of Milan's aperitivo tradition, with its generous portions of finger food, or opt for an informal trattoria for heartier portions of homemade fare. Local wine is often priced lower, too.

MILAN AND THE LAKES ON A SHOESTRING

Milan may be one of Italy's more expensive cities but you can easily spend a few days here without breaking the bank. Eating out – whether in the city or around the Lakes – doesn't have to be costly, and there are plenty of delightful parks and promenades to enjoy during your stay.

TOP 5 IDEAS FOR FREE WALKS

Cimitero Monumentale
A stroll through Milan's impressive cemetery.

Sentiero del Ponale
A scenic hiking and cycling route along Lake Garda's sheer cliffs.

Isola di San Giulio
The cobbled path of Lake Orta's delightful little lake island.

Strada Valeriana
This ancient trading route traces Lake Iseo's eastern shore.

Lungolago di Como
This scenic lakeside promenade is dotted with historic villas to snap along the way.

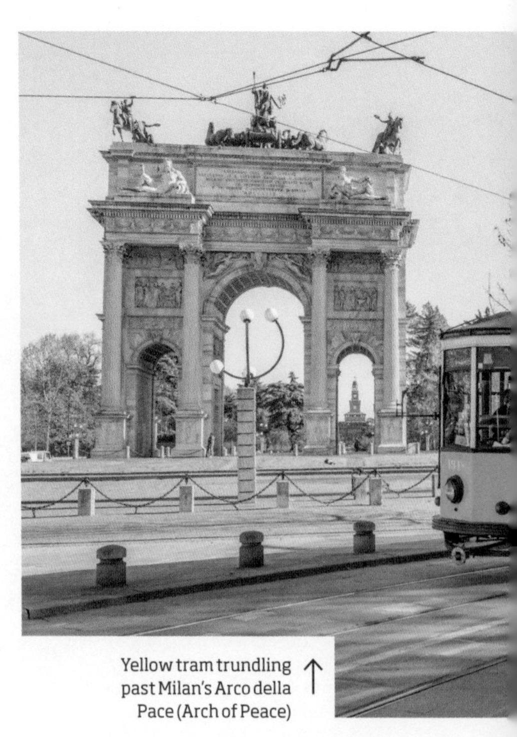

Yellow tram trundling past Milan's Arco della Pace (Arch of Peace) ↑

Churches and Museums

With the exception of the Duomo, entry to Milan's churches is free, including the delightful Sant'Ambrogio *(p104)*, with its interiors decorated with frescoes by Bernardino Luini. There's free entry to all state museums on the first Sunday of the month, too, and several museums offer complimentary entry year-round, including MUDEC *(mudec.it)*, Pirelli Hangar Bicocca *(p147)* and Lake Garda's Museo dell'Olio *(museum.it)*.

→

Frescos in Sant'Ambrogio and *(inset)* MUDEC

THE MILAN PASS

If you're staying in Milan for a long weekend, you may want to consider purchasing a Milan Pass *(themilanpass.com)*. It offers free or discounted entry to selected attractions, and vouchers for city tours, shops and restaurants. The pass also includes rides on the double-decker sightseeing bus, while the Milan Pass Full Edition covers the use of public transport.

All Aboard

A great way to see Milan is aboard a historic yellow tram. Part of the city's public transport system, trams cost the same as local buses, at just over €2 per passenger. Hop on tram #14, which travels through Chinatown *(p89)*, Brera *(p156)*, the historical centre and the Navigli district, with stations near major sights including the Duomo *(p56)*. Alternatively, take tram #1. This route weaves through the Montenapoleone district, passing the Teatro alla Scala *(p60)* and the iconic Arco della Pace, a triumphal arch dating back to the 1800s.

TOP 4 ECO-FRIENDLY TRAVEL TIPS

Keep to the path
Stay on designated hiking trails to protect delicate ecological environments.

Protect local species
Refrain from picking flowers or taking rocks and sand home.

Leave no trace
Deposit your rubbish properly and safely.

Respect the wildlife
Observe the local wildlife from a distance.

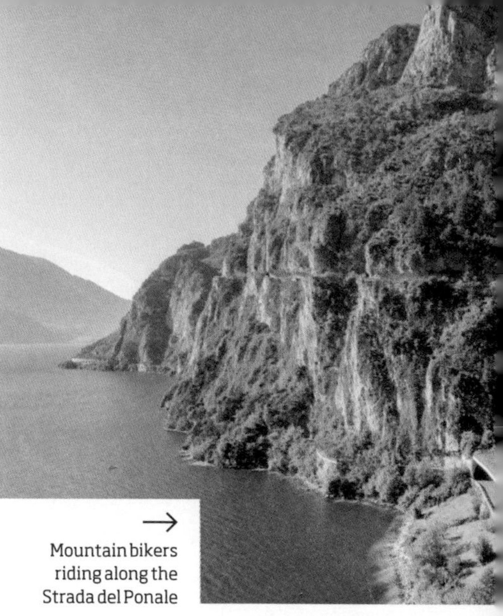

→ Mountain bikers riding along the Strada del Ponale

MILAN AND THE LAKES FOR OUTDOOR ACTIVITIES

Milan has several leafy spots ideal for a gentle stroll. In the Lakes, there's no shortage of water sports, from sailing to SUP, while scenic trails and cycling routes snake along the shores, offering breathtaking views.

Nature Trails

The Lakes are a hiker's paradise, with scores of scenic paths crisscrossing the surrounding mountains. There are walking trails to suit all abilities, from easy routes such as Lake Iseo's Strada Valeriana to more challenging trails such as the Cammino di San Carlo connecting Lake Maggiore *(p162)* to Lake Orta *(p186)*, around 18 km (11 miles). No matter which route you choose, you'll be rewarded with panoramic lake views.

Hikers looking across beautiful Lake Iseo

Cycling

Connecting the Darsena dockland to the Ticino River, Milan's Naviglio Grande *(p113)* is a pleasant spot for a relaxed city bike ride. The Lakes meanwhile are a prime destination for budding cyclists. Lake Garda's Strada del Ponale is a particularly lovely stretch, while Lake Como's Muro di Sormano is a good challenge for experienced cyclists.

PICTURE PERFECT

Strada del Ponale

The Strada del Ponale weaves through tunnels perched high above cliffs, unveiling awe-inspiring vistas at every turn – head here at sunset for the best photo ops.

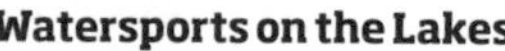

Watersports on the Lakes

Lake Garda is the Lakes' top destination for water sports, with the wind-swept northern basin offering a wealth of activities, including windsurfing, kite surfing and sailing. Nearby Lake Iseo is ideal for rowing and wakeboarding, while Lake Orta and Lake Como's Alto Lario are excellent locations for a spot for windsurfing. Keen to kayak? You can't beat Lake Maggiore on a sunny morning.

← Windsurfing on the pristine waters of Lake Como

Family Fun

Parco Sempione is Milan's largest park, with plenty of open space for children to blow off steam in the city. The Giardini Indro Montanelli in Porta Venezia, meanwhile, is home to a popular playground, and the verdant Parco Giussani, which is frequented by local residents and dog walkers, has a pleasant swimming pool.

↑ Working out in Giardini Indro Montanelli

A YEAR IN MILAN AND THE LAKES

JANUARY

△ **Corteo dei Re Magi** *(6 Jan)*. A celebration of the three wise men's visit to Bethlehem with floats, music and historical costumes.

FEBRUARY

Carnevale Ambrosiano *(late Feb/Mar)*. Named after Milan's patron saint, this carnival features street dancing, music and floats.

△ **Milan Fashion Week** *(late Feb/Mar)*. New autumn/winter collections are unveiled yearly.

MAY

Arte sul Naviglio Grande *(early May)*. Artists display their works along the Naviglio Grande.

△ **Concorso d'Eleganza Villa d'Este** *(late May)*. This exclusive contest on Lake Como features classic cars and motorcycles in the grounds of Villa d'Este and Villa Erba.

JUNE

Sagra di San Giovanni *(24 Jun)*. A historic festival with candlelit displays, a traditional regatta and an impressive fireworks display.

△ **Pride Week** *(late Jun)*. Milan celebrates the LGBTQ+ community with events ranging from dance performances to film screenings.

SEPTEMBER

Italian Grand Prix *(early Sep)*. This iconic motor racing contest takes place in Monza.

△ **Centomiglia** *(second weekend)*. Hundreds of boats compete in Lake Garda's sailing regatta.

Milan Fashion Week *(second half Sep)*. New spring/summer collections hit the runway.

OCTOBER

△ **Arte in Via Bagutta** *(first weekend Oct)*. Dozens of artists display their paintings, sculptures and drawings for two days along Milan's Via Bagutta.

MARCH

△ Milano-Sanremo *(third Sat)*. An annual one-day cycling race from Milan to Sanremo.

Giornate FAI *(late Mar)*. Historic, rarely accessible sites open their doors to the public across Italy, from palaces and castles to gardens and nature trails.

APRIL

Milan Marathon *(early Apr)*. Amateurs and top runners follow a loop course, taking in panoramic sights along the way.

△ Salone del Mobile *(second-half Apr)*. Innovative designs are exhibited at this furniture fair, with scores of events also taking place throughout the city.

JULY

△ Festival di Bellagio *(mid-Jun to mid-Aug)*. This classical music festival sees scores of concerts at venues in Bellagio.

AUGUST

Stresa Festival *(third week Jul–Sep)*. Internationally famous musicians perform in churches and historic buildings dotted around Lake Maggiore.

△ Notte di Fiaba *(late Aug)*. Fairy tales come to life, with shows, workshops, games and storytelling for children throughout the town of Riva del Garda.

NOVEMBER

△ Milan Music Week *(third week Nov)*. This annual week-long music festival features concerts, DJ sets and workshops, as well as artist interviews and panel events.

DECEMBER

Opening night at La Scala *(7 Dec)*. One of the most prestigious events in the world of opera.

△ Oh Bej! Oh Bej! *(7 Dec)*. A four-day Christmas fair held in and around the Castello Sforzesco grounds, selling all manner of items including crafts, toys, sweets, and local produce such as honey and roasted chestnuts.

1

A BRIEF HISTORY

From its foundation as a Roman trading centre, Milan has been conquered and occupied by several foreign rulers, who have left an indelible mark on the city, whether in the city's architecture or cuisine. Today, it is Italy's economic centre and is renowned globally as a major hub for fashion and design.

Prehistory and Roman Rule

In the 3rd–2nd millennium BCE, the area now covered by Milan was inhabited by the Ligurians. It was later settled by Indo-European populations and then, in the 5th century BCE, by the Etruscans. In around 400 BCE, the Gallic Insubre tribes defeated the Etruscans and created the foundations of Mediolanum (now Milan). In 222 BCE, the Romans conquered the Po River Valley and its cities. Thanks to its strategic geographic location, Mediolanum gained importance, eventually becoming the capital of the Western Roman Empire in 286 CE.

Did You Know?

Mediolanum derives from the Latin *medio* (in the middle) and *planus* (plain).

Timeline of events

400 BCE
Gauls settle in Milan.

222 BCE
Romans found the city of Mediolanum.

476 CE
Collapse of the Roman empire.

9th century CE
Milan becomes part of the Holy Roman Empire.

1176
The Lombard League defeats the imperial army of Frederick I Barbarossa at the Battle of Legnano.

Middle Ages

Following the fall of the Roman Empire in the mid-5th century, Milan was ransacked and ruled by several Germanic tribes, including the Lombards, who gave their name to the region of Lombardy. The city gained importance when it became part of the Germanic Holy Roman Empire, with several emperors crowned in Milan. By the 12th century, Milan had become a great economic centre but it weakened under Frederick I Barbarossa. Eventually, the powerful Milanese Visconti family rose in prominence, establishing the Duchy of Milan in the 14th century.

The Renaissance

Milan prospered during the Renaissance, largely due to two influential families: the Visconti and the Sforza. During the rule of Galeazzo II (1349–1378) and his son Gian Galeazzo Visconti (1378–1402), the city's famous cathedral, the Duomo, was commissioned. In the mid-15th century, the Sforza family came into power, developing the arts in the city, with Ludovico Sforza commissioning several of the city's most important works, including Leonardo da Vinci's famous mural of the *Last Supper*.

1 A map showing the Roman settlement of Mediolanum. ↑

2 Emperor Frederick I Barbarossa.

3 Artwork depicting the coronation of Gian Galeazzo Visconti, Duke of Milan.

4 Leonardo da Vinci discussing the Duomo's design.

1386

Construction of the Duomo begins.

1395

Gian Galeazzo Visconti establishes the Duchy of Milan.

1447

Sforza dynasty takes control of the city.

1498

Leonardo da Vinci begins painting the *Last Supper*.

1

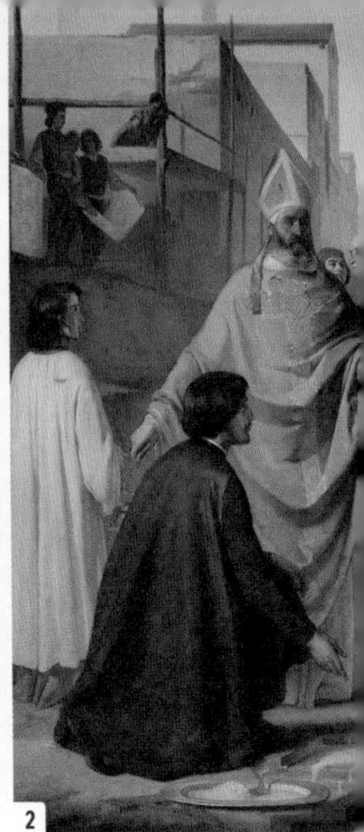

2

Foreign Rule

In the 16th century, Milan found itself under the rule of various foreign powers, primarily France and Spain. King Louis XII (1462–1515) of France claimed the city in 1499, ruling the Duchy of Milan until the early 16th century. The city was briefly taken by the Swiss before returning to the French in 1515. Shortly after, the Spanish Habsburgs seized control until 1706, when Austrian troops occupied the city during the War of Spanish Succession. In 1714, Lombardy was ceded to Austria under the Treaty of Utrecht and in 1740, Empress Maria Theresa of Austria came to power.

Enlightenment

Milan flourished in the 18th century during the Enlightenment, becoming a cultural and intellectual centre, with scholars, academics and thinkers like Cesare Beccaria exchanging ideas in the city's coffee houses. Educational institutions such as the Brera Academy, founded in 1776 by Empress Maria Theresa, became hubs for the arts and sciences. The Enlightenment also brought political ideals that challenged governance of the city,

↑ Cesare Beccaria and other co-founders of the publication *Il Caffè*

Timeline of events

1515

Milan is taken by Francis I of France.

1535

Milan becomes part of Habsburg Spain.

1776

Brera Academy is founded.

1778

La Scala Opera House is inaugurated.

helping reform the legal system and better education. This period of change and investment also saw Milan's architecture transform. Leading architect Giuseppe Piermarini designed the Teatro alla Scala and rebuilt the Palazzo Reale.

City Rebellion

Power struggles continued in Milan with the arrival of Napoleon's troops in 1796 and the creation of the Cisalpine Republic, a sister republic of France in northern Italy. In 1804, the city witnessed Napoleon's coronation as King of Italy followed by the construction of new buildings, including the Arco della Pace. A decade later, the Congress of Vienna handed Milan back to the Habsburgs after Napoleon's defeat but resentment of foreign rule grew within the city, which had become the focal point of Romanticism. Tensions peaked in 1848 with the Cinque Giornate di Milano revolt, or Five Days of Milan, when the Milanese briefly succeeded in driving Austrian troops out of the city. This marked a crucial moment in the wider context of the Risorgimento (Italian reunification), inspiring other regions to fight. The unified resistance eventually led to Italy gaining its independence in 1861.

1 King Louis XII of France. ↑

2 Duke Francesco Sforza laying the foundation stone of the Brera Academy.

3 Fighting during the Cinque Giornate di Milano (The Five Days of Milan).

1796

Milan becomes capital of the Cisalpine Republic.

1802

The city becomes the capital of the Napoleonic Italian Republic.

1848

Milan rises up against the Austrian Empire.

1861

Milan becomes part of the Kingdom of Italy.

1

Post-Unification

Milan played a key role in the country's development following the unification of Italy in the 19th century, becoming a major economic and industrial hub as well as a major centre for finance, fashion and culture. The construction of the Milan Central Railway Station in 1864 helped boost trade and commerce, and new infrastructure was built, such as the city's glittering Galleria Vittorio Emanuele II shopping arcade.

World Wars and Post-War Boom

The Industrial Era in Milan was marked by the growth of the manufacturing sector and the development of the automobile and aviation industries, aided by Italy's involvement in World War I. Shortly after, Benito Mussolini was appointed prime minister in 1922, becoming leader of the nation's fascist government. Italy entered World War II with Nazi Germany, and Milan, severely damaged by bombing raids, was the last large Italian city to remain under the control of the remaining fascists and the Germans. Italy switched to the Allies in 1943 and in April 1945, Mussolini and his lover Claretta Petacci were

SALÒ

Named after the inventor of the violin, Gaspere di Salò (1540–1609), this small town on Lake Garda became the headquarters for a Nazi puppet state in 1943. Known as the Republic of Salò, it was run by Mussolini at Hitler's behest in Axis-controlled northern Italy. Approximately 19 months later, it collapsed and Mussolini was forced to flee.

Timeline of events

1877
Galleria Vittorio Emanuele II is built.

1926
Stadio San Siro welcomes its first fans.

1943
The Nazis establish the puppet state of the Republic of Salò on Lake Garda.

1945
Mussolini and his lover Petacci are captured on Lake Como.

1958
Italy joins the EU.

captured on the shores of Lake Como as they tried to flee north, and later executed. Following this, Milan played a key role during the post-war years, when Italy experienced what is dubbed as the "Economic Miracle" of the 1950s and 1960s. The 1980s saw the development of the fashion industry that has made Milan one of the world leaders in this field.

1 Milan's Central Station, inaugurated in 1864.

2 Inside the city's 2015 Expo World Fair.

3 CityLife, one of Milan's newest neighbourhoods.

Milan Today

During the 2022 elections, the wider Lombardy region voted overwhelmingly for the right-wing Fratelli d'Italia party, although Milan remained the last stronghold of the centre-left, with the Democratic Party gaining 25 per cent of the vote. The country's right-wing coalition went on to win a majority to lead a new government, with Giorgia Meloni becoming the country's first female prime minister. Politics aside, Milan thrives as Italy's economic powerhouse and most cosmopolitan city. It is also at the forefront of sustainable urban living, with several initiatives implemented over the years, from the introduction of car-sharing services to the promotion of sustainable architecture and the creation of new green spaces.

1958–1963
Industrial output booms during Italy's Economic Miracle.

1965
The Duomo is finally completed.

1999
Italy adopts the Euro.

2015
Milan hosts the Expo World Fair.

2022
Giorgia Meloni becomes Italy's first female prime minister.

2023
Silvio Berlusconi's funeral takes place in the Duomo.

EXPERIENCE

Strolling through Galleria Vittorio Emanuele II

Duomo gargoyles overlooking the piazza below

HISTORIC CENTRE

The Historic Centre, also known as Centro Storico, has a conglomeration of architectural styles that reflects Milan's long and diverse history. During the Middle Ages, the city was an important commercial centre with the wonderfully preserved Piazza Mercantiat its core. Markets were held under the square's porticoes, while the 13th-century Palazzo della Ragione was once the judicial seat.

This commercial success continued into the 14th century, bringing with it investment in the city and the construction of several new buildings, including the beautiful Chiesa di Santa Maria and the now iconic Duomo. Commissioned by Gian Galeazzo Visconti, the magnificent Duomo replaced numerous churches in the area, which were demolished to make space. Work continued throughout the latter half of the 14th century despite the arrival of the Black Death and the strict quarantines imposed by the Visconti.

In the 19th century, Milan grew in importance on a national level following the Italian unification and the Historic Centre became the nucleus of the city. Later, in the 20th century, the area suffered the effects of the World Wars, but it bounced back rapidly in the postwar years, reclaiming its role as the beating heart of the city.

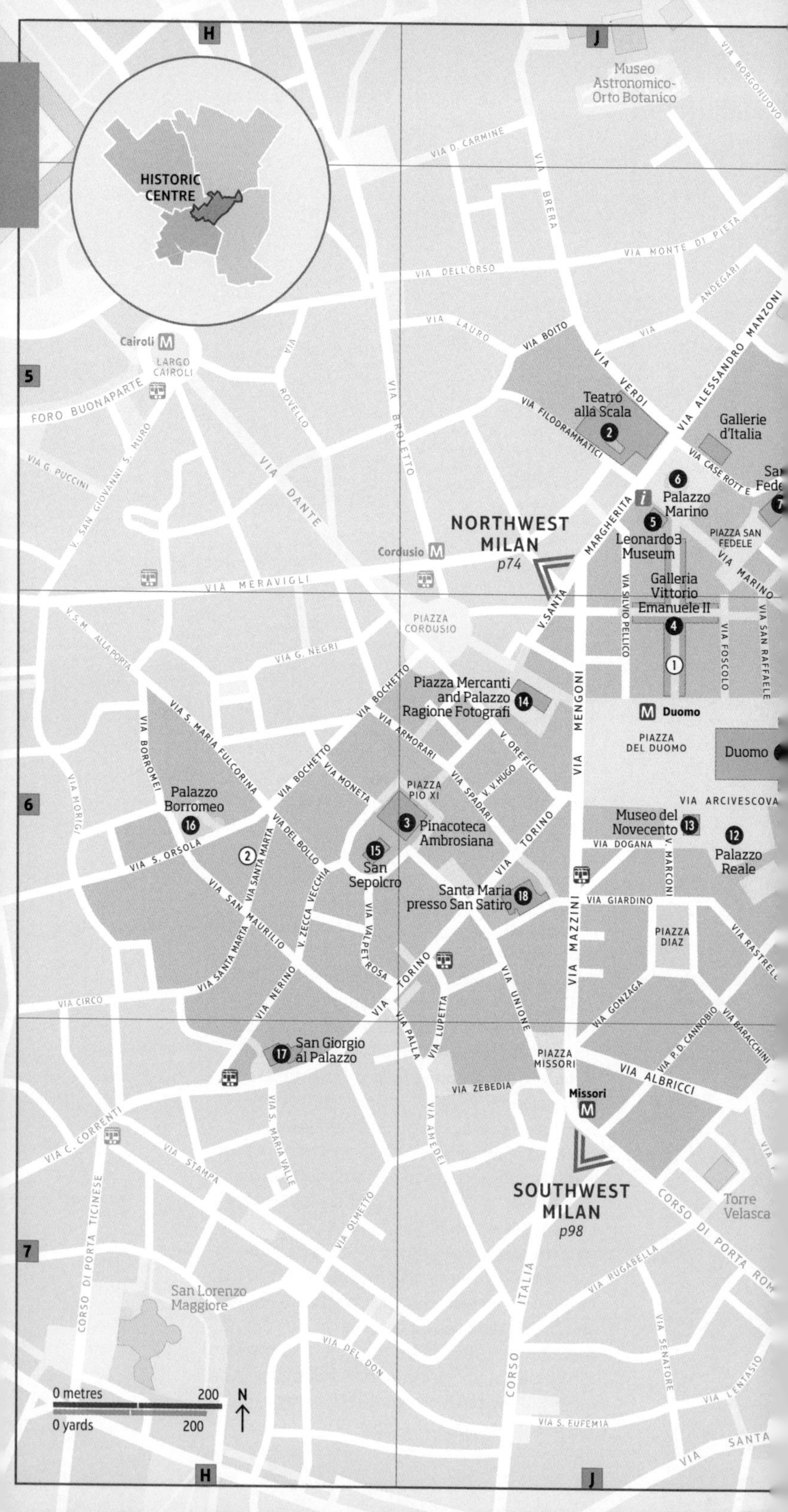

HISTORIC CENTRE
Museo Astronomico-Orto Botanico
Cairoli
LARGO CAIROLI
FORO BUONAPARTE
Teatro alla Scala
Gallerie d'Italia
Palazzo Marino
Leonardo3 Museum
NORTHWEST MILAN
p74
Cordusio
PIAZZA CORDUSIO
PIAZZA SAN FEDELE
Galleria Vittorio Emanuele II
Piazza Mercanti and Palazzo Ragione Fotografi
Duomo
PIAZZA DEL DUOMO
Duomo
PIAZZA PIO XI
Pinacoteca Ambrosiana
Palazzo Borromeo
San Sepolcro
Museo del Novecento
Palazzo Reale
Santa Maria presso San Satiro
PIAZZA DIAZ
San Giorgio al Palazzo
PIAZZA MISSORI
Missori
SOUTHWEST MILAN
p98
Torre Velasca
San Lorenzo Maggiore
0 metres 200
0 yards 200
N
VIA D. CARMINE
VIA BRERA
VIA MONTE DI PIETÀ
VIA DELL'ORSO
VIA LAURO
VIA BOITO
VIA VERDI
VIA ALESSANDRO MANZONI
VIA FILODRAMMATICI
VIA CASE ROTTE
VIA ROVELLO
VIA BROLETTO
VIA DANTE
VIA G. PUCCINI
V. SAN GIOVANNI S. MURO
VIA MERAVIGLI
V. SANTA MARGHERITA
VIA SILVIO PELLICO
VIA MARINO
VIA FOSCOLO
VIA SAN RAFFAELE
V.S.M. ALLA PORTA
VIA G. NEGRI
VIA BOCHETTO
VIA ARMORARI
V. OREFICI
VIA MENGONI
VIA S. MARIA FULCORINA
VIA BORROMEI
VIA MORIGI
VIA MONETA
VIA SPADARI
V. V. HUGO
VIA TORINO
VIA ARCIVESCOVADO
VIA DOGANA
V. MARCONI
VIA S. ORSOLA
VIA SANTA MARTA
VIA DEL BOLLO
VIA SAN MAURILIO
V. ZECCA VECCHIA
VIA VALPETROSA
VIA GIARDINO
VIA MAZZINI
VIA RASTRELLI
VIA SANTA MARTA
VIA NERINO
VIA CIRCO
VIA UNIONE
VIA GONZAGA
VIA P.D. CANNOBIO
VIA BARACCHINI
VIA PALLA
VIA LUPETTA
VIA ALBRICCI
VIA ZEBEDIA
VIA C. CORRENTI
VIA STAMPA
VIA S. MARIA VALLE
VIA AMEDEI
CORSO DI PORTA TICINESE
VIA OLMETTO
CORSO DI PORTA ROMANA
VIA RUGABELLA
CORSO ITALIA
VIA DEL DON
VIA SENATORE
VIA LENTASIO
VIA S. EUFEMIA
VIA SANTA
VIA BORGONUOVO
ANDEGARI

HISTORIC CENTRE
Must Sees
1 Duomo
2 Teatro alla Scala
3 Pinacoteca Ambrosiana
Experience More
4 Galleria Vittorio Emanuele II
5 Leonardo3 Museum
6 Palazzo Marino
7 San Fedele
8 Casa degli Omenoni
9 Casa Manzoni and Piazza Belgioioso
10 Piazza del Liberty and Corso Vittorio Emanuele II
11 San Gottardo in Corte
12 Palazzo Reale
13 Museo del Novecento
14 Piazza Mercanti and Palazzo Ragione Fotografi
15 San Sepolcro
16 Palazzo Borromeo
17 San Giorgio al Palazzo
18 Santa Maria presso San Satiro
Eat
① Cracco
Stay
② Hotel Santa Marta Suites
K
L
4
5
Montenapoleone
Palestro
San Babila
Museo Bagatti Valsecchi
Museo Poldi Pezzoli
Palazzo Morando
Villa Necchi Campiglio
Parco Villa Campiglio
Casa Manzoni and Piazza Belgioioso
NORTHEAST MILAN
p134
Basilica di San Babila
Piazza del Liberty and Corso Vittorio Emanuele II
SOUTHEAST MILAN
p118
Giardino della Guastalla
Ca' Granda
San Nazaro Maggiore
PIAZZA S.BABILA
PIAZZA BECCARIA
PIAZZA FONTANA
LARGO AUGUSTO
VIA ALESSANDRO MANZONI
VIA BORGOSPESSO
VIA DELLA SPIGA
VIA MARINA
VIA SENATO
CORSO VENEZIA
VIA MOZART
VIA MONTENAPOLEONE
VIA BIGLI
VIA SANT'ANDREA
VIA S. DAMIANO
VIA CECILIA
VIA P. VERRI
CORSO G. MATTEOTTI
CORSO MONFORTE
VIA SAN PIETRO ALL'ORTO
VIA RONCHETTI
VIA PIETRO MASCAGNI
VIA BORGOGNA
VIA SAN PAOLO
CORSO VITTORIO EMANUELE II
CORSO EUROPA
VIA DURINI
GALLERIA DEL CORSO
VIA BECCARIA
VIA PATTARI
PIAZZA FONTANA
VIA CAVALLOTTI
VIA LARGA
VIA D. SIGNORA
V. LAGHETTO
V. ANDREANI
VIA S. ANTONIO
VIA FESTA D. PERDONO
VIA FRANCESCO SFORZA

1

DUOMO

J6 Piazza Duomo M1, 3 Duomo 8am-7pm daily; museum: 10am-6:10pm Thu-Tue; baptistery: 9am-6pm daily; roof terraces: 9am-7pm daily duomomilano.it

Standing majestically in Piazza Duomo, the city's Gothic-style cathedral is an architectural marvel, with its intricate façade and marble-clad interiors featuring three huge stained-glass apse windows.

From its inception to the finishing touches, Milan's cathedral took almost 430 years to complete. Construction began in 1386, with the city's bishop, Antonio da Saluzzo, as its patron. Duke Gian Galeazzo Visconti invited Lombard, German and French architects to supervise the works and insisted they use Candoglia marble, which was transported along the Navigli canals. The official seal AUF (*ad usum fabricae*), stamped on the slabs, exempted them from customs duty. The cathedral was consecrated in 1418, yet remained unfinished until the 19th century, when Napoleon – crowned King of Italy here – had the façade completed.

The cathedral was consecrated in 1418, yet remained unfinished until the 19th century, when Napoleon - crowned King of Italy here - had the façade completed.

↑ Interior of the Duomo di Milano, the third-largest cathedral in the world

← Milan's skyline, with the Duomo's Gothic spires in the foreground

Timeline

1386 The first stone of the Duomo is laid.

1418 Pope Martin V consecrates the high altar.

1500 Central spire is inaugurated.

1617 Francesco Maria Richini begins work on the façade.

1774 The Madonnina is placed on the tallest spire.

1813 Façade completed with Gothic spires.

1981–4 Presbytery piers are restored.

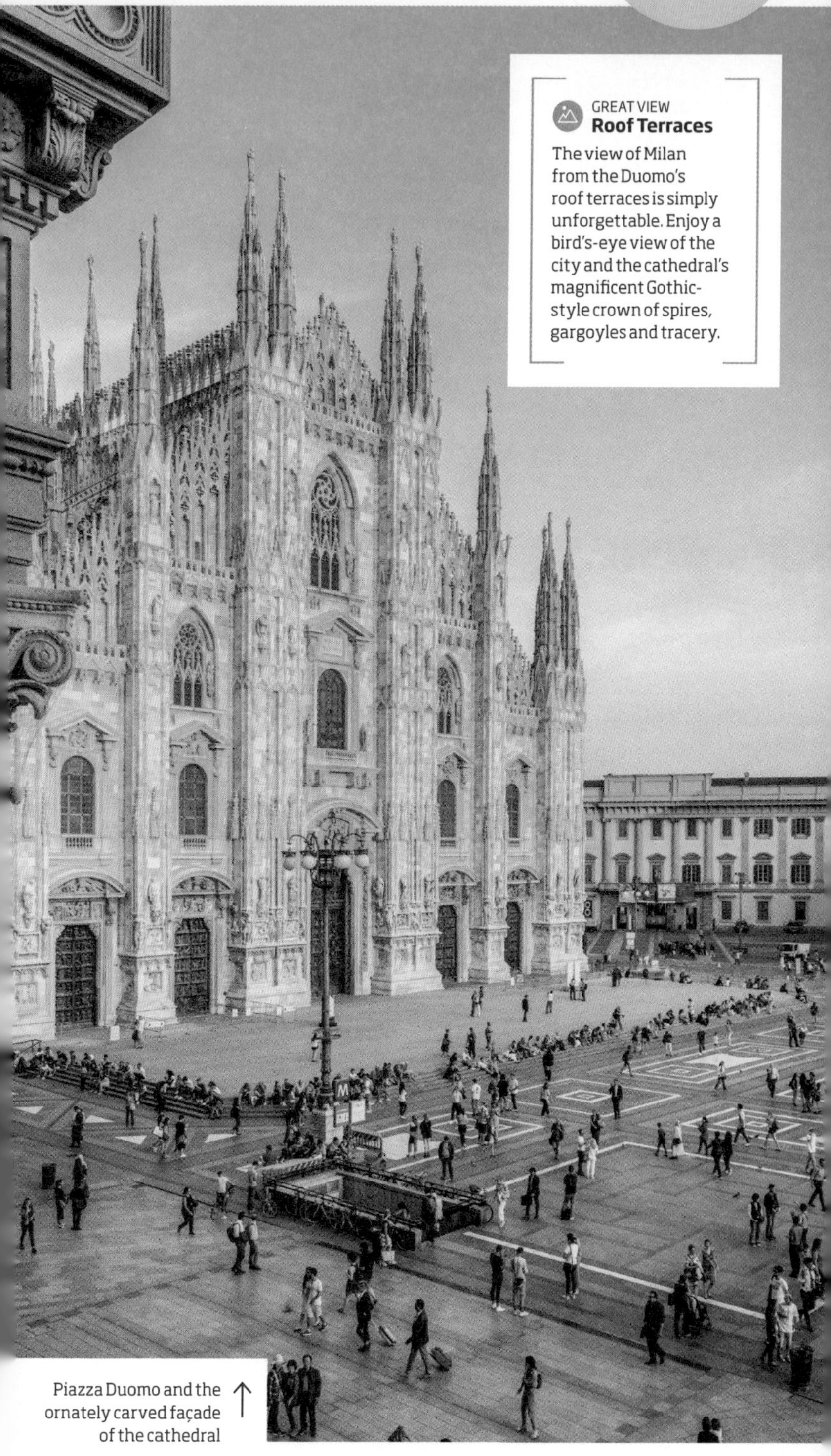

GREAT VIEW
Roof Terraces

The view of Milan from the Duomo's roof terraces is simply unforgettable. Enjoy a bird's-eye view of the city and the cathedral's magnificent Gothic-style crown of spires, gargoyles and tracery.

Piazza Duomo and the ornately carved façade of the cathedral ↑

Building the Duomo

For the Duomo to be built, a great Jubilee was proclaimed in 1390 in order to urge the Milanese to contribute money and manual labour to carry out the work. The initial plan was to build it in fired bricks, as the excavations in the northern sacristy have revealed, but in 1387 Duke Gian Galeazzo Visconti, who wanted the cathedral to be seen as a great symbol of his power, demanded that marble should be used instead and that the architectural style should be International Gothic. Construction continued over five centuries, resulting in the obvious mix of styles that characterizes the cathedral. Final touches were still ongoing in 1965, when the bronze doors were fitted.

↑ The vast nave of Duomo topped by tall cross vaults

Did You Know?

The Duomo is home to 3,500 statues, more than any other cathedral in the world.

The 4.16-m (13.6-ft) gilded statue of the Madonna was sculpted by Giuseppe Bini in 1774.

Most of the stained-glass windows depict scenes from the Bible, and date from the 19th century.

Flying buttresses

Crypt

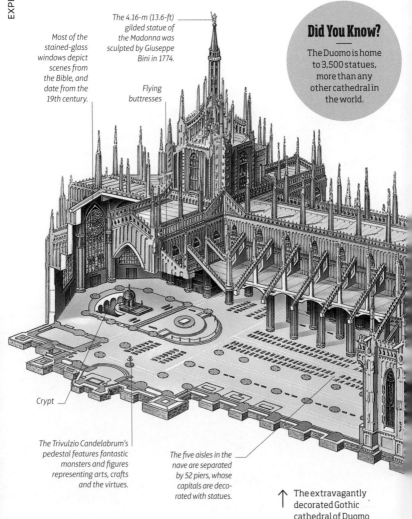

The Trivulzio Candelabrum's pedestal features fantastic monsters and figures representing arts, crafts and the virtues.

The five aisles in the nave are separated by 52 piers, whose capitals are decorated with statues.

↑ The extravagantly decorated Gothic cathedral of Duomo

Highlights

The Façade

Up to the first level, the façade is Baroque. It was completed in the 19th century with Neo-Gothic ogival windows and spires.

The Foundations of the Duomo

▶ Next to the sarcophagus of Archbishop Ariberto d'Intimiano is a plaque with the date of the foundation of the cathedral. The corresponding stained-glass window depicts the *Life of St John the Evangelist* (1473-7). The windows in the next three bays, showing scenes from the Old Testament, date from the 16th century.

The Meridian

Tall cross vaults cover the interior, and the aisles in the nave are separated by 52 piers (for the 52 weeks of the year). The capitals on the piers feature statues of saints. Behind the façade, embedded in the floor, is a meridian, installed in 1786 by the Brera astronomers. It marks astronomical noon, thanks to a ray of sunlight that enters from the first bay of the south aisle on the right-hand side.

Copper Pulpits

The Duomo has two 16th-century gilded copper pulpits with depictions from the Old and New Testaments, surmounted by organs painted by Giovanni Ambrogio Figino, Camillo Procaccini and Giuseppe Meda.

Carvings and Sculptures

▶ Behind the altar is a wooden choir with the *Life of Sant'Ambrogio*, carved in 1572-1620. A little further on is the statue of the flayed St Bartholomew, signed and dated 1562 by Marco d'Agrate.

The Crypt

At the beginning of the ambulatory, steps lead to the crypt (1606), where San Carlo Borromeo, the Archbishop of Milan from 1564 to 1584, is buried with a collection of church objects, and the Coro Jemale, a small 16th-century room, is decorated with fine stuccowork.

Artworks in the Apse

On the way to the lift is the apse with a stained-glass window, designed by Filippino degli Organi in 1402. There are also three 19th-century stained-glass windows by the Bertini brothers with episodes from the Old and New Testaments and the Apocalypse. The ambulatory ends at the northern portal of the sacristy, with *Christ the Lord and Judge* (1389), while the left-hand transept has the 5-m (16-ft) bronze Trivulzio Candelabrum, a 12th-century piece by the goldsmith Nicola da Verdun with scenes from the Old Testament.

Roof Terraces

There may be 250 steps to climb, but the view is well worth it. Take in magnificent panoramas of the city and the mountains to the north, as well as the Duomo spires and statues. Alternatively, opt for the elevator.

Museo del Duomo

The Cathedral Museum, founded in 1953, is at Via Arcivescovado 15. It has artworks, religious objects and a wooden model of the Duomo, begun in 1519.

THE HOLY NAIL OF THE CROSS

In the vault above the choir, a red light marks the location of the niche where a nail from Christ's Cross has been kept since 1461. The nail, which was once kept in the early medieval Santa Maria Maggiore, is in the shape of a horseshoe. It was found by St Helena and given to her son, Emperor Constantine. The nail was later donated to Sant' Ambrogio and carried by San Carlo in procession during the 1576 plague. Every year on 14 September, it is shown to the public when the Bishop of Milan is raised up to the level of the niche, which holds the nail in a decorated balcony, drawn by invisible pulleys.

A plaque confirms that the Duomo is dedicated to Maria Nascente.

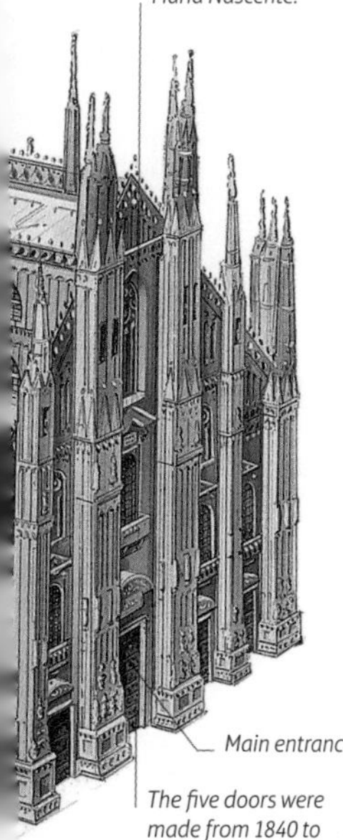

Main entrance

The five doors were made from 1840 to 1965. The central door features a bronze relief, The Flagellation *by Ludovico Pogliaghi.*

2

TEATRO ALLA SCALA

J5 Piazza della Scala 1, 3 Duomo 1, 61
9:30am-5:30pm daily; tours: 9:30am & 4pm daily
teatroallascala.org

Milan's renowned opera house sits discreetly on Via Filodrammatici, its Neo-Classical façade belying a rich interior. As well as opera, the theatre hosts ballet performances, symphonic concerts, and vocal and piano recitals.

Built by Giuseppe Piermarini in 1776-8, this opera house owes its name to the fact that it stands on the site of Santa Maria della Scala, a church built in 1381 for Regina della Scala, Bernabò Visconti's wife. The theatre opened in 1778; it was bombed in 1943 and rebuilt three years later. After an extensive restoration programme that saw the addition of a new stage tower designed by Mario Botta, La Scala reopened in 2004. To learn more about the history of La Scala and the theatre in general, visit the theatre museum, Museo Teatrale, which houses original scores and art.

INSIDER TIP
Free Screenings

Tickets for La Prima della Scala, a prestigious event held on 7 December marking the opening night of La Scala's opera season, are hard to come by but screenings are available to view across the city for free.

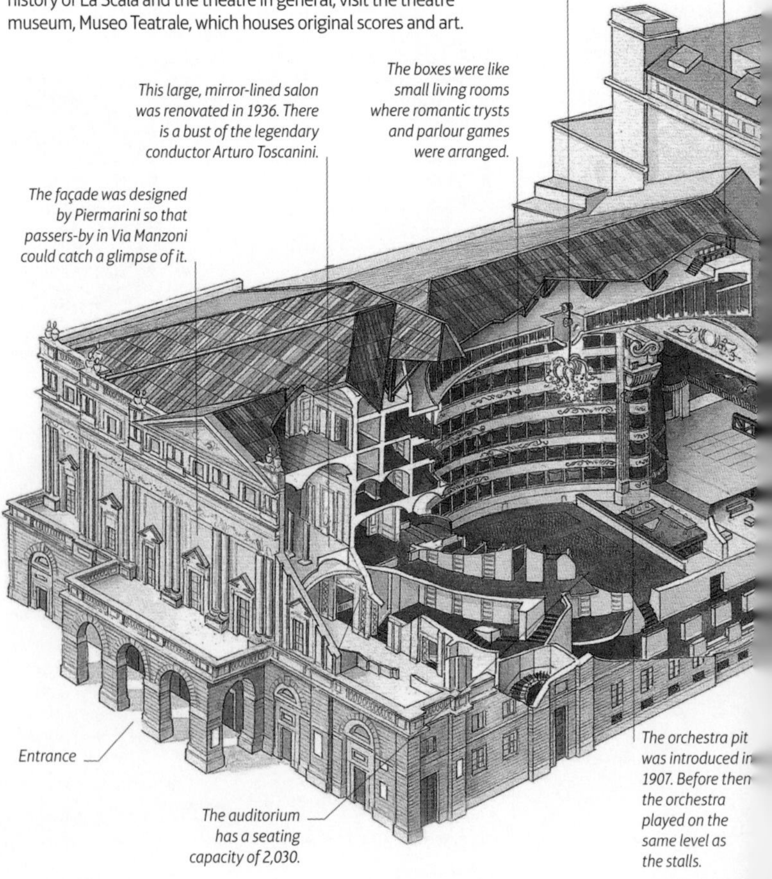

A tank, filled with water, placed over the wooden vault, was ready for use in case of fire.

The chandelier (1923), made of Bohemian crystal, holds 383 lightbulbs.

The boxes were like small living rooms where romantic trysts and parlour games were arranged.

This large, mirror-lined salon was renovated in 1936. There is a bust of the legendary conductor Arturo Toscanini.

The façade was designed by Piermarini so that passers-by in Via Manzoni could catch a glimpse of it.

Entrance

The auditorium has a seating capacity of 2,030.

The orchestra pit was introduced in 1907. Before then the orchestra played on the same level as the stalls.

Opulent interior of the world-famous opera house

The Teatro alla Scala's modest linear façade

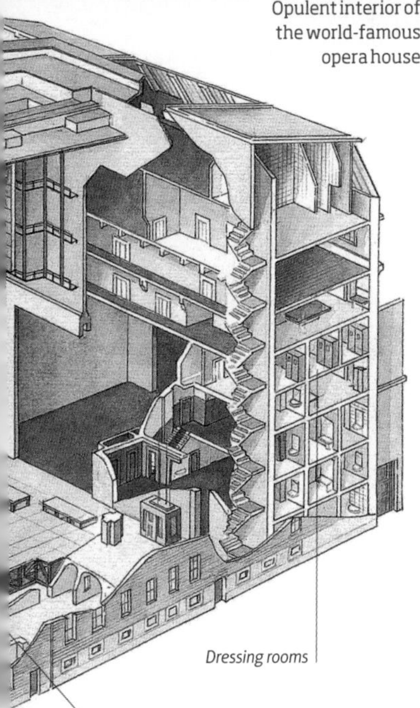
Dressing rooms
This is one of the largest stages in Italy, measuring 1,200 sq m (13,000 sq ft).

The vast Neo-Classical opera house and its various sections

THE BALLET SCHOOL

La Scala's Ballet School was founded in 1813. Originally there were 48 students who studied dance, mime or specialist disciplines. At the end of an eight-year course, the best students were awarded merits of distinction and became part of the theatre's *corps de ballet* with an annual stipend of €1.50. This rigorously disciplined school has produced such artists as Carla Fracci and Luciana Savignano.

3

PINACOTECA AMBROSIANA

J6 Piazza Pio XI 2 M1, 3 Duomo, 1 Cordusio 1, 2, 14, 16, 27 10am-6pm Thu-Tue (last adm: 5:30pm) ambrosiana.it

Housing masterpieces of Italian art, including works by Caravaggio, Raphael and Titian, the Pinacoteca Ambrosiana is one of Milan's most impressive galleries. It is also the site of the Biblioteca Ambrosiana – a grand library displaying Leonardo da Vinci's *Codex Atlanticus*.

The Ambrosiana art gallery was founded in 1618 by Cardinal Federico Borromeo, the cousin of San Carlo and his successor in charge of the archdiocese of Milan. Borromeo planned the gallery as part of a vast cultural project that included the Ambrosiana Library, opened in 1609, and the Accademia del Disegno (1620) for the training of Counter-Reformation artists. The gallery held 172 paintings – some of which already belonged to Borromeo, while others were purchased later after painstaking research by the cardinal. The collection was then enlarged thanks to private donations. Today, it has 24 rooms and is one of Milan's finest museums.

BIBLIOTECA AMBROSIANA

This was one of the first libraries open to the public. It houses over 750,000 printed volumes, 2,500 of which are incunabula (early printed works), and 36,000 manuscripts. Among them is the 5th-century *Ilias Picta*, Homer's Illiad; a Virgil anthology annotated by Petrarch and illuminated by Simone Martini; a volume of Aristotle with annotations by Boccaccio; as well as Arab, Syrian, Greek and Latin texts.

Did You Know?

The Pinacoteca Ambrosiana houses some unusual objects, including a template of Napoleon's boots.

→ Marble figures and artifacts on display at the Pinacoteca Ambrosiana

↑ Entrance to the historic building housing the Ambrosiana gallery and library

Gallery Guide

The Borromeo Collection, 15th–16th-Century Paintings

▶ The Borromeo Collection features Venetian and Leonardo-esque paintings. The room known as Aula Leonardi is home to one of the most famous works in the museum, *Basket of Fruit*, painted by Caravaggio in the late 1500s on a used canvas. In the same room hangs Leonardo da Vinci's *Portrait of a Musician*.

The Galbiati Wing

▼ The Sala della Medusa and the Sala delle Colonne feature Renaissance paintings and a collection of objects, the most curious of which are Lucrezia Borgia's blonde hair and Napoleon's gloves. A short passageway leads to the Spiriti Magni courtyard, decorated with statues of illustrious artists. The three rooms that follow contain 16th-century Italian and Venetian paintings.

De Pecis Collection and 19th Century

The largest section of the Pinacoteca Ambrosiana, donated by Giovanni Edoardo De Pecis in 1827, consists mostly of Italian and Flemish paintings and includes a series of small Neoclassical bronze pieces and a *Self Portrait* by sculptor Antonio Canova, inspired by Roman portraiture. German and Flemish art from the 15th to 17th centuries are here, as well as the *Dantesque Stained Glass* by Giuseppe Bertini, the Duomo master glassblower.

Sculpture

▶ There are ancient Roman, Romanesque and Renaissance pieces as well as the highly elegant bas-reliefs by Agostino Busti - known as "*il Bambaia*" - sculpted for the tomb of Gaston de Foix around 1516.

EXPERIENCE MORE

4   

Galleria Vittorio Emanuele II

J6 Piazza della Scala, Piazza del Duomo M 1, 3 Duomo 02-8845 5555 Summer: 10am-11pm daily; winter: 10am-9pm daily; guided tours: 10am-dusk (call ahead) 1 Jan, 1 May, 2 Jun, 25 & 26 Dec

The Galleria is an elegant arcade lined with cafés, bookshops, luxury retailers and a famous restaurant, Savini. The oldest shopping centre in Italy, its construction began in 1865, overseen by the renowned Italian architect Giuseppe Mengoni. It was opened two years later by King Vittorio Emanuele II, after whom it was named. The gallery was designed as part of an ambitious urban renewal project and served to connect Piazza del Duomo and Piazza della Scala. Its design was soon replicated in many other Italian cities, most notably in Naples, Rome and Turin.

On the floor in the central octagonal area, directly under the 47-m- (154-ft-) high glass dome, is the heraldic symbol of the Savoy family, a white cross on a red ground. Around it are the arms of four major Italian cities: the bull of Turin, the wolf of Rome, the lily of Florence and the red cross on a white ground (Milan). On the vault are vast mosaics of Asia, Africa, Europe and America.

Guided walks are available all year round and can be booked from the office in Via Silvio Pellico.

TREND-SETTING MALLS

The grand design for Milan's Galleria Vittorio Emanuele II was inspired by similar mall-style buildings in Europe that opened in the early 19th century, including the Galerie Vivienne in Paris and the Burlington Arcades in London.

5  

Leonardo3 Museum

J5 Piazza della Scala, Entrance Galleria M 1, 3 Duomo 1, 2 61 9:30am-9pm leonardo3.net

Leonardo da Vinci's many talents are celebrated at this small museum in central Milan. Opened in 2013, the Leonardo3 Museum is home to more than 200 interactive 3D models across seven rooms. They have all been made by engineers working in the museum's dynamic research department, dedicated to meticulously following Leonardo's drawings to reproduce his machines.

The models on display include the first working prototype of Leonardo's self-propelling cart, a flying machine and a mechanical eagle. Exhibits feature studies of the *Mona Lisa* and physical reconstructions of the refectory of Santa Maria delle Grazie *(p84)*. Audio guides are available in eight languages.

6 Palazzo Marino

J5 Piazza della Scala M1, 3 Duomo To the public

This palazzo was designed in 1558 by Galeazzo Alessi for the banker Tommaso Marino, but remained unfinished until 1892, when the architect Luca Beltrami completed the façade. From Via Marino on the right you can see the richly decorated, porticoed courtyard of honour.

According to tradition, the palazzo, home of the Milan Town Hall since 1860, was the birthplace of Marianna de Leyva, the famous nun of Monza described by Alessandro Manzoni in *The Betrothed* as the "Signora".

← Crowded arcade of the Galleria Vittorio Emanuele II

→ San Fedele's façade, faced by a bronze statue of Alessandro Manzoni

7 San Fedele

J5 Piazza San Fedele 02-86 35 22 15 M1, 3 Duomo 1 61 7:30am-4pm Mon & Tue, 7:30am-6pm Wed-Fri, 2-7pm Sat, 10am-noon & 2-7:30pm Sun

This church is the Milanese seat of the Jesuit Order, commissioned by San Carlo Borromeo from Pellegrino Tibaldi in 1569. Construction was continued by Martino Bassi, and the dome, crypt and choir were designed by Francesco Maria Richini (1633–52). With its austere architecture and nave without aisles, this is a typical Counter-Reformation church.

The façade is being restored, but the interior has three interesting paintings. By the first altar on the right is *St Ignatius's Vision* by Giovan Battista Crespi, known as "il Cerano" (c 1622). A *Transfiguration* by Bernardino Campi (1565) is in the atrium after the second altar on the left; Campi also painted the *Blessed Virgin and Child,* by the second altar. These last two works came from Santa Maria della Scala, which was demolished to make room for the La Scala opera house *(p60)*.

The wooden furniture is also worth a closer look: the confessionals (1596) have scenes from the life of Christ carved by Giovanni Taurini, and the cupboards in Richini's sacristy (1624–28) are by Daniele Ferrari (1639). A statue of Alessandro Manzoni *(p66)*, whose death certificate is kept in San Fedele, stands in the square.

8 Casa degli Omenoni

K5 Via Omenoni 3 M1, 3 Duomo 1 To the public

Eight telamones, which the Milanese call *omenoni* ("large men"), are the most striking feature of this house-cum-studio, built by the sculptor Leone Leoni in 1565. The artist collected many works of art, including paintings by Titian and Correggio and Leonardo da Vinci's famous *Codex Atlanticus (p62)*.

A reference to Leoni can be seen in the relief under the cornice, in which Calumny is torn up by *leoni* (lions).

Did You Know?

Six statues on Palazzo degli Omenoni have names referring to tribes defeated by the Romans.

Casa Manzoni and Piazza Belgioioso

J5, K5 Via Morone 1 02-8646 0403 3 Montenapoleone 1 10am-6pm Tue-Fri, 2-6pm Sat (guided tours only) Public hols

This is the house where Italian author Alessandro Manzoni lived from 1814 until his death in 1873 after a fall on the steps of San Fedele *(p65)*. The interior includes Manzoni's studio on the ground floor, where he received Garibaldi in 1862 and Verdi in 1868. Next to this is the room where poet and author Tommaso Grossi had his notary office, and on the first floor is Manzoni's bedroom.

The house is now the seat of the National Centre for Manzoni Studies, which was founded in 1937. It includes a library with works by Manzoni and critical studies of his oeuvre, as well as the Lombard Historical Society Library with over 40,000 volumes.

The brick façade overlooks Piazza Belgioioso, designed by Piermarini in 1777–81 for Prince Alberico XII di Belgioioso d'Este. Its façade bears heraldic emblems and the interior houses a fresco by Martin Knoller.

ALESSANDRO MANZONI

Writer Alessandro Manzoni (1785-1873) was born into a wealthy Milanese family and is best known for *I Promessi Sposi* (*The Betrothed*), a historical novel set in 1628-31. Considered one of the greatest novels in Italian literature, it is a splendid portrait of Milan under Spanish rule during the 1600s and serves vivid descriptions of a city devastated by the plague of 1630. Manzoni rewrote it several times and had three different editions published (1820, with the title *Fermo e Lucia*, 1827 and 1840).

Piazza del Liberty and Corso Vittorio Emanuele II

K6 1, 3 Duomo, 1 San Babila 15, 23 60, 61, 73

Once past the arch at the end of Piazza Belgioioso, go through Piazza Meda (1926), then past Corso Matteotti and Via San Paolo to Piazza del Liberty. This small square owes its name to the Art Nouveau (Liberty) façade on No 8, restored by Giovanni and Lorenzo Muzio in 1963 with architectural elements from the Trianon café-concert, a building dating from 1905 which was moved from Corso Vittorio Emanuele II. (Go along Via San Paolo to reach Corso Vittorio Emanuele II).

This is Milan's main commercial street, and was once called "Corsia dei Servi" (Servants' Lane). It follows the course of an ancient Roman street and in 1628 was the scene of bread riots, described by Manzoni in *The Betrothed*. Near San Carlo al Corso, at No 13, is the *Omm de preja* (local dialect for *uomo di pietra* or "man of stone") statue, a copy of an ancient Roman work. It is also called "Sciur Carera", a misspelling of the first word of a Latin inscription under the statue *("Carere debet omni vitio qui in alterum dicere paratus est"*, meaning "you must be free from the faults that you are ready to find in others").

San Gottardo in Corte

J6 Via Pecorari 2 02-8646 4500 1, 3 Duomo 3, 12, 15, 16, 24, 27 54 10am-6pm Thu-Tue

Azzone Visconti, lord of Milan, ordered the construction of this church in 1336 as the ducal chapel in the Broletto Vecchio (Courthouse) courtyard. The interior was rebuilt in Neo-Classical style by Piermarini. On the left-hand wall is a *Crucifixion* by the school of Giotto.

Azzone Visconti's funerary monument, by Giovanni di Balduccio, is in the apse: the reclining statue of Visconti is

←

Exhibits chronicling the life and works of Alessandro Manzoni at Casa Manzoni

flanked by the figures of two women. The octagonal brick bell tower with small stone arches and columns is by Francesco Pecorari (c 1335).

Museo del Novecento's modern façade and *(inset)* admiring the 20th-century artworks on display ↑

Palazzo Reale

J6 Piazza del Duomo 02-8846 5230 M 1, 3 Duomo 1, 2, 3, 12, 24, 27 54, 60 Tue-Sun (to 10:30pm Thu)

The seat of the commune administration in the 11th century, this building was drastically rebuilt by Azzone Visconti in 1330–36. At the height of its importance, it was the headquarters of the lords of Milan. Galeazzo Maria Sforza's decision to move the palace, however, ultimately led to the decline of the Palazzo Reale.

In 1598, it housed the first permanent theatre in Milan. Made of wood, the theatre was rebuilt in 1737 and Mozart played here as a child. In 1776, it was tragically destroyed by a fire.

The present Neo-Classical appearance dates from 1778, when Giuseppe Piermarini made it into a residence for Archduke Ferdinand of Austria. In 1920 Vittorio Emanuele III granted the place temporarily to the city of Milan, and in 1965 the city purchased the building to use as offices and museums and for important temporary exhibitions by sculptors and painters such as Claude Monet and Pablo Picasso.

STAY

Hotel Santa Marta Suites

The rooms here feature antique styling with modern twists. The roof offers superb views.

H6 Via Santa Marta 4 santamartasuites.it

€€€

13  

Museo del Novecento

J6 Via Marconi 1 02-8844 4061 M 1, 3 Duomo 1, 2, 3, 12, 14, 24, 27 54 Hours vary, call ahead

The construction of the Arengario palazzo began in the late 1930s as part of a modernization plan for the city. The name *arengario* refers to the place where medieval town councils were held.

The building now houses the Museo del Novecento, which traces the history of 20th-century Italian art with sections devoted to Futurism, Metaphysical Art, Arte Povera and Abstractionism. Works by 20th-century Milanese artists are also featured. Architect Italo Rota's design includes an exterior steel and glass bridge to connect the building to the Palazzo Reale.

Piazza Mercanti and Palazzo della Ragione Fotografia

J6 M1 Cordusio, 1, 3 Duomo 1, 2, 3, 12, 14, 16, 24, 27 54 Palazzo della Ragione Fotografia 9:30am-7:30pm Tue-Sun palazzodellaragione fotografia.it

This corner of the city was the seat of public and civic activities in medieval Milan and also housed the prison. Palazzo della Ragione was built in 1233 by the chief magistrate (and virtual ruler) Oldrado da Tresseno, who is portrayed in a relief by Antelami on the side facing the square. This courthouse is also known as "Broletto Nuovo" to distinguish it from the older Broletto Vecchio near Palazzo Reale. Markets were held under the porticoes, while the Salone dei Giudici on the first floor was used as the law court.

Piazza Mercenti is built around a medieval well, and on one side of the square is the Loggia degli Osii, built by Matteo Visconti in 1316. Next is the Palazzo delle Scuole Palatine (1645), which features statues of St Augustine and the Latin poet Ausonius. The Palazzo dei Panigarola (to the right), rebuilt in the 15th century, was used to register public documents.

In a secluded corner of the square, the Palazzo della Ragione Fotografia occupies a historic 13th-century building. The restored space now hosts some of the city's best photography exhibitions.

In Via Mercanti is the Palazzo dei Giureconsulti, dominated by the Torre del Comune, built by Napo Torriani in 1272.

San Sepolcro

H6 Piazza San Sepolcro M1, 3 Duomo 1, 2, 14 Sep-Jul: 10am-5pm Mon-Fri

San Sepolcro was founded in 1030 in the area of the ancient Roman Forum and rebuilt in 1100 at the time of the second Crusade. The striking Neo-Romanesque façade was built in 1897, while the interior is Baroque. There are two terracotta groups by Agostino De Fondutis (16th century): *Christ Washing His Disciples' Feet* and *The Flagellation of Christ with Caiaphas and St Peter*. The only extant part of the 1030 church is the Romanesque crypt, with a sculpture group of the *Deposition* by the De Fondutis school in the apse.

PICTURE PERFECT
Medieval Piazza Mercanti

Stand in front of the 16th-century pit in Piazza Mercanti around sunset for a great shot, capturing the beauty of this medieval piazza's fine architecture at golden hour.

Palazzo Borromeo

H6 Piazza Borromeo 7 M1 Cordusio 1, 2, 3, 14, 16, 27 Courtyard only

This early 15th-century residence was badly damaged

Bromante's innovative stuccowork apse, Santa Maria presso San Satiro

←

The 16th-century well at the centre of Piazza Mercanti

by the 1943 bombings and the only remaining original architectural element is the ogival portal, with leaf decoration and the Borromeo family's coat of arms. The partly rebuilt second courtyard has porticoes on three sides and on the fourth is the original decoration with the family motto *Humilitas*. This courtyard leads to the 15th-century Sala dei Giochi, which is decorated with frescoes of the games played by the aristocracy of the time, including the Game of Tarot.

17

San Giorgio al Palazzo

H7 Piazza San Giorgio 2 02-805 7148 2, 14 7:30am-noon & 3:30-6pm daily

Founded in 750, this church was named after an ancient Roman *palatium* that stood here. It was radically changed in 1623 and 1800–21 by the architects Richini and Cagnola respectively, and little remains of the original or Romanesque (1129) structures. The third chapel in the right-hand aisle contains paintings by Bernardino Luini (1516) with scenes from the Passion. On the vault there is a fresco of the Crucifixion.

18

Santa Maria presso San Satiro

J6 Via Speronari 3 02-874 683 M1, 3 Duomo 1, 2, 3, 14, 16, 24, 27 54 7:30am-noon & 3-6:30pm Mon-Fri, 3:30-7pm Sat, 7:30am-noon & 3-7pm Sun

The original nucleus of this church, founded by archbishop Ansperto da Biassono, dates from 876. The only remnant is the Sacello della Pietà (Chapel of Pity), which was altered by the architect, Bramante, in the 15th century, and the Lombard Romanesque bell tower. In 1478, Bramante was asked to rebuild the church to salvage a 13th-century fresco on the façade, which was said to have miraculous powers. Bramante set it on the high altar, solving the problem of lack of space by creating a sort of *trompe l'oeil* apse of only 97 cm (38 in) with stuccowork and frescoes. The transept leads to the Chapel of San Satiro with a terracotta *Pietà* (c 1482). In the right-hand aisle is the baptismal font decorated by De Fondutis.

EAT

Cracco

Celebrity chef Carlo Cracco serves delicious Milanese food with a twist (think risotto with mascarpone, kohlrabi, herring and bitter cocoa) at this Michelin-starred restaurant. There's also an excellent bakery and a well-stocked wine cellar.

J6 Galleria Vittorio Emanuele II Sat & Mon D, Sun ristorantecracco.it

€€€

A SHORT WALK
PIAZZA DEL DUOMO

Distance 2 km (1 mile) **Time** 30 minutes
Nearest metro 1, 3 Duomo

Piazza del Duomo, designed by Giuseppe Mengoni and opened in 1865 after protracted difficulties, is the ideal starting point for a visit to Milan's historic centre. The area is usually packed with visitors fascinated by the "great machine of the Duomo", as Alessandro Manzoni describes the cathedral in *The Betrothed*. Along this route, you'll see numerous spots where the Milanese like to meet for an aperitif, especially on Sunday morning. Corso Vittorio Emanuele II, meanwhile, attracts a younger crowd with its cinemas and many shops.

The church of **San Fedele** (p65), *a typical example of Counter-Reformation architecture, is popular with the old Milanese aristocracy.*

Casa degli Omenoni (p65)

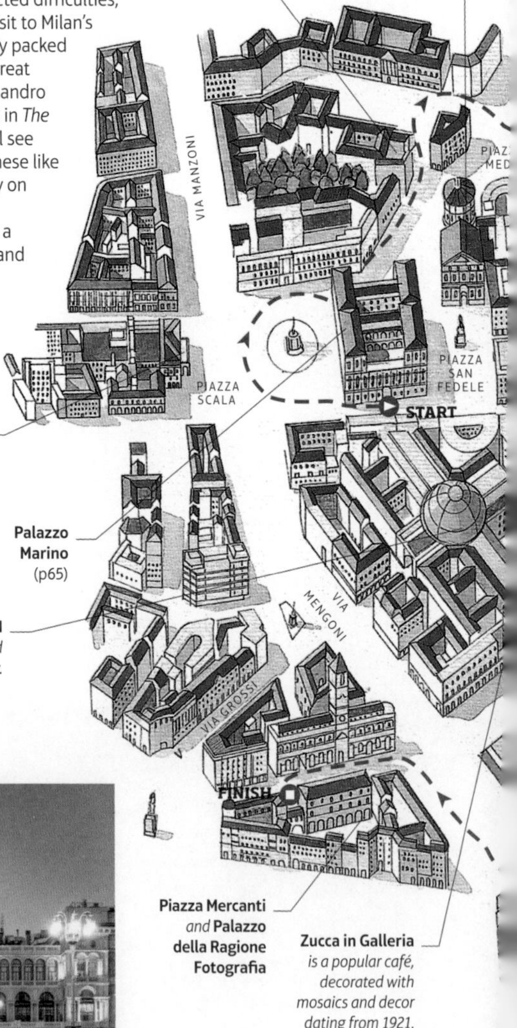

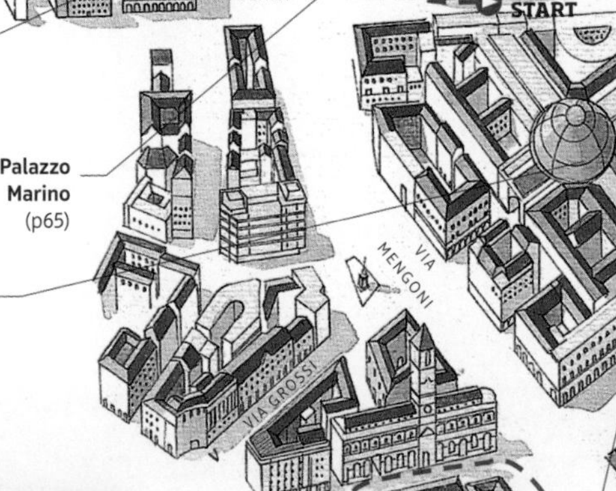

Teatro alla Scala (p60) *was the first monument in Milan to be rebuilt after the 1943 bombings.*

Palazzo Marino (p65)

Galleria Vittorio Emanuele II *was one of the first iron and glass constructions in Italy.*

Piazza Mercanti *and* **Palazzo della Ragione Fotografia**

Zucca in Galleria *is a popular café, decorated with mosaics and decor dating from 1921.*

←

Façade of the Galleria Vittorio Emanuele II shopping arcade

In the middle of Piazza Meda is a large rotating disc, sculpted by Arnaldo Pomodoro (1980).

San Carlo *was built in 1838–47.*

Locator Map
For more detail see p54

Piazza del Liberty (p66) *was named after the Art Nouveau ("Liberty" in Italian) façade at No 8. It was restored after the 1943 bombing.*

The third-largest church in the world after St Peter's and Seville Cathedral, the **Duomo** (p56) *towers over the large square named after it.*

Piazza Fontana *was the target of terrorism in 1969: a bomb in the Banca dell'Agricoltura killed 16 people. In the centre of the square is a fountain designed by Piermarini in 1783.*

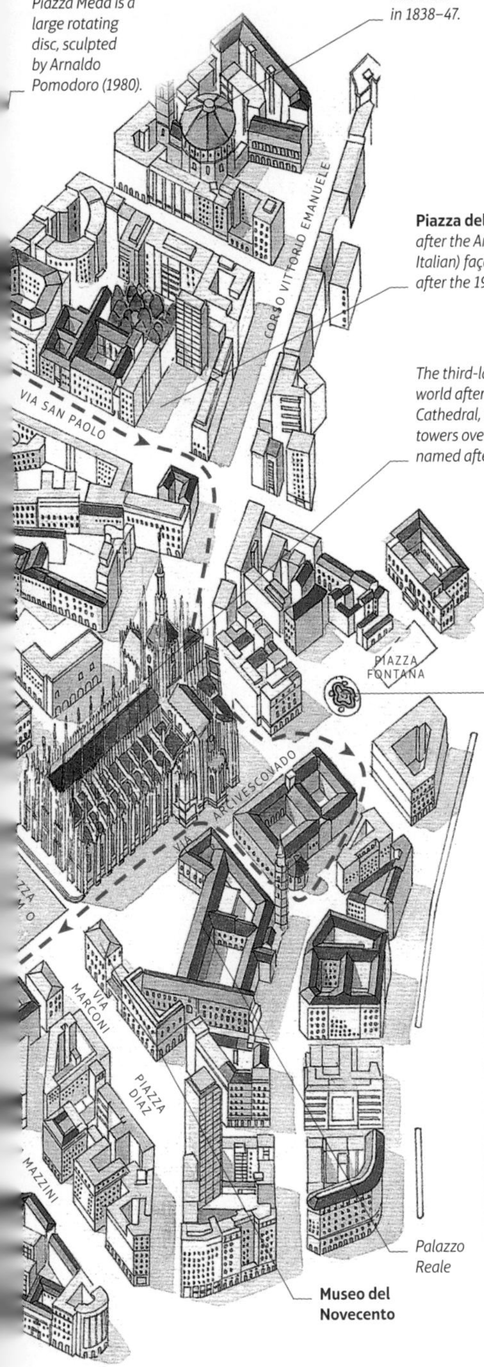

0 metres 100
0 yards 100
N

Palazzo Reale

Museo del Novecento

↑ The beautiful 18th-century Neo-Classical fountain at the centre of Piazza Fontana

A SHORT WALK
MILAN'S HIDDEN GLORIES

Distance 3 km (2 miles) **Time** 45 minutes
Nearest metro 1, 3 Duomo

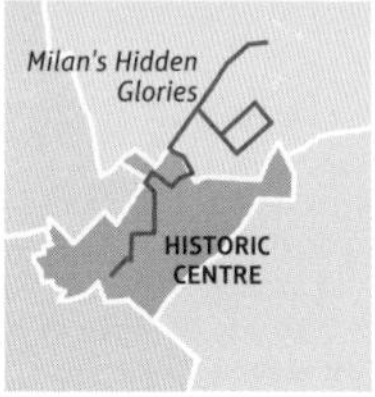

Milan's beauty is not immediately obvious. With a few exceptions, such as the Duomo and the Galleria, the city's glories are hidden. This walk will take you to the heart of Milan's historic centre, from church gems to fantastical façades tucked just off busy thoroughfares, and from designer boutiques to the town-houses of Milan's 19th-century elite.

Locator Map
For more detail see p54 and p136

↑ The 9th-century church of Santa Maria presso San Satiro

The magnificent **Grand Hotel et de Milan** *is where Giuseppe Verdi died in 1901.*

The splendid **Teatro alla Scala** *(p60) opera house is adjoined by the Museo Teatrale.*

The **Galleria Vittorio Emanuele II**, *a 19th-century shopping arcade, has a glass-roofed atrium.*

The **Duomo's** *roof offers spectacular panoramic views.*

Encased by modern buildings, the jewel-box church of **Santa Maria presso San Satiro** *(p69) can be hard to find (it's down an alley off Via Torino).*

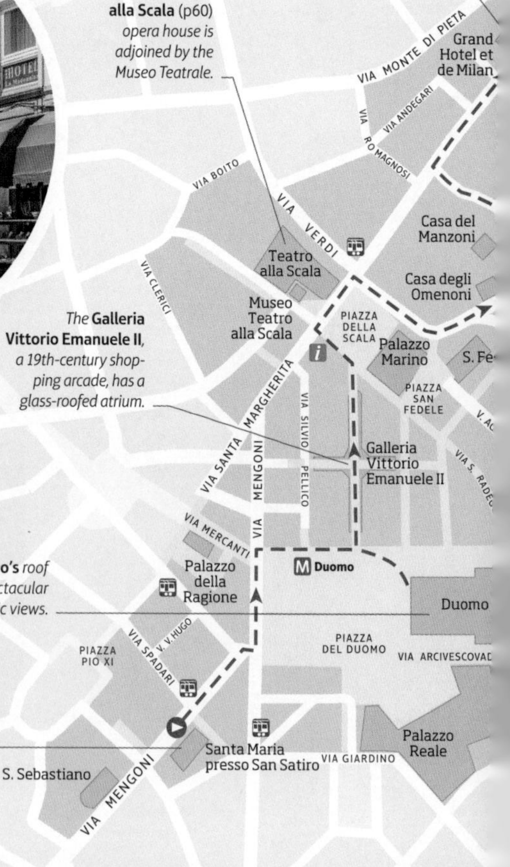

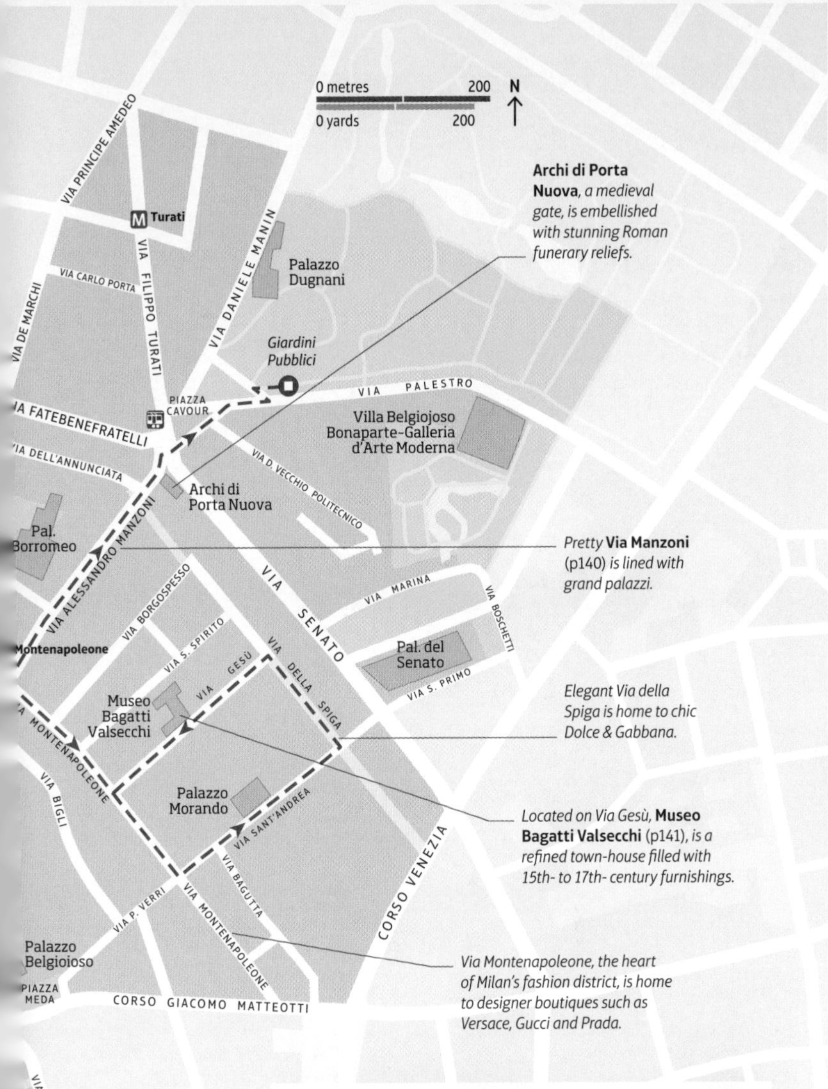

0 metres 200
0 yards 200
N

Archi di Porta Nuova, *a medieval gate, is embellished with stunning Roman funerary reliefs.*

Pretty **Via Manzoni** *(p140) is lined with grand palazzi.*

Elegant Via della Spiga is home to chic Dolce & Gabbana.

Located on Via Gesù, **Museo Bagatti Valsecchi** *(p141), is a refined town-house filled with 15th- to 17th- century furnishings.*

Via Montenapoleone, the heart of Milan's fashion district, is home to designer boutiques such as Versace, Gucci and Prada.

Turati
Via Principe Amedeo
Via Carlo Porta
Via Filippo Turati
Via Daniele Manin
Via de Marchi
Palazzo Dugnani
Giardini Pubblici
Via Palestro
Piazza Cavour
Via Fatebenefratelli
Via dell'Annunciata
Villa Belgiojoso Bonaparte-Galleria d'Arte Moderna
Via D. Vecchio Politecnico
Archi di Porta Nuova
Pal. Borromeo
Via Alessandro Manzoni
Via Senato
Via Marina
Via Boschetti
Via Borgospesso
Montenapoleone
Via S. Spirito
Via Gesù
Via della Spiga
Pal. del Senato
Via S. Primo
Museo Bagatti Valsecchi
Via Montenapoleone
Via Bigli
Palazzo Morando
Via Sant'Andrea
Corso Venezia
Via Bagutta
Via P. Verri
Via Montenapoleone
Palazzo Belgioioso
Piazza Meda
Corso Giacomo Matteotti
Via S. Paolo
Via Pattari

The Versace store in the heart of Milan's fashion district

The imposing Castello Sforzesco at night

NORTHWEST MILAN

Dominating the area that lies northwest of the Duomo is the imposing red-brick Castello Sforzesco, whose construction began in the woods outside of the city walls during the 14th century. The fortress was built to defend the Historic Centre from attacks and barracks were later added to accommodate the several foreign powers that ruled Milan throughout the centuries, including the Spanish, Austrians and French, leading to the castle being seen as a symbol of tyranny by the Milanese.

The area surrounding the fortress also became a canvas for rulers to flex their power. It was during the reign of Napoleon that the Neoclassical Arco della Pace was built. His French influence extended further along Corso Sempione, north of Parco Sempione, which was modelled on Paris's grand, leafy boulevards. Later, in the 19th century, the area attracted attention and investment. The now deteriorating castle was saved from demolition by Luca Beltrami who transformed it into a museum centre. Piazza Affari, south of Castello Sforzesco, became the home of Borsa Valori, Italy's most important stock exchange, while further west the Corso Magenta residential district around Santa Maria delle Grazie was constructed. In the 20th century, international migration to the area north of Parco Sempione saw the establishment of Chinatown, adding to the diverse and cultural identity of the district today.

NORTHWEST MILAN

Must Sees

❶ Castello Sforzesco
❷ Leonardo da Vinci's Last Supper

Experience More

❸ Santa Maria delle Grazie
❹ CityLife
❺ Casa degli Atellani and Vigna di Leonardo
❻ Parco Sempione
❼ Acquario Civico
❽ Arena Civica
❾ Arco della Pace
❿ Triennale Design Museum
⓫ Corso Sempione
⓬ Fieramilanocity
⓭ Meazza (San Siro) Stadium
⓮ Chinatown
⓯ Corso Magenta
⓰ Palazzo Litta
⓱ Civico Museo Archeologico
⓲ San Maurizio
⓳ Piazza Cordusio
⓴ Certosa di Garegnano
㉑ Piazza Affari
㉒ Via Brisa

Eat

① Ravioleria Sarpi
② Little Lamb
③ Savana

Drink

④ Mit Café
⑤ Rufus Cocktail Bar
⑥ Café Etniko

Stay

⑦ Hotel Tiziano
⑧ Antica Locanda dei Mercanti
⑨ Hotel Palazzo delle Stelline

Shop

⑩ Officina Profumo-Farmaceutica di Santa Maria Novella
⑪ ViaTivoli
⑫ Figus Designer
⑬ Camicissima

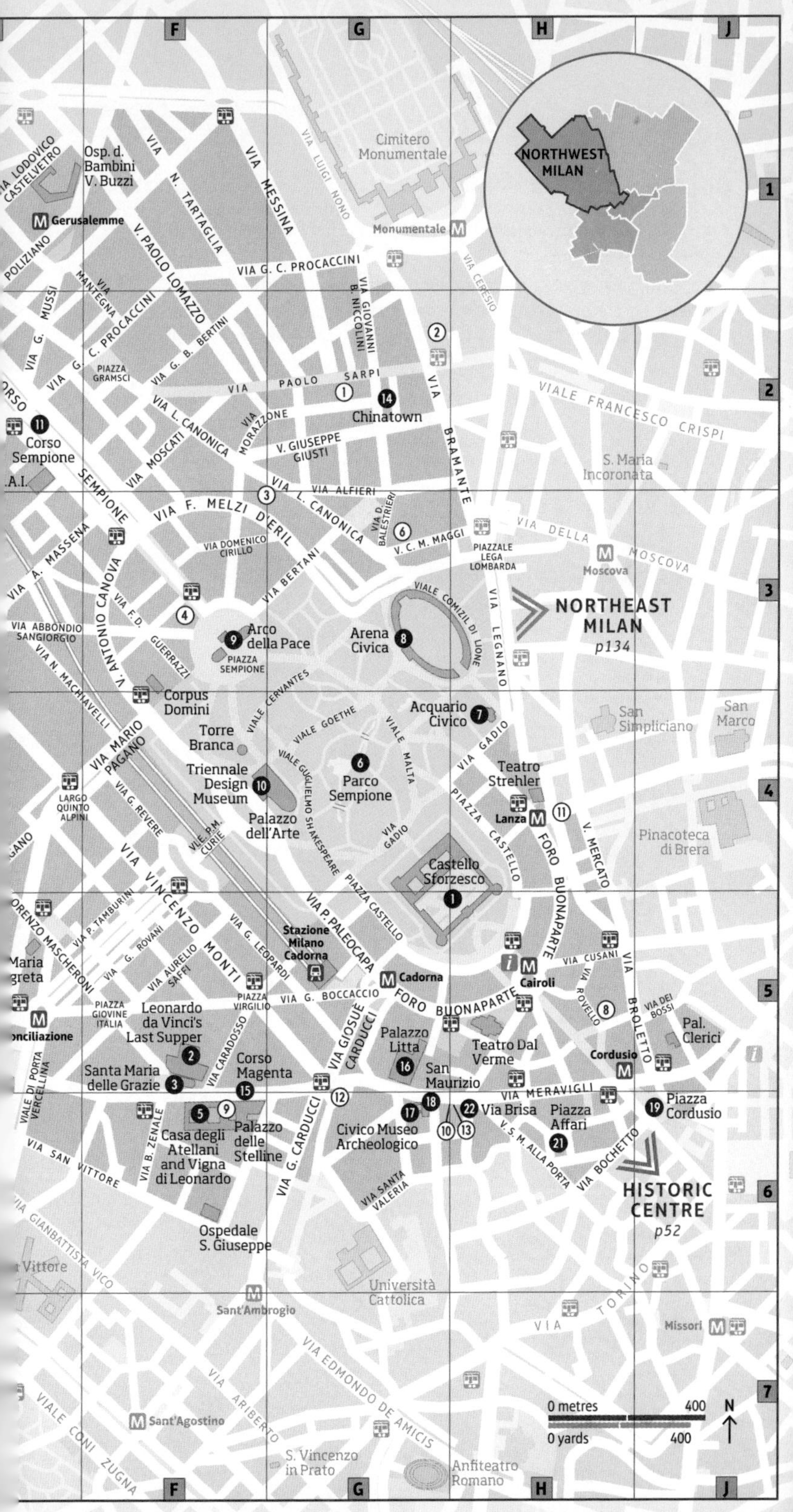

F
G
H
J
1
2
3
4
5
6
7
NORTHWEST MILAN
NORTHEAST MILAN
p134
HISTORIC CENTRE
p52
Cimitero Monumentale
Monumentale
Gerusalemme
Osp. d. Bambini V. Buzzi
Chinatown
Corso Sempione
Arco della Pace
Arena Civica
Acquario Civico
Torre Branca
Triennale Design Museum
Palazzo dell'Arte
Parco Sempione
Castello Sforzesco
Teatro Strehler
Lanza
Moscova
S. Maria Incoronata
San Simpliciano
San Marco
Pinacoteca di Brera
Corpus Domini
Stazione Milano Cadorna
Cadorna
Cairoli
Cordusio
Pal. Clerici
Leonardo da Vinci's Last Supper
Santa Maria delle Grazie
Corso Magenta
Palazzo Litta
San Maurizio
Teatro Dal Verme
Via Brisa
Piazza Affari
Piazza Cordusio
Casa degli Atellani and Vigna di Leonardo
Palazzo delle Stelline
Civico Museo Archeologico
Ospedale S. Giuseppe
Università Cattolica
Sant'Ambrogio
Missori
Sant'Agostino
S. Vincenzo in Prato
Anfiteatro Romano
Conciliazione
VIA MESSINA
VIA PAOLO SARPI
VIA BRAMANTE
VIALE FRANCESCO CRISPI
VIA DELLA MOSCOVA
VIA LEGNANO
FORO BUONAPARTE
VIA VINCENZO MONTI
VIA EDMONDO DE AMICIS
VIA TORINO
0 metres 400
0 yards 400
N

CASTELLO SFORZESCO

H5 Piazza Castello M1 Cairoli, Cadorna, 2 Lanza, Cadorna 1, 4 50, 57, 61, 94 Castello courtyards: 7am-7:30pm daily (winter: to 6pm); Musei Civici: 9am-5:30pm Tue-Sun (last adm: 5pm) 1 Jan, Easter, Easter Mon, 1 May, 25 Dec milanocastello.it

With its imposing courtyards and landscaped grounds, this historic fortress and cultural complex houses several of the city's state museums, with displays shedding light on Milan's rich history and cultural heritage.

Built in 1368 by Galeazzo II Visconti as a fortress, the Sforza castle was enlarged in the 14th century by Gian Galeazzo and then by Filippo Maria, who transformed it into a splendid ducal palace. It was partly demolished in 1447 during the Ambrosian Republic. Francesco Sforza, who became lord of Milan in 1450, and his son Ludovico il Moro made the castle the home of one of the most magnificent courts in Renaissance Italy, graced by Bramante and Leonardo da Vinci. Under Spanish and Austrian domination, the Castello went into gradual decline as it resumed its original military function. It was saved from demolition by the architect Luca Beltrami, who from 1893 to 1904 restored it and converted it into an important museum centre *(p80)* dedicated to preserving the arts.

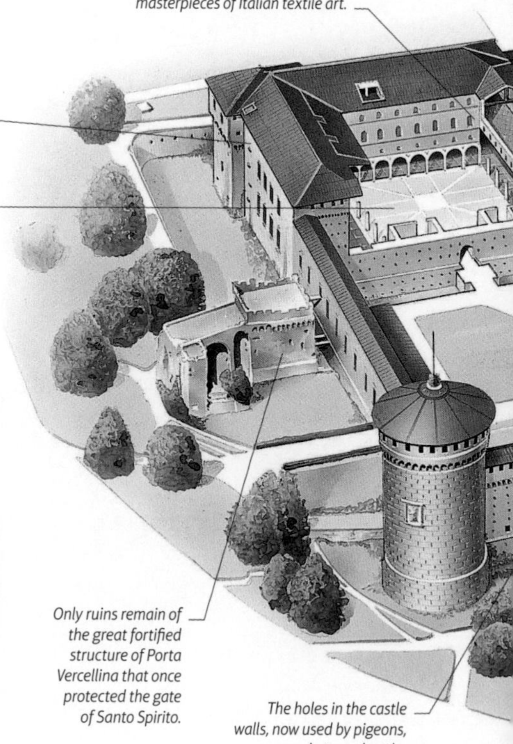

The 12 Trivulzio Tapestries designed by Bramantino, depicting the months and signs of the zodiac, are masterpieces of Italian textile art.

The Torre Castellana was where Ludovico il Moro kept his treasury. It was "guarded" by a figure of Argus, in a fresco by Bramantino at the Sala del Tesoro entrance.

The Cortile della Rocchetta was the last refuge in the event of a siege. The oldest wing (1456–66), opposite the entrance to the Corte Ducale, was the apartment of Ludovico and his wife before he became duke.

Only ruins remain of the great fortified structure of Porta Vercellina that once protected the gate of Santo Spirito.

The holes in the castle walls, now used by pigeons, were made to anchor the scaffolding used for maintenance work.

Did You Know?

The Filarete Tower collapsed in 1521 when the gunpowder kept there exploded.

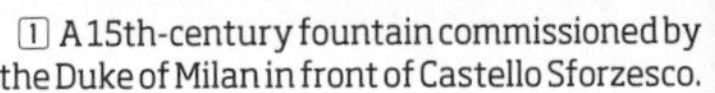

1 A 15th-century fountain commissioned by the Duke of Milan in front of Castello Sforzesco.

2 The castle's open, pebbled courtyards, surrounded by scenic arcades.

3 Ceiling of a hall in the castle's Museum of Ancient Art, featuring a biscione serpent consuming a human figure, the emblem of the House of Visconti.

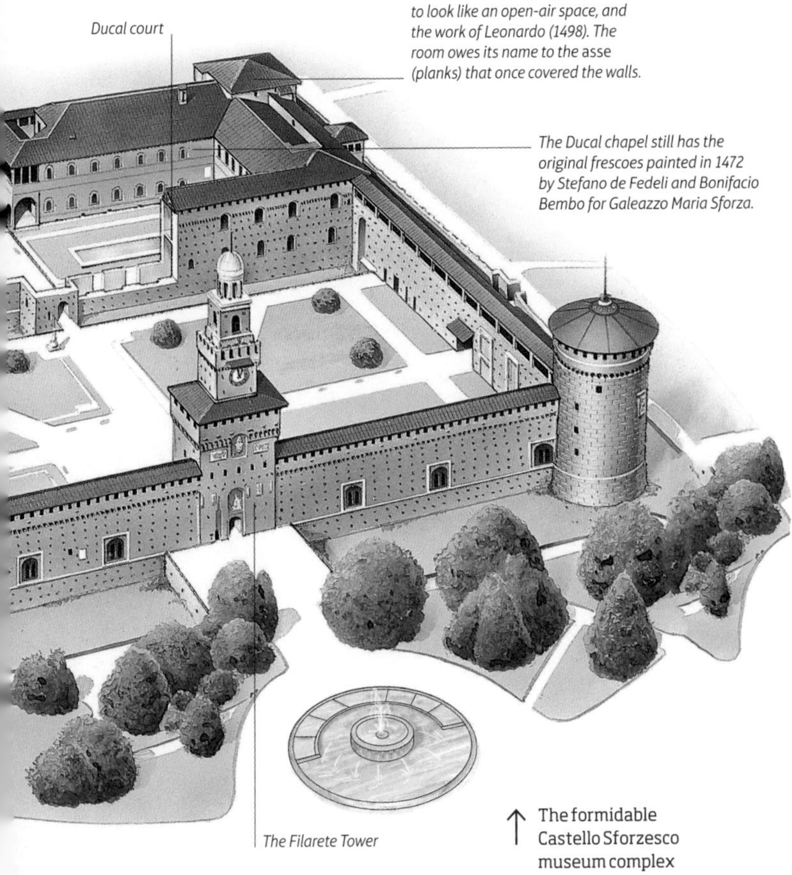

Ducal court

Sala delle Asse is a pergola painted to look like an open-air space, and the work of Leonardo (1498). The room owes its name to the asse (planks) that once covered the walls.

The Ducal chapel still has the original frescoes painted in 1472 by Stefano de Fedeli and Bonifacio Bembo for Galeazzo Maria Sforza.

The Filarete Tower

↑ The formidable Castello Sforzesco museum complex

↑ Biblical tableaux in the Civiche Raccolte d'Arte Antica

EXPLORING THE CIVIC MUSEUMS

Since 1896, the Castello Sforzesco has housed the Civic Museums, with one of the largest collections of art in Milan. The Corte Ducale is home to the Raccolte di Arte Antica and the art and sculpture gallery, as well as a furniture collection, while the Rocchetta holds decorative arts such as ceramics and the Trivulzio Tapestries. The photography archive and the Achille Bertarelli Collection, featuring about 700,000 prints, books and photographs from the 19th century, are here too. Major institutions, such as the Art Library and the Trivulziana Library, are in the same building.

INSIDER TIP
Visit for Free

Art aficionados on a budget can explore the Civic Museums for free by visiting after 2pm on the first or third Tuesday of the month. Alternatively, you can plan your trip for the first Sunday of the month, when access is free all day.

Civiche Raccolte d'Arte Antica

The displays making up the collections of Ancient Art are arranged in chronological order (except for Room 6) in rooms facing the Corte Ducale.

In Room 1 is the Sarcophagus of Lambrate (late 4th century) and a bust of the Empress Theodora (6th century). The main attraction in Room 2 is the *Mausoleum of Bernabò Visconti*, sculpted by Bonino da Campione in 1363 for the lord of Milan. He is portrayed on horseback between Wisdom and Fortitude.

Room 3 has a window with a 14th-century Tuscan *Benedictory Christ*. Room 4 is given over to Giovanni di Balduccio, with fragments from the façade of Santa Maria di Brera (14th century). A passage leads to the Cappelletta, dominated by a 14th-century wooden Crucifix.

Room 6 features reliefs from the Porta Romana (1171) narrating the *Return of the Milanese after Being Driven out of Town by Barbarossa* and *St Ambrose Expelling the Arians*. In Room 7 is the *Gonfalone* (Standard) of Milan designed by Giuseppe Meda in 1566.

The Sala delle Asse is known for its fine fresco decoration on the vault, designed by Leonardo da Vinci in 1498. Next is the Sala dei Ducali, dominated by Agostino di

→ Bonino da Campione's *Mausoleum of Bernabò Visconti*

ARTWORK RESTORATION

The Sala delle Asse is an exceptional display of Leonardo da Vinci's creativity. The artist decorated the tempera-on-plaster *trompe l'oeil* of intricate vines on the vaulted ceiling in 1498, but is said to have left an original, unfinished sketch of twisting roots while fleeing the French invasion of Milan in 1499. Restoration work was paused in 2020 to mark the 500th anniversary of Leonardo's death, but the room is regularly closed to allow preservation work to continue.

Duccio's relief of *St Sigismund on a Journey* from the Malatesta Temple in Rimini. Left is the door to the ducal chapel, with a braided Virgin, *Madonna del Coazzone*, a 15th-century work attributed to Pietro Antonio Solari.

Late 15th-century sculpture is featured in the Sala delle Colombine, with the Visconti coat of arms and motto, *A Bon Droit*. One of the finest works here is Antonio Mantegazza's *Kneeling Apostles*.

The 1463 Portale del Banco Mediceo (portal) in the Sala Verde is attributed to Filarete. This room also has some fine armour. The last room, the Sala degli Scarlioni, has a famous sculpture: Gaston de Foix's funerary monument crafted by Agostino Busti, known as "Il Bambaia".

In the Ospedale Spagnolo is the Museo della Pietà Rondanini, which houses Michelangelo's, the *Rondanini Pietà*, depicting the Mother of Christ supporting the heavy body of her Son.

Furniture Collection and Pinacoteca

"From the Sforza to Design" is the name given to this collection showcasing the traditions from which Milanese furniture design has grown. Beginning with court and church furniture from the 15th to the 16th centuries and Baroque inlaid furniture, alongside collections from aristocratic Milanese families, the collection ends with 20th-century pieces by important Milanese designers such as Giò Ponti and Ettore Sottsass.

The art gallery houses works in chronological order from the mid-15th to the 18th centuries. It begins in Room 20, the former Falconry Tower, with 14th- and 15th-century Italian paintings, while Rooms 21 and 22 contain works by Milanese artists such as Vincenzo Foppa. Room 23 contains major works such as Mantegna's *Madonna in Glory* and *Saint John* (1497), Antonello da Messina's *Saint Benedict* (c 1470–73), Lorenzo Veneziano's *Resurrection* (1371), Giovanni Bellini's *Madonna and Child* (c 1460–65) and *Madonna of Humility* by Filippo Lippi (1430).

Room 24 features Correggio's *Portrait of a Man Reading* along with examples of Cremonese Mannerism, an Italian art movement founded during the Renaissance period. In Room 25, Venetian paintings are displayed, including examples by Titian and Tintoretto, which contrast with pieces from the 16th-century schools of Brescia and Bergamo. Room 26, the former Salone della Cancellaria, houses works by "plague painters" such as Morazzone and Il Cerano (Crespi), finishing with two views of Venice by Canaletto.

Applied Arts Collection

Return to the entrance for access to the first floor to see a collection of old musical instruments, which includes a Flemish double virginal with ottavino. Between these two rooms is the impressive Sala della Balla (ballroom), with Bramantino's splendid Trivulzio Tapestries (1503–09), representing the 12 months of the year. On the second floor (Rooms 28–32) is a large collection of fine Italian and European glass, ceramics, majolica and porcelain, ivory works, gold medieval jewellery and scientific instruments.

Lastly, in the basement of the Corte Ducale are a Prehistoric and an Egyptian section with funerary cult objects, including a tomb from around 640 BCE.

↑ String instruments on display in the Applied Arts Collection

Christ's last meal in Leonardo's magnificent *Last Supper* painting

LEONARDO DA VINCI'S LAST SUPPER

F5 Piazza Santa Maria delle Grazie 2 M1, 2 Cadorna 16 18 8:15am-7pm Tue-Sun (book ahead online) Public hols cenacolovinciano.org

This masterpiece was painted by Leonardo da Vinci for Ludovico il Moro in the refectory of Santa Maria delle Grazie *(p84)* in 1495–7. Titled the *Last Supper*, the artwork portrays the moment just after Christ has uttered the words, "One of you will betray me", capturing the expressions and body language of his disciples in impressively vivid detail.

Leonardo da Vinci's *Last Supper* depicts Jesus composed in the centre, and all the disciples around the table shocked and protesting. That is, except Judas (fifth from the left) who drops his bread and recoils in guilty horror.

The fragility of the blotchy and faded image means that visits are limited to 15 minutes, but it is amazing there is anything left at all. Leonardo painted in tempera to achieve the subtle nuances in his work, rather than the standard, longer-lasting fresco technique in which pigment is mixed with the plaster, and the work began to deteriorate almost immediately. Later, a door was knocked through the picture, then Napoleon's troops used the wall for target practice and, in 1943, the monastery was destroyed by a bomb. Fortunately, the work, protected by sandbags, survived. There have been many attempts to restore the *Last Supper,* beginning in 1726, but in retouching the picture further damage was done. The seventh restoration ended in spring 1999: although it lacks the splendour of the original, it is at least genuine.

On the opposite wall of the refectory is Donato Montorfano's fresco of the *Crucifixion*, commissioned by the Dominican monks in 1495. In this dense composition, the despairing Mary Magdalene hugs the cross while the soldiers on the right throw dice for Christ's robe. On either side of the *Crucifixion*, under the cross, Leonardo added the signed portraits – now almost invisible – of Ludovico il Moro, his wife Beatrice and their children.

↑ A sketch of Judas by Leonardo, preserved in Windsor's Royal Library

← Donato Montorfano's *Crucifixion*, on the opposite wall of the refectory

SKETCHES OF THE APOSTLES

The *Last Supper* is famous for the gesturing hands of the Apostles, so expressive that they seem to "speak". It's thought that Leonardo wandered around Milan in search of faces to use for the Apostles. The agitation of the Apostles appears to be a deliberate contrast to the serene figure of Christ.

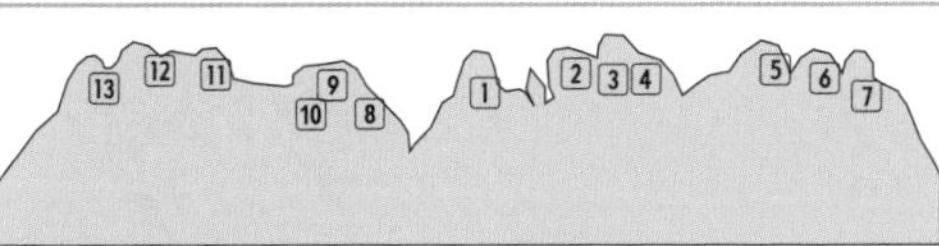

CHRIST AND THE APOSTLES

1 Christ
2 Thomas
3 James the Greater
4 Philip
5 Matthew
6 Thaddaeus
7 Simon
8 John
9 Peter
10 Judas
11 Andrew
12 James the Lesser
13 Bartholomew

EXPERIENCE MORE

Santa Maria delle Grazie

F5 Piazza Santa Maria delle Grazie M1, 2 Cadorna 16 02-4676 111 9am-12:20pm & 3-5:30pm Mon-Sat, 3-5:50pm Sun

Construction of this church, designed by Guiniforte Solari, began in 1463 and was completed in 1490. Two years later, Ludovico il Moro asked Bramante to change the church into the family mausoleum: Solari's apse section was demolished and replaced by a Renaissance apse. After il Moro lost power in 1500, the Dominicans continued to decorate the church, later assisted by the court of Inquisition, which had moved here in 1558. Restoration was undertaken only in the late 19th century. In 1943, a bomb destroyed the main cloister, but the apse and the room containing Leonardo da Vinci's *Last Supper (p82)* were miraculously left intact; restoration work has continued since then.

On the exterior, Solari's brick façade is worthy of note. The doorway was designed by Bramante; it is preceded by a porch supported by Corinthian columns and the lunette has a painting by Leonardo with the Madonna between Ludovico and his wife, Beatrice d'Este. The sides and polygonal apse are also of interest.

As you enter the church, you notice the difference between Solari's nave, which echoes Lombard Gothic architecture, and Bramante's design for the apse, which is larger, better lit and almost bare of decoration. The painting decoration of the aisle walls is by Bernardino Butinone and Donato Montorfano (1482–6).

The Della Torre chapel is the first one in the right-hand aisle: the altar has a 15th-century fresco, while to the left is the tomb of Giacomo Della Torre. The fourth chapel, dedicated to Santa Corona, has frescoes by Gaudenzio Ferrari. In the next chapel is a *Crucifixion* by Giovanni Demìo (1542).

The apse, decorated only with graffiti to maintain the purity of the architectural volumes, is a perfect cube crowned by a hemisphere. It was built to house the tomb of Ludovico il Moro and Beatrice d'Este, but the work never reached Santa Maria delle Grazie (it is now in the Charterhouse of Pavia). The dome is rich with Marian symbols, while the Doctors of the Church appear in the roundels in the pendentives. The carved and inlaid wooden stalls of the choir are lovely.

A door on the right leads to a cloister, known as Chiostrino delle Rane because of the frogs *(rane)* in the central basin. The cloister leads to the old sacristy, with

LEONARDO DA VINCI IN MILAN

Leonardo arrived in Milan in 1482 to work with Ludovico Sforza, the ruler of the city and a patron of the arts. He presented Sforza with a long letter detailing his abilities, and successfully performed with a horse-head shaped lyre that he had designed and made by hand. Their relationship grew and Sforza later commissioned the *Last Supper (p82)* in 1495.

its painted wardrobes, one of which conceals a secret underground passageway, used by Ludovico to come from the Castello on horseback.

Back in the church, the chapels in the north aisle begin with the Madonna delle Grazie chapel, with Cerano's *Madonna Freeing Milan of the Plague* (1631) on the entrance archway. The altarpiece, *Madonna delle Grazie*, dates from the 15th century. The sixth chapel has a *Holy Family with St Catherine* by Paris Bordone, and the first chapel contains the cloak of St Catherine of Siena.

4 

CityLife

C3 Piazza Tre Torri
5 Tre Torri 1, 78, 19, 68
city-life.it

Created in the early 2000s as part of a redevelopment plan, the avant-garde CityLife neighbourhood is now a symbol of Milan's sustainable and modern urban life.

Located in the heart of the city, it features three office towers, known as the Straight, the Curved and the Crooked, designed by renowned architects Arata Isozaki, Daniel Libeskind and Zaha Hadid respectively. Standing up to 209 m (685 ft) tall, the buildings are a key part of the city's skyline and are surrounded by 17 ha (43 acres) of green space and the largest pedestrianized area in Milan.

There are several residential buildings, designed by Libeskind and Hadid, which are home to Italian celebrities and football stars. There is also a large shopping centre with a cinema. The public park displays numerous art installations and features a golf course, playgrounds and 5 km (3 miles) of bike lanes.

The wide brick façade of Santa Maria delle Grazie

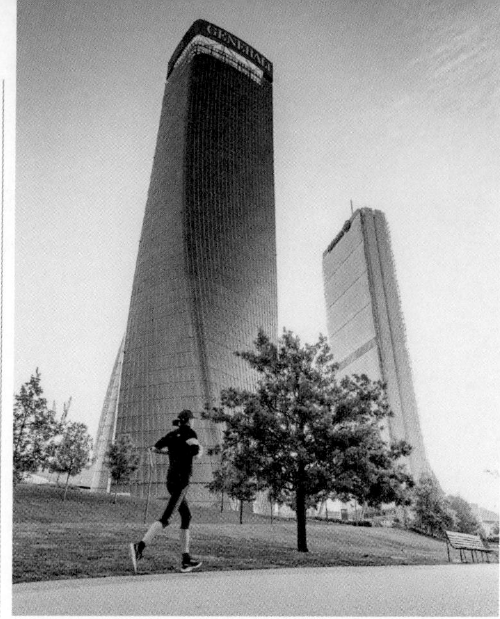

↑ Jogging past soaring skyscrapers in CityLife neighbourhood's public park

5   

Casa degli Atellani and Vigna di Leonardo

F6 Corso Magenta 65
1, 2 Cadorna 16, 19
9am-6pm Tue-Sun 1 Jan, 1 May, 2 Jun, 25 & 26 Dec
vignadileonardo.com

Ludovico il Moro Sforza, duke of Milan, wanted to create a residential neighbourhood where he could establish his most loyal followers. In 1490, he gave houses to the Atellani family of Sforza courtiers and to Leonardo da Vinci. In 1498, he also gave Leonardo a vineyard. Casa degli Atellani is one of the few traces left of Ludovico's Renaissance dream. Over the course of the 20th century, it was transformed by Piero Portaluppi, a major Milanese architect, while still retaining its grandeur. Both the house and the vineyard in the garden are open to the public.

STAY

Hotel Tiziano

A 1930s building with a garden, gym and kids' area. Pets are welcome.

D4 Via Tiziano 6
minihotel.it

Antica Locanda dei Mercanti

Stay in luxurious rooms with private terraces.

H5 Via San Tomaso 6
locanda.it

Hotel Palazzo delle Stelline

Rooms here centre around a 15th-century cloister and garden.

F6 Corso Magenta 61
hotelpalazzostelline.it

DRINK

Touted as Italy's capital of elegant drinking and aperitivo, Milan is the birthplace of beloved cocktails such as Negroni sbagliato, Ginrosa and the Milanese. Enjoy a tipple at one of these popular bars in the northwest, offering both classic cocktails and modern variations.

Mit Café
F3 Corso Sempione 3 mitmilano.it

Rufus Cocktail Bar
E5 Via Alberto da Giussano 2 rufus cocktailbar.com

Café Etniko
G3 Via Carlo Maria Maggi 14 345 012 2227

6

Parco Sempione

G4 Piazza Castello-Piazza Sempione (eight entrances around perimeter) Ferrovie Nord, Cadorna M1 Cadorna, Cairoli, 2 Lanza, Cadorna 1, 4, 12, 14, 19, 27 18, 43, 57, 58, 61, 94 Mar-Oct: 6:30am-11:30pm daily; Nov-Feb: 6:30am-9pm daily

Although it covers an area of 47 ha (116 acres), this park is only a part of the old Visconti ducal garden, enlarged by the Sforza in the 15th century to make a 300-ha (740-acre) hunting reserve. The area was partly abandoned during Spanish rule, and in the 1800s part of it was used to create a parade ground extending as far as the Arco della Pace.

The present-day layout was the work of Emilio Alemagna, who in 1890–93 designed it along the lines of an English garden. In World War II, the park was used to cultivate wheat, but after the reconstruction period it returned to its former splendour as a locals' haunt, especially in spring and summer, when it plays host to numerous entertainment events. Walking through the park after dark is not advisable.

Among the trees are the monuments to Napoleon III created by Francesco Barzaghi, De Chirico's Metaphysical construction *Mysterious Baths*, a sulphur water fountain near the Arena and the Torre del Parco, a 108-m (354-ft) tower made of steel tubes in 1932 after a design by Giò Ponti.

Did You Know?

Parco Sempione is said to be haunted by Dame Nera, a ghost dressed all in black.

 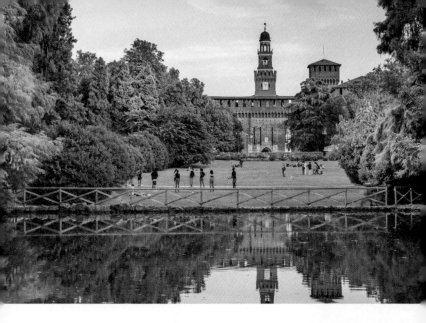

Acquario Civico

H4 Viale Gadio 2 M2 Lanza 2, 4, 12, 14 57 10am-5:30pm Tue-Sun acquariodimilano.it

The Civic Aquarium was built by Sebastiano Locati for the 1906 National Exposition. Its

←

Visitors relaxing in the lush Parco Sempione, the park by Castello Sforzesco

36 tanks house about 100 species (fish, crustaceans, molluscs and echinoderms) typical of the Mediterranean sea and Italian freshwater fauna. There are also rare tropical fish on display. The aquarium museum is home to the Hydrobiological Station, which has a library specializing in the subject.

The aquarium building itself (1906) is a fine example of Art Nouveau architecture and is decorated with Richard-Ginori ceramic tiles and statues of aquatic animals, dominated by Oreste Labò's statue of Neptune.

Arena Civica

G3 Via Legnano, Viale Elvezia M2 Lanza 2, 4, 12, 14 57 For events and exhibitions only

This impressive Neo-Classical amphitheatre, designed in 1806 by Luigi Canonica, was – together with the Arco della Pace, Caselli Daziari and Foro Buonaparte – part of a project to transform the Castello Sforzesco area into a monumental civic centre. Napoleon was present at the Arena inauguration, and it was the venue for various cultural and sports events, from horse and mock Roman chariot races to hot-air balloon launchings, mock naval battles and festivities. With a seating capacity of 30,000, it has also been a football stadium, but San Siro *(p89)* is now the more important ground. The Arena is mainly a venue for athletics (it has a 500-m, 1,640-ft track), concerts and civil weddings.

Arco della Pace

F3 Piazza Sempione 1, 19 43, 57, 61

Work on this Neo-Classical monument was begun by Luigi Cagnola in 1807 to celebrate Napoleon's victories. It was originally called the Arch of Victories, but construction was interrupted and not resumed until 1826 by Francis I of Austria, who had the subjects of the bas-reliefs changed to commemorate the peace of 1815 instead. The Arch of Peace was inaugurated on 10 September 1838 on the occasion of Ferdinand I's coronation as ruler of the Lombardy-Veneto kingdom.

The arch is dressed in Crevola marble and has bas-reliefs depicting episodes of the restoration after Napoleon's fall. On the upper level are personifications of the rivers in the Lombardy-Veneto kingdom: the Po, Ticino, Adda and Tagliamento.

At the top of the monument stands the huge bronze Chariot of Peace, by Abbondio Sangiorgio, surrounded by four Victories on horseback. The chariot originally faced France. However, when Milan was ceded to Austria in 1815, it was turned to face the centre of the city, and was the site of the triumphal entrance into Milan of Vittorio Emanuele II, first king of Italy upon unification in 1861.

→

The grand Arco della Pace, with its bas-reliefs and statues

Triennale Design Museum

F4 Viale Alemagna 6 M1,2 Cadorna 61 11am-8pm Tue-Sun triennale.org

The stately Palazzo dell'Arte, southwest of Parco Sempione, was built by Giovanni Muzio in 1932–3 as a permanent site for the International Exhibition of Decorative Arts. The Triennale show was founded in 1923 to foster the development of Italian arts and architecture.

The building now houses the Triennale Design Museum, offering both a permanent collection and temporary exhibitions showcasing Milan as a centre for cutting-edge design. The museum includes an excellent decorative arts bookstore and a research library with specialized and rare research resources in the fields of architecture, art and fashion. The popular DesignCafé is worth a visit to take in the surroundings and Michelin-starred cuisine. Next to the museum is the Teatro dell'Arte, which was redesigned in 1960.

11

Corso Sempione

E2 1,19 37,43,57

Modelled on the grand boulevards of Paris, Corso Sempione was the first stage of a road built by Napoleon to link the city with Lake Maggiore, Switzerland and France via the Simplon Pass.

The first section, starting at the Arco della Pace *(p87)*, is pedestrianized. The Corso is lined with late 19th-century and early 20th-century houses and is the main thoroughfare in a vast quarter. The initial stretch (towards the park) is considered an elegant area, with good shops, bars and restaurants, the headquarters of Milanese banks and Italian state radio and TV, RAI (at No 27). Opposite, at No 36, is a residence designed by Giuseppe Terragni and Pietro Lingeri in 1935, one of the first examples of Rationalist architecture in Milan.

The semicircular Via Canova and Via Melzi d'Eril cross the Corso, every angle of which offers a different view of the Arco della Pace.

Fieramilanocity

B1 Largo Domodossola 1 M5 Portello, 1, 5 Lotto 27 37, 48, 68, 78 For exhibitions only fieramilano.it

The Fiera Campionaria, or Trade Fair, was founded in 1920 to stimulate the domestic market in postwar Italy. It was originally located near Porta Venezia , but in 1923 was moved to the ground behind the Castello Sforzesco *(p78)*. It was fitted out with permanent pavilions and buildings, many of which were damaged or destroyed in World War II. Some original Art Nouveau buildings have survived at the entrance in Via Domodossola and the Palazzo dello Sport (sports arena). The old main entrance to

↓ The unusual sloping roof of the Fieramilano exhibition centre.

↑ San Siro Stadium, teeming with fans cheering for the Italian football team

2026

The year San Siro stadium hosts the Winter Olympics' opening ceremony.

the Fiera is in Piazza Giulio Cesare, which is dominated by a Four Seasons fountain, placed there in 1927.

One of the leading exhibition centres in Europe, the Fiera di Milano is a symbol of Milanese industriousness. It hosts 78 specialist international shows attracting 2.5 million visitors every year.

Rho, a town located just outside Milan, now holds most trade fairs at an innovative centre known as Fieramilano.

Meazza (San Siro) Stadium

B3 Stadium: Piazzale A Moratti; museum: gate 14 M5 San Siro Stadio 16 49 9:30am-7pm daily sansirostadium.com

Named after Giuseppe Meazza, the famous footballer who played for the local teams, Inter and AC Milan, Italy's top stadium is commonly known as San Siro, after the surrounding district. It was built in 1926, rebuilt in the 1950s with a capacity of 85,000, and then renovated in 1990, when another ring of tiers and a roof were added. The stadium and changing rooms can be visited on the museum tour.

Chinatown

G2 Via Paolo Sarpi M5 Monumentale 62, 91, 92

The history of Milan's Chinese district goes as far back as the 1920s, when a group of people from the Zhejiang region of China arrived in the city. They settled around Via Canonica and Via Paolo Sarpi to sell goods including silk, clothing and leather. By the 1990s, further Chinese immigration brought new generations to the area. Today, the Oriental Mall, a five-storey shopping centre, sells fragrant spices and teas, while the pedestrianized main street offers sweet bubble tea and steaming dumplings. Early each year, Chinatown comes alive with the colourful Chinese New Year parade featuring dragons, music and energetic dance performances.

EAT

Ravioleria Sarpi

Sample freshly made Italian-Chinese ravioli and dumplings to go.

G2 Via Paolo Sarpi 27 laravioleria sarpi.com

Little Lamb

Dunk vegetables or meat into huge bowls of simmering broth at this Chinese barbecue and hotpot restaurant.

G2 Via Paolo Sarpi 8 327 298 1339

Savana

This Eritrean restaurant serves meat and vegetarian dishes with traditional *injera* (spongy flatbread).

G3 Via Canonica Luigi 45 ristorante eritreo.com

SHOP

Officina Profumo-Farmaceutica di Santa Maria Novella
Find your signature scent at this traditional Italian perfume shop founded in the 1200s.

G6 Corso Magenta 11 eu.smnovella.com

ViaTivoli
ViaTivoli has a curated collection of women's clothing, including floral scarves and colourful outfits.The owner pays particular attention to the selection of textiles and stocks lots of organic fabrics.

H4 Corso Magenta 32 viativoli.it

Figus Designer
This artisanal leather workshop crafts beautiful bags and accessories in a variety of colours. Everything in the store is handmade in Milan using traditional Italian techniques.

G5 Corso Magenta 31 figusdesigner.com

Camicissima
Add a touch of impeccable Italian style to your wardrobe and choose from the wide selection of button-down shirts for men.

H6 Corso Magenta 5 camicissima.it

15

Corso Magenta

F5 M1 Conciliazione, 1, 2 Cadorna 16, 27 18

This street, with its elegant shops and historic buildings, is one of the loveliest quarters in Milan. At No 65, just past Santa Maria delle Grazie, is a building incorporating the remains of the Atellani residence, where Leonardo da Vinci stayed while working on the *Last Supper*. Piero Portaluppi carried out the work on No 65 in 1919. In the garden at the back there are some vines, said to be remnants of the vineyard that Ludovico il Moro gave to the great artist. The next building (No 61), Palazzo delle Stelline, originally a girls' orphanage, is now a convention centre and houses the Fondazione Stelline, which holds art exhibitions. The Fondazione also has a garden, created from the land given to Leonardo. At the corner of Via Carducci, which was built over the original course of the Naviglio canal, is Bar Magenta. The medieval city gate, Porta Vercellina, once stood at this junction.

Palazzo Litta

G5 Corso Magenta 24 M1, 2 Cadorna 16, 27 18, 50, 58, 94 During cultural events only

Considered one of the best examples of 18th-century Lombard architecture, Palazzo Litta was first built in 1648 for Count Bartolomeo Arese by Francesco Maria Richini. At the end of the century the interior was embellished and, in 1763, the pink façade was built at the request of the heirs, the Litta Visconti Arese. Since 1905 the building has housed the State Railway offices. Inside are sumptuous rooms looking onto a 17th-century courtyard. The staircase, designed by Carlo Giuseppe Merlo in 1740, is decorated

The Corso Magenta, with its elegant shops and historic buildings, is one of the loveliest quarters in Milan.

→ A tram on busy Corso Magenta, one of Milan's most striking streets

with the family coat of arms (a black and white check). It leads up to the Sala Rossa (Red Room), named after the colour of its wallpaper (a copy of the original). Set in the floor is a pearl, there to commemorate a tear said to have been shed during a meeting between the Duchess Litta and Napoleon.

The next room is the Salone degli Specchi, with large mirrors *(specchi)* lining the walls. The Salotto della Duchessa is the only room in the palazzo that still has its original 18th-century wallpaper. The Teatro Litta stands to the left of the palazzo, the oldest theatre in the city.

Civico Museo Archeologico

G6 Corso Magenta 15 M1, 2 Cadorna 16, 27 18, 50, 58, 94 10am-5:30pm Tue-Sun museo archeologicomilano.it

The Archaeological Museum is well worth a visit for the finds and to see the only remaining part of the city's Roman walls. At the entrance, graphic reconstructions illustrate urban planning and architecture in Milan from the 1st to the 4th century CE. The visit begins in a hall on the right, with clay objects, including a collection of oil lamps. This is followed by Roman sculpture. One of the most interesting pieces in the series of portraits dating from Caesar's era to late antiquity (1st–4th century CE), is the *Portrait of Maximian* (mid-3rd century CE). At the end of this room is a huge fragment of a torso of Hercules from the Milanese thermae, dating from the first half of the 2nd century CE. Behind this are some 3rd-century CE floor mosaics found in Milanese houses.

By the window are two of the most important works in the museum: the Parabiago Patera and the Diatreta Cup. The Patera is a gilded silver plate with a relief of the triumph of the goddess Cybele, mother of the gods, on a chariot pulled by lions and surrounded by the Sun and Moon and sea and Zodiac divinities (mid-4th century CE). The marvellous Diatreta Cup, also dating from the 4th century CE, comes from Novara and consists of a single piece of coloured glass, with finely wrought, intricate decoration. Winding around the cup is the inscription *Bibe vivas multis annis* ("Drink and you will live many years"). The entrance hall leads to a courtyard, where you will see the Torre di Ansperto, a Roman tower, from the ancient Maximianian walls. Leading from the courtyard is a three-storey exhibition space displaying early medieval, Etruscan and Greek collections. The basement houses art from Gandhar and Caesaera (Israel), as well as Roman and Mediolanum flooring.

→ The 4th-century Diatreta Cup in the Civico Museo Archeologico

INSIDER TIP
Museum Access

The three-day Tourist Museum Card (€12) gives you access to the permanent collections of all civic museums in Milan, as well as discounts on other city events and attractions *(www.vivaticket.com)*.

↑ The second hall of San Maurizio, with intricate frescoes, and *(inset)* the church's exterior

San Maurizio

G6 Corso Magenta 13 M1, 2 Cadorna 16, 27 50, 58, 94 02-866 660 (Santa Maria alla Porta) 10am-5pm Tue-Sat

In 1503, Gian Giacomo Dolcebuono began construction of this church, which was intended for the most powerful closed order of Benedictine nuns in Milan. It was designed with one hall for the public and another for the nuns.

In the first hall, to the right of the altar, is the opening through which the nuns receive the Body of Christ. Most of the decoration was done by Bernardino Luini. He painted the frescoes in the first hall, including the *Life of St Catherine* (third chapel to the right) and those on the middle wall. The second chapel on the right was decorated by Callisto Piazza, the chapels to the left by pupils of Luini. On the altar is an *Adoration of the Magi* by Antonio Campi. The middle wall of the second hall, occupied by the choir, has frescoes by Foppa, Piazza, an *Annunciation* attributed to Bramantino and *Episodes of the Passion*. Concerts are held here in the winter.

Piazza Cordusio

J6 M1 Cordusio 1, 2, 3, 12, 14, 16, 27

This oval-shaped piazza was named after the *Curtis Ducis*, the main seat of the Lombard duchy. The area, Milan's financial district, was laid out from 1889 to 1901. Buildings include Luca Beltrami's Assicurazioni Generali building, Casa Dario, and the main offices of UniCredit, designed by Luigi Broggi.

Certosa di Garegnano

B1 Via Garegnano 28 14 40 7:30am-6:30pm daily Thu am

The church that forms the heart of this important Carthusian monastery, dedicated to Our Lady of the Assumption, was founded in 1349 by Archbishop Giovanni Visconti. Sadly, the Certosa is well known because the main cloister was ruined by the construction of the A4 motorway.

The courtyard is of impressive size, with the monks' houses, each with a kitchen garden, around the sides. The rules imposed by the semi-closed order required each monk to live independently. The complex was rebuilt in late Renaissance style in 1562; the façade, completed in 1608, was decorated with obelisks and statues, crowned by a statue of Our Lady. A porticoed atrium with an exedra-shaped vestibule provides a harmonious introduction to the complex.

Vincenzo Seregni designed the interior in the 1500s. The aisleless nave is crowned by a barrel vault flanked by blind arcades. The church is famous for the frescoes by Daniele Crespi, a leading 17th-century Lombard artist. He reputedly painted the entire cycle *(The Legend of the Foundation of the Order)* to thank the Carthusian monks for offering refuge after he had been charged with murder. The cycle begins by the first arch on the right, continues on the wall behind the façade, designed by Simone Peterzano, and is resumed on the vault, where there are four medallions. In the first bay on the left, Crespi included a self-portrait of himself as a servant blowing a horn, and added the date (1629) and his signature in a scroll.

Simone Peterzano painted the frescoes in the presbytery and apse (1578), with scenes from the life of Mary. The chapel on the right has two macabre 17th-century paintings informing novices of the various forms of torture they might encounter while spreading Christianity. On leaving, look at the 14th-century cloister on the right, the only surviving part of the original monastery.

Piazza Affari

H6 M 1 Cordusio
3, 16, 27

The heart of the financial district, this square was laid out in 1928–40 to house the city's markets (especially farm produce). The Borsa Valori, Italy's most important Stock Exchange, stands here. Founded in 1808, it is housed in a building designed by Paolo Mezzanotte in 1931. Ruins of a 1st-century BCE Roman theatre were found in the basement area.

Via Brisa

H6 M 1, 2 Cadorna
16, 27 50, 58

Excavations carried out after the 1943 Allied bombing of this street revealed Roman ruins that were probably part of Maximian's grand imperial palace: the foundation of a round hall surrounded by apsidal halls and preceded by a narthex. Note the columns that raised the pavement to allow warm air to enter and circulate through the palace.

MILAN'S ROMAN HISTORY

Conquered in 222 BCE, Milan was an important city of the Roman empire due to its geographical location. Known back then as Mediolanum, meaning "central place", it was home to the region's administrative buildings and the grand imperial palace, the remains of which can still be seen today around Via Brisa.

↓ Borsa Valori, Italy's main Stock Exchange, on Piazza Affari

A SHORT WALK

AROUND THE CASTELLO SFORZESCO

Distance 3 km (2 miles) **Time** 45 minutes **Nearest metro** 1 Cairoli

The Castello Sforzesco and Parco Sempione today are the result of late 19th-century restoration. Architect Luca Beltrami thwarted attempts to demolish the castle by converting it into a museum centre. He restored many of its original elements, which can be admired on a stroll around the complex. In the early 1800s, the Arco della Pace and the Arena were built in the Parco Sempione, which was landscaped as an "English" garden by Emilio Alemagna. In 1906, the opening of the Galleria del Sempione was marked with an International Exposition.

This amphitheatre, **Arena Civica** (p87), *was built in 1806. Originally it was filled with water from the Naviglio canals and used for boating displays.*

The **Civic Aquarium** *was built in 1906 as an educational centre. The building still has its original tiles* (p86).

Parco Sempione, *a 47-hectare (116-acre) English-style garden, was designed by Emilio Alemagna in 1893. It contains a number of historic buildings and monuments* (p86).

↑ The triumphant Arch of Peace, based on Rome's Septimius Severus arch

Napoleon built **Corso Sempione** (p88), *which leads to the Castello, modelling it on the Champs-Elysées in Paris.*

The **Arch of Peace** *was inaugurated by Francis I in memory of the peace declared in 1815* (p87).

↑ Castello Sforzesco and the 19th-century Parco Sempione

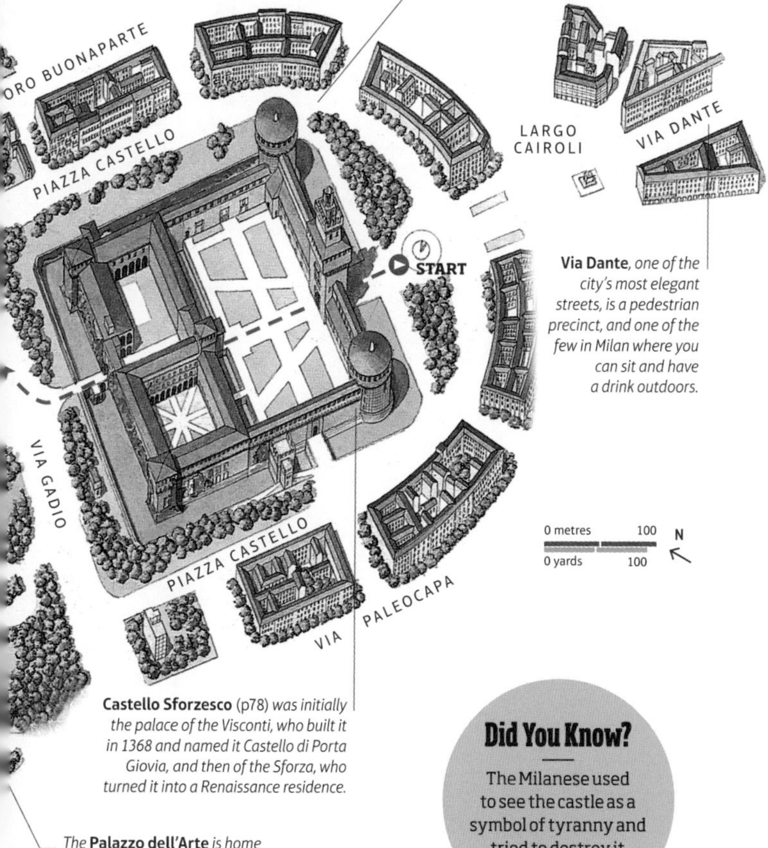

Locator Map
For more details see p76

The **Foro Buonaparte** *is a semicircular boulevard lined with imposing late 19th-century buildings.*

Via Dante, *one of the city's most elegant streets, is a pedestrian precinct, and one of the few in Milan where you can sit and have a drink outdoors.*

Castello Sforzesco (p78) *was initially the palace of the Visconti, who built it in 1368 and named it Castello di Porta Giovia, and then of the Sforza, who turned it into a Renaissance residence.*

The **Palazzo dell'Arte** *is home to the Triennale Design Museum* (p88), *which features decorative art, fashion and handicrafts.*

Did You Know?

The Milanese used to see the castle as a symbol of tyranny and tried to destroy it multiple times.

A LONG WALK

MILAN'S HISTORIC PAST

Distance 5 km (3 miles) **Time** 1 hour
Nearest Metro 1, 3 Duomo

Milan is a city that tends to keep its history largely buried under a modern, business-orientated veneer. The following walk seeks out the remnants of Roman, medieval and Renaissance Milan while paying homage to the city's most famous adopted son, Leonardo da Vinci. The Renaissance master has left a distinctive stamp on the city. Examples of his genius are scattered all around town, from the *Last Supper* fresco to models of his inventions to the surviving canals that were once part of a vast and intricate waterway system Leonardo helped plan.

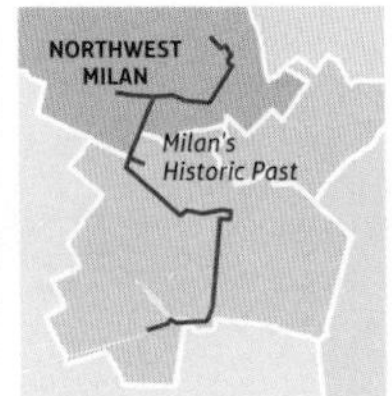

Locator Map
For more detail see p76 and p100

Located on Corso Magenta is the church of **Santa Maria delle Grazie** (p84), *which houses Leonardo's da Vinci's* Last Supper.

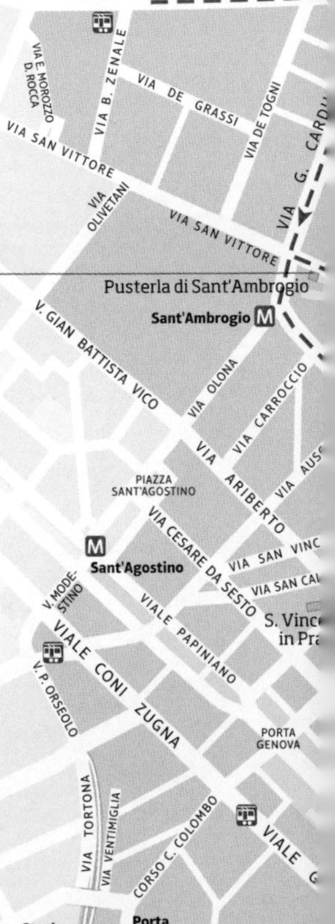

At the bottom of Via Carducci is the **Pusterla di Sant'Ambrogio**, *a remnant of the medieval city gates.*

Down the alley of Vicolo dei Lavandai is a canal of stone washbasins covered by a tiled roof.

To the southwest of the Darsena is the **Naviglio Grande** (p113).

↑ Santa Maria delle Grazie, a UNESCO World Heritage Site

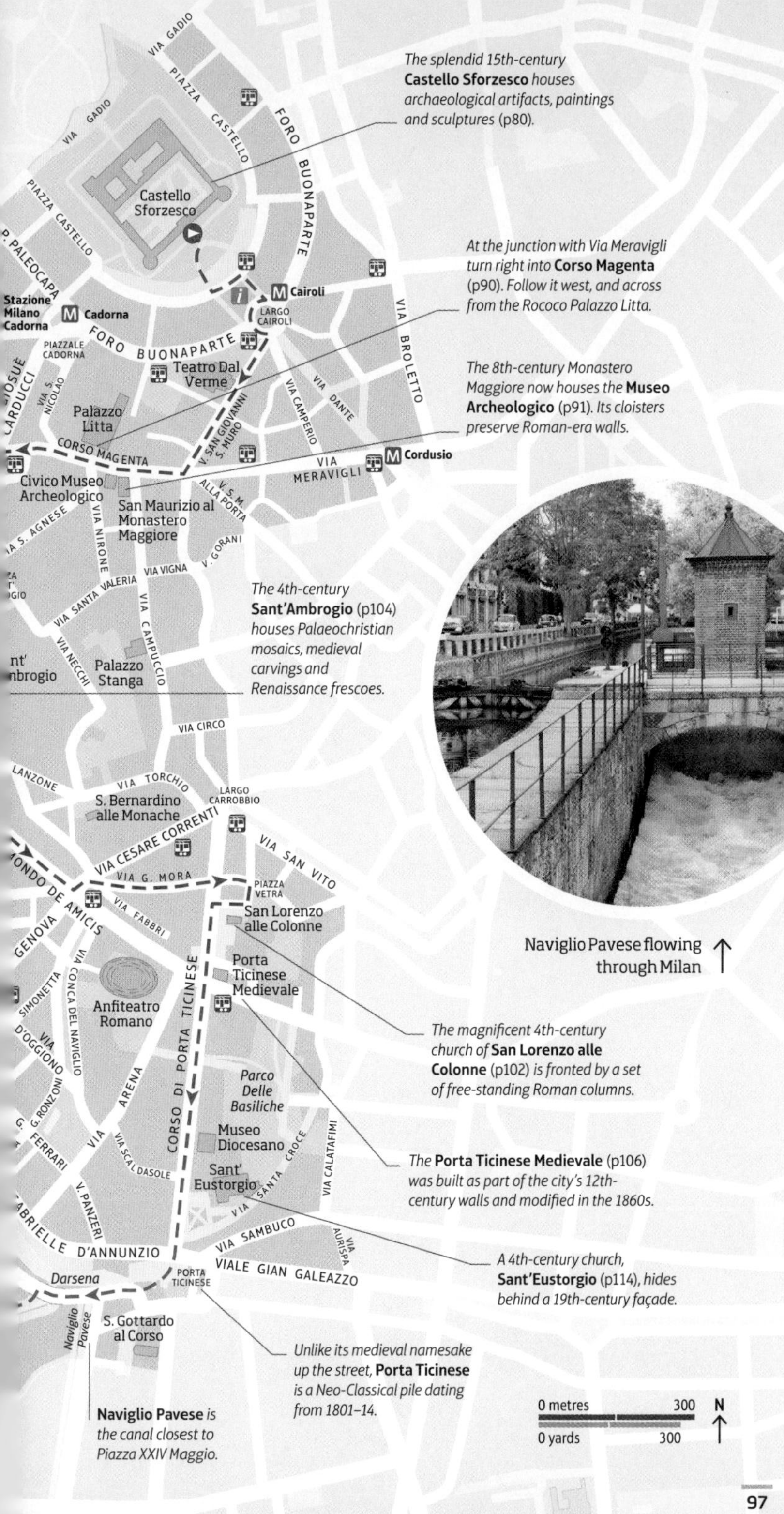
The splendid 15th-century **Castello Sforzesco** houses archaeological artifacts, paintings and sculptures (p80).
At the junction with Via Meravigli turn right into **Corso Magenta** (p90). Follow it west, and across from the Rococo Palazzo Litta.
The 8th-century Monastero Maggiore now houses the **Museo Archeologico** (p91). Its cloisters preserve Roman-era walls.
The 4th-century **Sant'Ambrogio** (p104) houses Palaeochristian mosaics, medieval carvings and Renaissance frescoes.
The magnificent 4th-century church of **San Lorenzo alle Colonne** (p102) is fronted by a set of free-standing Roman columns.
The **Porta Ticinese Medievale** (p106) was built as part of the city's 12th-century walls and modified in the 1860s.
A 4th-century church, **Sant'Eustorgio** (p114), hides behind a 19th-century façade.
Unlike its medieval namesake up the street, **Porta Ticinese** is a Neo-Classical pile dating from 1801–14.
Naviglio Pavese is the canal closest to Piazza XXIV Maggio.
Via Gadio
Piazza Castello
Foro Buonaparte
Castello Sforzesco
P. Paleocapa
Stazione Milano Cadorna
Cadorna
Cairoli
Largo Cairoli
Piazzale Cadorna
Teatro Dal Verme
Via Broletto
Via Dante
Via Camperio
V. San Giovanni S. Muro
Via S. Nicolao
Palazzo Litta
Corso Magenta
Via Meravigli
Cordusio
Civico Museo Archeologico
San Maurizio al Monastero Maggiore
V. S. M. alla Porta
Via S. Agnese
Via Nirone
V. Gorani
Via Vigna
Via Santa Valeria
Via Campuccio
Via Necchi
Palazzo Stanga
Via Circo
Lanzone
Via Torchio
Largo Carrobbio
S. Bernardino alle Monache
Via Cesare Correnti
Via San Vito
Via G. Mora
Piazza Vetra
Via Fabbri
San Lorenzo alle Colonne
Porta Ticinese Medievale
Corso di Porta Ticinese
Genova
Simonetta
Via Conca del Naviglio
Anfiteatro Romano
Via D'Oggiono
G. Ronzoni
Via Arena
Parco Delle Basiliche
Museo Diocesano
Via Calatafimi
Via Santa Croce
G. Ferrari
Via Scaldasole
Sant' Eustorgio
V. Panzeri
Via Sambuco
Via Aurispa
D'Annunzio
Viale Gian Galeazzo
Darsena
Porta Ticinese
Naviglio Pavese
S. Gottardo al Corso
0 metres 300
0 yards 300
N

Naviglio Pavese flowing through Milan

The intricately adorned celing in San Vittore al Corpo

SOUTHWEST MILAN

Religious complexes once covered this district, preventing further building until the early 19th century. The suppression of the monasteries in the late 18th century paved the way for the urbanization of the area between the medieval and Spanish walls, crossed by two large avenues, Corso Italia and Corso di Porta Ticinese.

Beyond Porta Ticinese, which leads to the southern part of Milan, is Corso San Gottardo. The area is bordered by the inner ring road, which follows the course of the medieval walls, and the outer ring road, which replaced the Spanish walls. Further on is the Navigli canals quarter, with the Naviglio Grande and the Pavese, the last vestiges of what was once a major network for communications and commerce. Barges used the Naviglio Grande to transport the Candoglia marble used to build the Duomo and, in the 1950s, the material for postwar reconstruction. Today, the area around the canals is lined with lively bars and restaurants, with market stalls selling antiques on weekends.

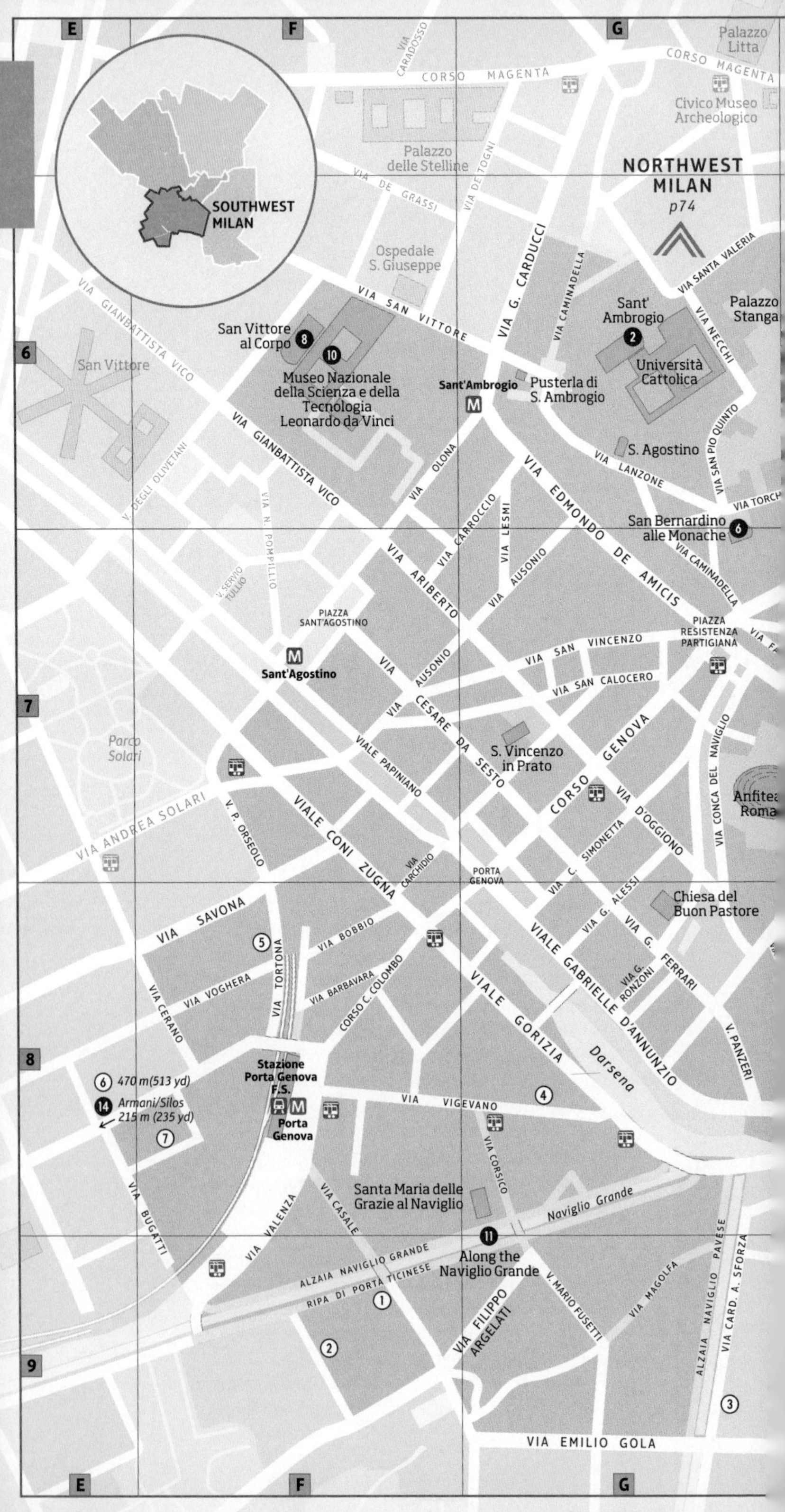

SOUTHWEST MILAN
NORTHWEST MILAN p74
Palazzo Litta
Civico Museo Archeologico
Palazzo delle Stelline
Ospedale S. Giuseppe
San Vittore al Corpo
Museo Nazionale della Scienza e della Tecnologia Leonardo da Vinci
Sant'Ambrogio
Pusterla di S. Ambrogio
Sant' Ambrogio
Università Cattolica
Palazzo Stanga
S. Agostino
San Bernardino alle Monache
San Vittore
Piazza Sant'Agostino
Sant'Agostino
Piazza Resistenza Partigiana
Parco Solari
S. Vincenzo in Prato
Chiesa del Buon Pastore
Porta Genova
Darsena
Stazione Porta Genova F.S.
Porta Genova
470 m(513 yd)
Armani/Silos 215 m (235 yd)
Santa Maria delle Grazie al Naviglio
Along the Naviglio Grande
Naviglio Grande
Corso Magenta
Via Caradosso
Via de Grassi
Via de Togni
Via San Vittore
Via G. Carducci
Via Caminadella
Via Santa Valeria
Via Necchi
Via Gianbattista Vico
Via Olona
Via Lanzone
Via San Pio Quinto
Via Torchio
Via Edmondo de Amicis
V. degli Olivetani
Via N. Pompillio
V. Servio Tullio
Via Carroccio
Via Lesmi
Via Ausonio
Via Ariberto
Via San Vincenzo
Via San Calocero
Via Cesare da Sesto
Viale Papiniano
Corso Genova
Via Conca del Naviglio
Via d'Oggiono
Via C. Simonetta
Via G. Alessi
Via G. Ferrari
Via G. Ronzoni
V. Panzeri
Via Andrea Solari
V. P. Orseolo
Viale Coni Zugna
Via Carchidio
Viale Gabrielle d'Annunzio
Via Savona
Via Tortona
Via Bobbio
Via Barbavara
Corso C. Colombo
Via Voghera
Via Cerano
Viale Gorizia
Via Vigevano
Via Corsico
Via Bugatti
Via Valenza
Via Casale
Alzaia Naviglio Grande
Ripa di Porta Ticinese
Via Filippo Argelati
V. Mario Fusetti
Via Magolfa
Alzaia Naviglio Pavese
Via Card. A. Sforza
Via Emilio Gola

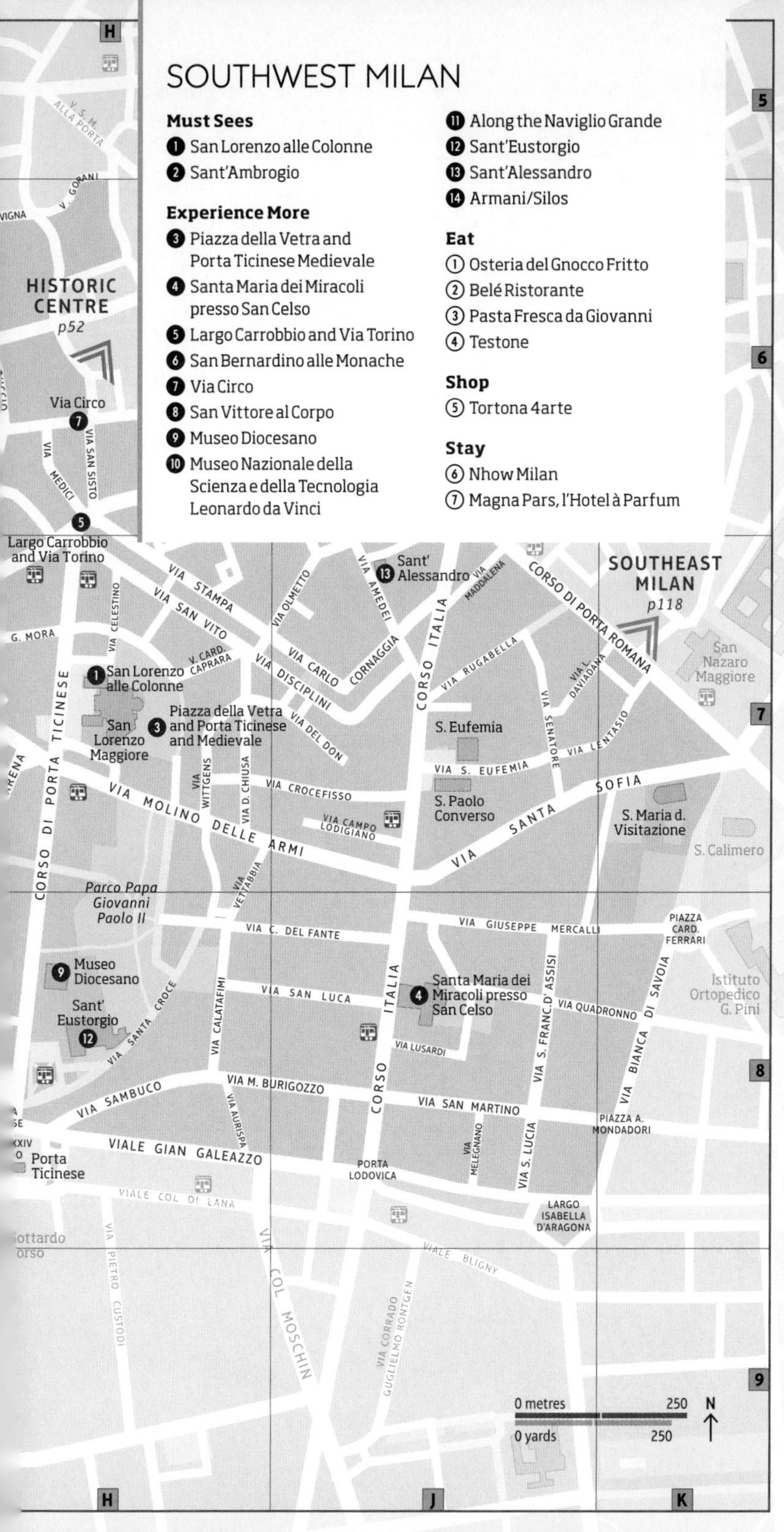

SOUTHWEST MILAN
Must Sees
1 San Lorenzo alle Colonne
2 Sant'Ambrogio
Experience More
3 Piazza della Vetra and Porta Ticinese Medievale
4 Santa Maria dei Miracoli presso San Celso
5 Largo Carrobbio and Via Torino
6 San Bernardino alle Monache
7 Via Circo
8 San Vittore al Corpo
9 Museo Diocesano
10 Museo Nazionale della Scienza e della Tecnologia Leonardo da Vinci
11 Along the Naviglio Grande
12 Sant'Eustorgio
13 Sant'Alessandro
14 Armani/Silos
Eat
① Osteria del Gnocco Fritto
② Belé Ristorante
③ Pasta Fresca da Giovanni
④ Testone
Shop
⑤ Tortona 4arte
Stay
⑥ Nhow Milan
⑦ Magna Pars, l'Hotel à Parfum
HISTORIC CENTRE p52
SOUTHEAST MILAN p118
Via Circo
Largo Carrobbio and Via Torino
San Lorenzo alle Colonne
San Lorenzo Maggiore
Piazza della Vetra and Porta Ticinese and Medievale
Sant' Alessandro
S. Eufemia
S. Paolo Converso
S. Maria d. Visitazione
San Nazaro Maggiore
S. Calimero
Parco Papa Giovanni Paolo II
Museo Diocesano
Sant' Eustorgio
Santa Maria dei Miracoli presso San Celso
Istituto Ortopedico G. Pini
Porta Ticinese
PORTA LODOVICA
PIAZZA CARD. FERRARI
PIAZZA A. MONDADORI
LARGO ISABELLA D'ARAGONA
VIA STAMPA
VIA SAN VITO
VIA OLMETTO
VIA AMEDEI
VIA MADDALENA
CORSO DI PORTA ROMANA
CORSO ITALIA
VIA CARLO CORNAGGIA
VIA DISCIPLINI
VIA DEL DON
VIA RUGABELLA
VIA L. DAVIADANA
VIA SENATORE
VIA LENTASIO
VIA S. EUFEMIA
VIA SANTA SOFIA
VIA CROCEFISSO
VIA CAMPO LODIGIANO
VIA MOLINO DELLE ARMI
VIA WITTGENS
VIA D. CHIUSA
VIA VETTABBIA
CORSO DI PORTA TICINESE
VIA CELESTINO
G. MORA
V. CARD. CAPRARA
VIA MEDICI
VIA SAN SISTO
VIA C. DEL FANTE
VIA GIUSEPPE MERCALLI
VIA SAN LUCA
VIA CALATAFIMI
VIA SANTA CROCE
VIA S. FRANC. D'ASSISI
VIA QUADRONNO
VIA BIANCA DI SAVOIA
VIA LUSARDI
VIA SAMBUCO
VIA M. BURIGOZZO
VIA AURISPA
VIA SAN MARTINO
VIA MELEGNANO
VIA S. LUCIA
VIALE GIAN GALEAZZO
VIALE COL DI LANA
VIA COL MOSCHIN
VIA PIETRO CUSTODI
VIA CORRADO GUGLIELMO RONTGEN
VIALE BLIGNY
V. S. M. ALLA PORTA
V. GORANI
VIGNA
0 metres 250
0 yards 250
N

1

SAN LORENZO ALLE COLONNE

H7 Corso di Porta Ticinese 39 02-8940 4129 M3 Missori 3 94 9am-12:30pm & 3-6pm Mon-Fri, 9am-1pm & 3-7pm Sat & Sun; Cappella di Sant'Aquilino: 8:30am-6:30pm Mon-Sat, 9am-7pm Sun

A mix of architectural styles, San Lorenzo alle Colonne is one of Milan's oldest churches. A highlight here is the Chapel of St Aquilino, its interiors embellished with medieval frescoes and Byzantine mosaics.

Dating from the 4th century, San Lorenzo is thought to have been the ancient imperial palatine chapel. The church was built with materials from a nearby Roman amphitheatre. The plan, with exedrae and women's galleries, is unlike Lombard architecture and reveals the hand of Roman architects and masons. Some art historians also note the influence of Byzantine art. After several fires, the church was reconstructed in the 11th and 12th centuries and was rebuilt after the dome collapsed in 1573, but the original quatrefoil plan has been preserved. The Chapel of Sant'Aquilino contains some of the best mosaics in northern Italy.

CHAPEL ARCHITECTURE

Constructed between 390 and 430 CE, the Chapel of St Aquilino is thought to have once served as an imperial mausoleum, its walls adorned entirely with mosaics. The architect behind this building studied the sun's trajectory, strategically positioning the windows to allow rays to pierce the southeast window, illuminating a mosaic scene before gently lighting the floor below where the imperial sarcophagus presumably rested.

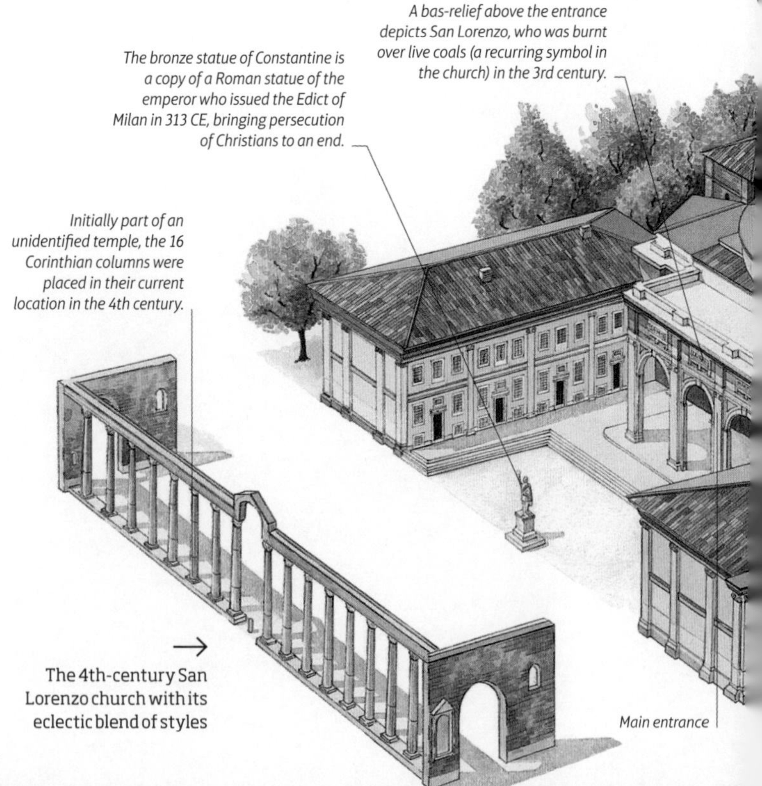

Cappella di San Sisto features 17th-century frescoes painted by Gian Cristoforo Storer.
A bas-relief above the entrance depicts San Lorenzo, who was burnt over live coals (a recurring symbol in the church) in the 3rd century.
The bronze statue of Constantine is a copy of a Roman statue of the emperor who issued the Edict of Milan in 313 CE, bringing persecution of Christians to an end.
Initially part of an unidentified temple, the 16 Corinthian columns were placed in their current location in the 4th century.
Main entrance

→ The 4th-century San Lorenzo church with its eclectic blend of styles

The church's façade fronted by the striking bronze statue of Constantine ↑

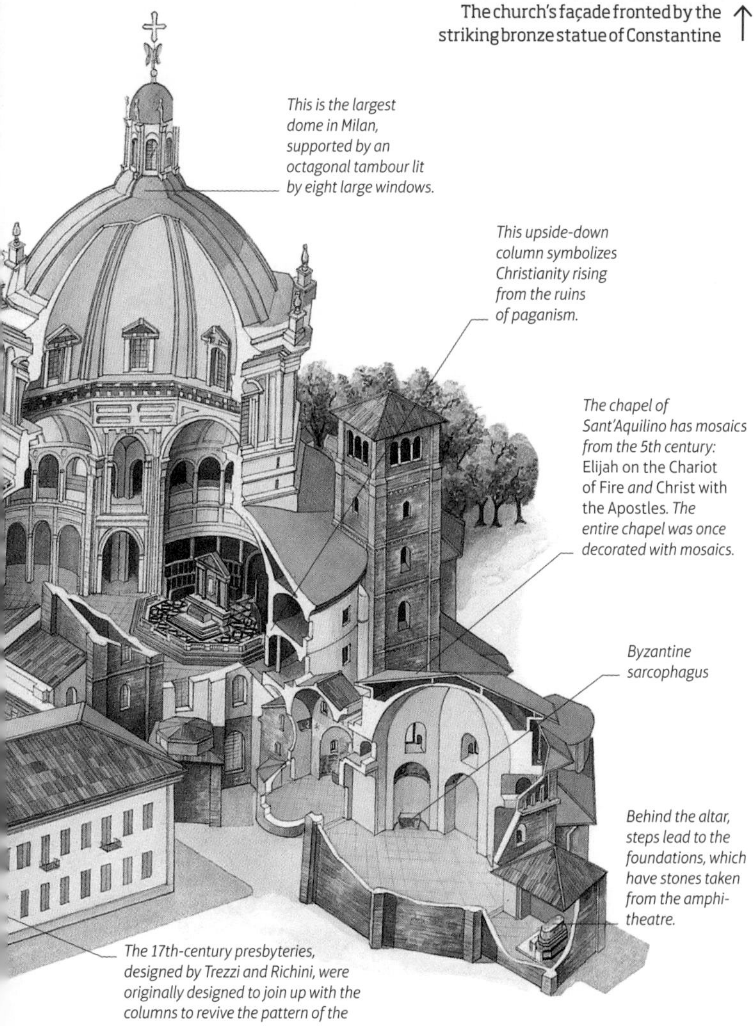

This is the largest dome in Milan, supported by an octagonal tambour lit by eight large windows.

This upside-down column symbolizes Christianity rising from the ruins of paganism.

The chapel of Sant'Aquilino has mosaics from the 5th century: Elijah on the Chariot of Fire *and* Christ with the Apostles. *The entire chapel was once decorated with mosaics.*

Byzantine sarcophagus

Behind the altar, steps lead to the foundations, which have stones taken from the amphitheatre.

The 17th-century presbyteries, designed by Trezzi and Richini, were originally designed to join up with the columns to revive the pattern of the ancient quadriporticus.

2

SANT'AMBROGIO

G6 19 Rue Balzac M2 Sant'Ambrogio Apr–Jun & Sep: 9:30am–6pm daily; Jul & Aug: 9:30am–7pm daily; Oct–Mar: 10am–5:15pm daily 1 Jan, 1 May, 25 Dec basilicasantambrogio.it

A religious focal point of southwest Milan, this impressive red-brick basilica was built in honour of Milan's patron saint and former bishop, St Ambrose, who was buried in the crypt.

The basilica was built by Bishop Ambrogio (Ambrose) in 379–86 CE on an early Christian burial ground as part of a programme to reorganize the Christian face of Milan. The church was dedicated to Ambrogio, a defender of Christianity against Arianism, after his burial here. The Benedictines began to enlarge it in the 8th century. Reconstruction of the entire church began in the 11th century. Sadly, the basilica was badly damaged by bombs in 1943. Most of its present-day appearance is the result of rebuilding in the 10th and 12th centuries by the Benedictines from the nearby monastery, who made it a model of Lombard Romanesque religious architecture. In 1937–40 and in the postwar period, the Romanesque structure and delicate colours were restored. From the Pusterla (gate), there is a marvellous view of the church, with its two bell towers and atrium, flanked by the rectory and museum.

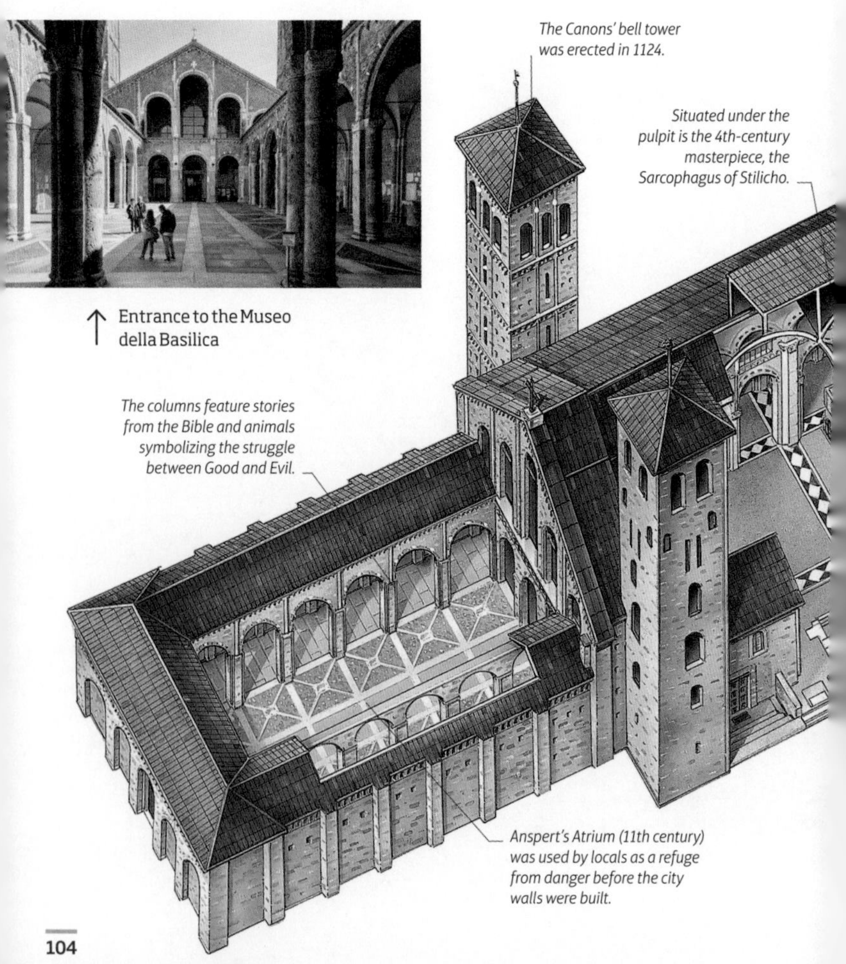

The Canons' bell tower was erected in 1124.
Situated under the pulpit is the 4th-century masterpiece, the Sarcophagus of Stilicho.
The columns feature stories from the Bible and animals symbolizing the struggle between Good and Evil.
Anspert's Atrium (11th century) was used by locals as a refuge from danger before the city walls were built.

↑ Entrance to the Museo della Basilica

PATRON SAINT OF BEEKEEPERS

St Ambrose is commonly known as the patron saint of Milan but he is also recognized as the patron saint of beekeepers. Legend has it that as an infant, his cradle was attacked by a swarm of bees. The bees are said to have covered his face but rather than stinging him, the hive left a drop of honey on his lips instead. This was taken as a sign that he would become a "honey-tongued" orator and deliver great sermons in adulthood.

The ciborium is the small 10th-century baldachin that protects the Golden Altar.

The apse mosaic dates from the 4th–8th centuries and was restored after the 1943 bombings.

Apse

Museum entrance

The golden altar was made by Volvinius (9th century) for the remains of Sant'Ambrogio.

The Chapel of San Vittore in Ciel d'Oro was named after the vault's gold (oro) mosaics.

Illustration of the basilica of Sant'Ambrogio

Highlights

Pusterla di Sant'Ambrogio

▶ The Pusterla di Sant'Ambrogio, one of the minor gates on the medieval walls, was rebuilt in 1939. It has a museum with old weapons and instruments of torture.

Anspert's Atrium

The present-day atrium, dating from the 12th century, houses finds and tombstones from this area.

The Interior

▼ The nave provides the best view of the interior, revealing the basilica in all its splendour. At the beginning of the nave is the *Serpent's Column*, said to have been erected by Moses in the desert. Beside it, to the left, excavations show the level of the original 4th-century floor. Next to the presbytery is the stairway to the crypt. Under the Golden Altar, an urn (1897) has the remains of Sts Ambrogio, Gervasio and Protasio.

The South Aisle

At the entrance in the south aisle are the monks' chapels, built in different eras, including St George's chapel and the Baroque chapel of the Holy Sacrament, which contain stunning altarpieces and frescoes.

The North Aisle

This aisle has a porphyry font by Franco Lombardi with the *Conversion of St Augustine* (1940), the saint baptized by Sant' Ambrogio in Milan.

Museo della Basilica

▶ The Basilica Museum has six rooms featuring objects and works of art from the church.

Università Cattolica del Sacro Cuore

Located in the former Benedictine monastery is the university, founded by Agostino Gemelli in 1921.

EXPERIENCE MORE

Piazza della Vetra and Porta Ticinese Medievale

H7 2, 3, 14, 15 94

The vast area of greenery dominated by a column bearing the statue of San Lazzaro (1728) is known as Piazza della Vetra but it is also referred to as Parco delle Basiliche, because it lies between the basilicas of San Lorenzo and Sant'Eustorgio. The name "Vetra" seems to derive from the Latin *castra vetera*, which probably alluded to the Roman military camps positioned here to defend the nearby imperial palace. The name was also given to a canal that was once on the northern side of the square and was lined with tanners' workshops (the tanners were known as *vetraschi*). Until 1840, the square was used for the public hangings of condemned commoners and those accused of witchcraft, while nobles were decapitated in front of the law court, the Broletto (p68).

TABERNACLE OF PORTA TICINESE

Milan's medieval fortifications were originally decorated with votive statues, placed on top of the main gates in the 12th century. One of them was the small tabernacle above the main arch of Porta Ticinese, bearing representations of the Virgin and Baby and St Ambrose, as well as St Lawrence, St Peter, and St Eustorgius. In order to better preserve the statues, the originals were moved to the Museo d'Arte Antica inside the Castello Sforzesco (p80) in 1961 and replaced with marble copies.

During the Roman era there was a small port here, at the point where the Seveso and Nirone rivers converged in the navigable Vettabbia canal.

This square is worth visiting just for the magnificent view of the apses of the basilicas. In the 12th century, when the city walls were enlarged to include San Lorenzo, the Roman gate at present-day Largo Carrobbio was replaced by the "new" medieval Porta Ticinese. A moat ran around the new walls and along present-day Via Molino delle Armi, which was named after the water mills (*molini*) used mostly to forge weapons.

Porta Ticinese was remodelled after 1329 by Lord of Milan, Azzone Visconti, (1302–1339) and decorated with a tabernacle of the *Madonna and Child with St Ambrose Proffering the Model of the City* by the workshop of Giovanni di Balduccio (14th century). This city gate – the only one, along with Porta Nuova on Via Manzoni, still standing – was fortified with two towers in 1865.

At the junction with Via San Sisto is the deconsecrated 17th-century church of San Sisto. In 1976 it became the museum-studio of sculptor Francesco Messina.

4

Santa Maria dei Miracoli presso San Celso

J8 Corso Italia 37 15 94 10am-noon & 4-5:30pm Mon-Wed, Fri & Sun (to 6pm Sun) www.santamariadeimiracolie-sancelso.it

In 1493, construction began on a sanctuary dedicated to Santa Maria dei Miracoli. It was first designed by Gian Giacomo Dolcebuono and subsequently by Vincenzo Seregni and Alessi. The late 16th-century façade bears sculptures by Stoldo Lorenzi and Annibale Fontana. The late Renaissance interior, constructed and redesigned throughout the 16th century, features a pavement by Martino Bassi and was frescoed by Cerano and Procaccini. Under the cupola is the high altar in semi-precious stones. On the Altar of the Madonna is Fontana's *Our Lady of the Assumption*.

There are fine works of art in the various chapels including a painting (1606) by Procaccini, the *Holy Family with St Jerome* altarpiece (1548) by Paris Bordone, Antonio Campi's *Resurrection* (1560) and an altarpiece by Bergognone.

By the right-hand transept is the entrance to San Celso, a Romanesque church built in the 11th century over the remains of a 4th-century church. It was founded to mark the spot where St Ambrose discovered the remains of the martyrs Celso and Nazaro. The church is decorated with 11th- to 15th-century frescoes and columns with carved capitals.

Largo Carrobbio and Via Torino

H6 2, 3, 14 Studio Museo Francesco Messina: Via San Sisto 4 www.studiomuseofrancesco messina.com For restoration

The bustling Carrobbio square, which connects Via Torino and Corso di Porta Ticinese, is thought to have been named after the *quadrivium*, a crossroads of four streets, or after *carrubium*, a road reserved for carts. At the junction with Via San Sisto is the deconsecrated 17th-century church of San Sisto. In 1976 it became the museum-studio of sculptor Francesco Messina. He died in 1990 and the building now houses a collection of his bronze and coloured plaster sculpture pieces, as well as graphic art.

Largo Carrobbio is located at one end of Via Torino, a major commercial street that developed after the merger of the old city districts. These once contained the workshops of oil merchants, silk weavers, hatters and famous armourers – as is reflected in the surrounding street names.

The 16th-century Palazzo Stampa, built by nobleman and politician Massimiliano Stampa, stands in Via Soncino. When the Sforza dynasty died out in 1535, Stampa introduced Spanish dominion to the city by hoisting the flag of Charles V on the Castello Sforzesco *(p78)* in exchange for land and privileges. The imperial eagle still stands on the palazzo tower, over the bronze globe representing the dominions of Charles V.

↑ Bronze sculptures and graphic art by Francesco Messina, in San Sisto

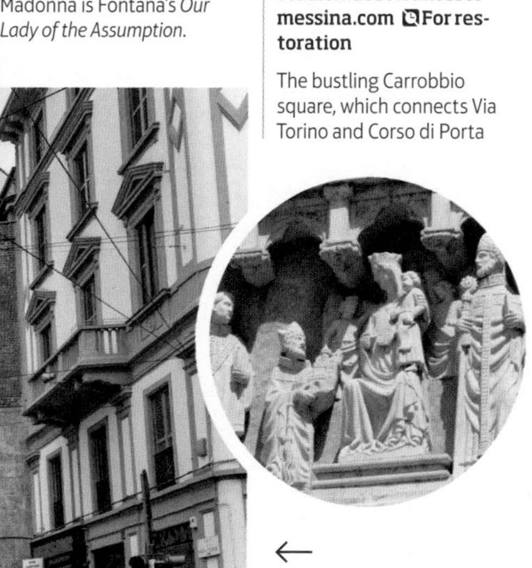

← Porta Ticinese and *(inset)* marble carvings of the Virgin and Baby

San Lorenzo alle Colonne, fronted by 16 Corinthian columns

↑ The peaceful courtyard in Santa Maria Maddalena al Cerchio, near Via Circo

San Bernardino alle Monache

G7 Via Lanzone 13 02-8645 0895 2, 3, 14 94 3:30-5:30pm Fri, 10:30am-12:30pm Sun

The church is the only remaining building in a Franciscan nuns' convent dating from the mid-15th century and attributed to the Lombard architect Pietro Antonio Solari. The church was named after the preacher Bernardino da Siena, whose relics are kept here. It was partly rebuilt in 1922. The narrow, elegant brick façade is decorated with majolica bowls and a fine elaborate cornice with small arches.

The interior houses fine 15th-century frescoes painted by the school of Vincenzo Foppa, and others dating from the early 16th century. Of note is *Madonna and Child with Saint Agnes*.

Austere exterior of San Bernardino alle Monache

Via Circo

H6 2, 3, 14 50, 58

The area extending from Largo Carrobbio to Corso Magenta is very rich in 3rd- and 4th-century ruins, particularly mosaics and masonry, much of it now part of private homes. This was the period when the Roman emperor Maximian lived in Milan: his splendid palace was near Via Brisa. In order to create a proper imperial capital, he built many civic edifices to gain the favour of the Milanese: the Arena, the thermae and the huge Circus used for two-horse chariot races. The Circus, 505 m (1,656 ft) long, was one of the largest constructions in the Roman Empire. The only remaining parts are the end curve, visible at the junction of Via Cappuccio and Via Circo, and one of the entrance towers, which became the bell tower of San Maurizio in Corso Magenta.

The Circus, active long after the fall of the Roman Empire, was the venue of the coronation of the Lombard king Adaloaldo in 615, while in the Carolingian period it became a vineyard, as the place name of nearby Via Vigna indicates. At No 7 Via Cappuccio, the 18th-century Palazzo Litta Biumi has incorporated, to the left of the central courtyard, the delightful 15th-century nuns' convent Santa Maria Maddalena al Cerchio, which

THE CIRCUS AND CHARIOT RACES

Chariot races were one of the favourite forms of entertainment in the Roman empire. Often organized to celebrate war victories, they were held in specially built circuses like the Circus Maximus in Rome and the Circus of Milan. Taking part in the races was dangerous - collisions and injuries were common, particularly when taking sharp corners at speed. Charioteers were also at risk of being trampled and dragged by their own horses, so many wore protective gear and carried a knife to cut loose from the reins.

has been partly rebuilt. Its name, a corruption of the Latin *ad circulum*, refers to the Circus over which it was built. The hood of the nuns' habit *(cappuccio)* is probably the origin of the name of the street where the convent is located. Further along, at No 13, is Palazzo Radice Fossati (a private house), of medieval origin, with a 13th-century portal and 18th-century frescoes inside.

On Via Sant'Orsola you come to Via Morigi, named after a famous Milanese family who once lived here; all that remains of their residence is a 14th-century tower with a small loggia. The nearby square is dominated by the 14th-century Torre dei Gorani, another tower crowned by a loggia with small stone columns.

8

San Vittore al Corpo

F6 Via San Vittore 25 02-4800 5351 M2 Sant'Ambrogio 50, 58, 94 10am-noon & 2-5pm daily

The original basilica on this site was founded in the 4th century, next to the mausoleum of Emperor Valentinian II, who died in 392. The church was rebuilt in the 11th and 12th centuries by Benedictine monks, and again altered in 1560 by the Olivetans, who replaced the monks. The architect (either Alessi or Seregni) reversed the orientation and made it one of Milan's most sumptuous churches, with splendid late 16th-century paintings. The Baroque Arese Chapel (1668), designed by Gerolamo Quadrio, and the right-hand apse, with scenes from the life of St Gregory by Camillo Procaccini (1602), are of particular interest. Moncalvo frescoed the angel musicians on the cupola in 1619. The wooden choir stalls, with carvings of episodes from St Benedict's life, date from 1583; above them are three canvases on the same subject by Giovanni Ambrogio Figino. Last, the chapel of Sant'Antonio Abate was entirely frescoed in 1619 by Daniele Crespi.

700

The number of artworks in Museo Diocesano's permanent collection.

9

Museo Diocesano

H8 Corso di Porta Ticinese 95 3, 9 94 10am-6pm Tue-Sun museodiocesano.it

The mission of the Museo Diocesano is to recover and highlight the artistic heritage of the Milan diocese, which extends as far north as the towns of Varese and Lecco.

This museum of religious art is housed in the cloisters of Sant'Eustorgio, next to the basilica. It features works of art dating from the 4th to the 21st centuries, from paintings from the private collections of past Milanese archbishops to items rescued from tiny village churches. Two of the highlights are the frescoes of the *Stations of the Cross* by late 19th-century artist Gaetano Previati and the section devoted to Milan's patron saint, Sant'Ambrogio. Guided tours of the museum are held between July and September. Book ahead online.

→ The 16th-century *Ancona of the Passion* in Museo Diocesano

←
A scale-model of a historic sailing ship in the Science and Technology Museum

10 Museo Nazionale della Scienza e della Tecnologia Leonardo da Vinci

F6 Via San Vittore 21 M2 Sant'Ambrogio 50, 58, 94 10am-5pm Tue-Sat (to 6pm Sat), 9:30am-6:30pm Sun museoscienza.org

The Science and Technology Museum is housed in the former Olivetan monastery of San Vittore (16th century) – partly designed by Vincenzo Seregni – which was turned into a military hospital and then a barracks after monasteries were suppressed in 1804. In 1947 it became the home of the museum. Parts of the ancient Roman foundation of the San Vittore fort and of the vast octagonal mausoleum of Emperor Valentinian II are still visible in the two courtyards.

The museum has one of the world's leading science and technology collections. The extensive exhibition space is housed in different buildings. The former monastery contains the technological sections on metallurgy, casting and transport, as well as science sections featuring physics, optics, acoustics and astronomy. Another section shows the development of calculation, from the first mechanical calculating machine, invented by Pascal in 1642, to IBM computers. There is also a section on time measurement, with a reconstruction of a 1750 watchmaker's workshop. The printing section shows the 1810 automatic inking method by which 800 sheets an hour could be printed.

The cinema photography section shows how the claw device, used to make motion-picture film move, was developed from a sewing machine needle conceived by Singer in 1851. In the rooms dedicated to telephones and television is a reconstruction of the 1856 pantelegraph, the ancestor of the fax machine.

Another highlight is the section on locomotive engineering. The history of trains begins with the first locomotive in Italy, used for the Naples–Portici line in 1839, and ends with 1970s models.

A pavilion in Via Olona houses the air and sea transport section, featuring

→
The bustling Naviglio Grande area, famous for its nightlife

two historic pieces: the bridge of the transatlantic liner *Conte Biancamano* and a naval training ship.

The Leonardo da Vinci Gallery displays models of the machines invented by the genius, alongside his drawings. Some models, like those of the rotating crane and the helical airscrew, which demonstrate principles of physics and applied mechanics, can be operated by the public.

Along the Naviglio Grande

G9 Alzaia Naviglio Grande

Now one of the liveliest quarters in Milan, the Navigli area formed the city's port district until the 19th century. Work on the Naviglio Grande canal first began in 1177, followed by the Pavia, Bereguardo, Martesana and Paderno canals. A system of locks allowed boats to travel along the canals on different levels (Candoglia marble was taken to the Duomo of Milan in the 14th century in this way).

Ludovico il Moro improved this network of canals with the help of Leonardo da Vinci in the 15th century. Barges arrived laden with coal and salt and departed with handmade goods and textiles. Some sections of the canals, which once extended for 150 km (93 miles), were filled in during the 1930s, and navigation ceased altogether in 1979. Thanks to the Navigli canals, in 1953 Milan was ranked the 13th port in Italy despite being landlocked.

Today, the big barges have become nightclubs. All along the Naviglio are blocks of flats painted in the typical "Milan yellow" and built with balconies running around courtyards. Among the places of note here is the beautiful church of Santa Maria delle Grazie al Naviglio, which faces the water.

INSIDER TIP

Mercatone dell'antiquariato

Antique lovers should not miss Milan's biggest open-air market, which lines the Naviglio Grande. Held on the last Sunday of every month, stalls sell furniture, paintings and ceramics.

EAT

Osteria del Gnocco Fritto

This restaurant is known for its pasta and its fried gnocchi, a crispy delicacy from the Emilia region served with a side of cheese or cured meats.

F9 Via Pasquale Paoli 2 gnoccofrittomilano.it

Belé Ristorante

The gourmet Belé Ristorant focuses on experimental revisitations of traditional Italian dishes. Try the spicy duck appetizer.

F9 Via Angelo Fumagalli 3 Mon beleristorante.com

Pasta Fresca da Giovanni

This small restaurant specializes in fresh pasta, including ravioli, tortellini and tagliatelle.

G9 Via Ascanio Sforza 31 Tue pastafrescadagiovanni.altervista.org

Testone

A rustic Italian, Testone is the best place in Milan to try *torta al testo*, a type of Umbrian focaccia cooked on a special pan and served with a variety of different toppings. Vegetarian options are also available.

G8 Via Vigevano 6 magnatestone.it

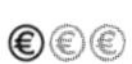

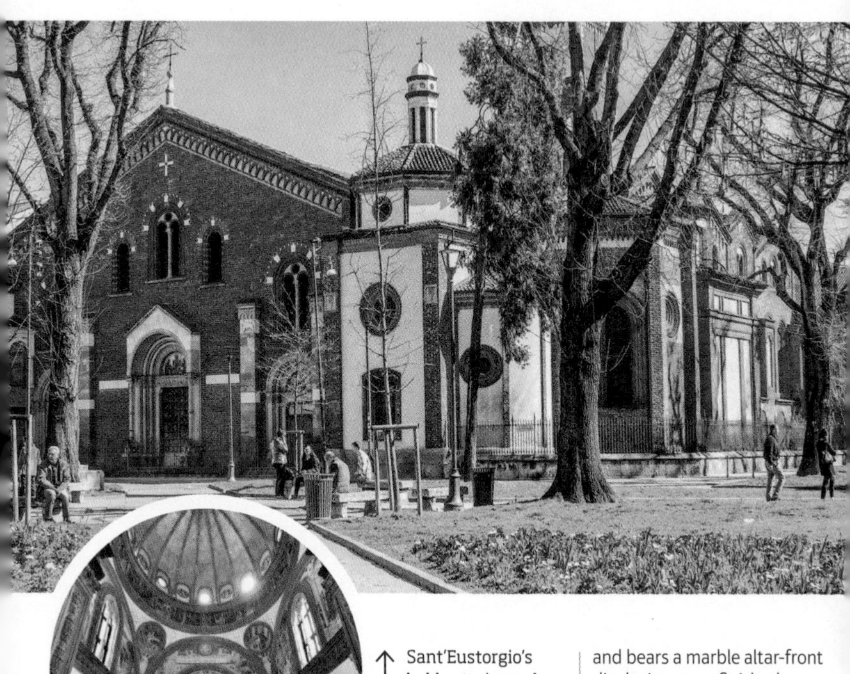

↑ Sant'Eustorgio's bold exterior and *(inset)* the Portinari Chapel dome within

12

Sant'Eustorgio

H8 Piazza Sant'Eustorgio 1 02-5810 1583 3, 9, 15, 29, 30 94 7:45am-noon & 3:30-6:30pm Tue-Sun; Portinari Chapel: 10am-6pm Tue-Sun

In the 11th century, work began on building a basilica over one founded by St Eustorgius in the 4th century, to house the relics of the Magi. The main structure of the present-day church was built in the 1300s.

On the right-hand side of the façade, which was rebuilt in 1865, there are several chapels dating from the 13th–15th centuries. The Brivio chapel houses Tommaso Cazzaniga's tomb of Giovanni Stefano Brivio (1486). The middle bas-relief depicts the *Adoration of the Magi*, and the altarpiece is a triptych by Bergognone. In the Baroque Crotta-Caimi chapel is a fine sarcophagus by 15th-century sculptor Protaso Caimi, and a depiction of *St Ambrose on Horseback*. The Visconti chapel has beautiful 14th-century frescoes: on the vault are the Evangelists and a *St George and the Dragon*, as well as the *Triumph of St Thomas*. The Torriani chapel, dedicated to St Martin, is frescoed with symbols of the Evangelists.

In the south transept is the large late Roman sarcophagus that once housed the relics of the Magi, and on the altar is a Campionese-school marble triptych of the journey of the Magi (1347). The Magi are also the subject of the fresco, attributed to Luini. The high altar houses the remains of St Eustorgius and bears a marble altar-front displaying an unfinished Passion of Christ.

Behind the altar, a passage leads to the Portinari Chapel, commissioned by banker Pigello Portinari as his tomb, and to house the body of St Peter Martyr. The first

THE RELICS OF MAGI

Emperor Constantine donated the relics in around 315 and they were taken to Milan by Bishop Eustorgius. Legend has it that the sarcophagus was so heavy the cart was forced to stop at the city gates, where the original Sant'Eustorgio basilica was founded and the Apostle Barnabas baptized the first Milanese Christians. Barbarossa moved the relics to Cologne in 1164. Some were returned in 1903, an event still celebrated at Epiphany with a procession.

example of a 15th-century central-plan church in Milan, it exemplifies the clarity of the architect Bramante's vision and features typical Lombard decoration attributed to painter Vincenzo Foppa. Under the dome is the tomb of St Peter Martyr (1339) by sculptor Giovanni di Balduccio, held up by the eight Virtues and showing scenes of his ministry. The small chapel on the left has an urn containing the saint's skull.

Sant'Alessandro

J7 Piazza Sant'Alessandro 02-8645 3065 M3 Missori 2, 3, 12, 15, 24, 27 9:30am-12:30pm Mon-Fri; 4-7:30pm Sat & Sun

Lorenzo Binago built this church in 1601 for the Barnabiti family. The interior has lavish Baroque furnishings and decoration; the frescoes were painted by Moncalvo and Daniele Crespi. In the presbytery is the *Life of St Alexander* by Filippo Abbiati and Federico Bianchi. The high altar (1741) is beautifully decorated with large semi-precious stones.

Next to the church are the Scuole Arcimbolde, schools for the poor founded in 1609 by the Barnabiti family. Opposite is Palazzo Trivulzio, rebuilt by Ruggeri in 1713, with the family coat of arms on the middle window. This family founded the Biblioteca Trivulziana, the library now in the Castello Sforzesco *(p80)*.

Nearby Via Palla leads to the Tempio Civico di San Sebastiano, begun by Pellegrino Tibaldi in 1577 and completed in the 1700s. Its interior features works by the Italian Baroque painters Legnanino, Montalto and Federico Bianchi.

Armani/Silos

E8 Via Bergognone 40 M2 Porta Genova 2, 9, 14, 19 68, 90, 91 11am-7pm Wed-Sun (to 9pm Thu & Sat) armanisilos.com

This large and stark former industrial building – built in 1950 for the preservation of cereals – was opened to the public in 2015. Here, visitors can enjoy a selection of garments created between the 1980s and the present day by the fashion designer Giorgio Armani.

The collection, showcased over four floors, explores and illustrates the aesthetics of the famous stylist and is divided not chronologically but into the themes that have inspired his creative work, including unusual patterns, fabrics and colours. This permanent collection confirms the role of Milan as one of the world's premier fashion capitals.

SHOP

Tortona 4arte

Browse a collection of advertising posters and furniture from the 1960s, neon signs and lamps at this mid-century modern store.

F8 Via Tortona 4 tortona4arte.com

STAY

Nhow Milan

A designer hotel housed in a former industrial building, Nhow has a rooftop bar and a range of colourful suites.

E8 Via Tortona 35 nh-hotel.com

Magna Pars, l'Hotel à Parfum

Set in a former perfume factory, this boutique hotel has its own signature fragrance and a relaxing spa.

F8 Via Vincenzo Forcella magnapars.it

A photography exhibition on display at Armani/Silos

Sant'Alessandro's interior has lavish Baroque furnishings and decoration; the frescoes were painted by Moncalvo and Daniele Crespi.

A SHORT WALK

FROM SANT'AMBROGIO TO SAN LORENZO

Distance 2 km (1 mile) **Time** 25 minutes **Nearest metro** 2 Sant'Ambrogio

Situated just outside the Roman walls, this area was occupied by early Christian cemeteries and imperial age buildings such as the Arena and Circus. Though little remains of this ancient heritage, the columns of the triumphal entrance to the basilica of San Lorenzo can still be seen on a gentle stroll around the area. Nine kings of Italy were crowned in Sant'Ambrogio in the 9th–15th centuries, with four buried here. Napoleon came here in 1805, and Ferdinand of Austria in 1838, after their respective coronations in the Duomo. On the feast day of Sant'Ambrogio, 7 December, the Oh Bej! Oh Bej! fair is held outside Castello Sforezesco.

Did You Know?

Inside Sant'Ambrogio is a black bronze snake, which is rumoured to have healing powers when touched.

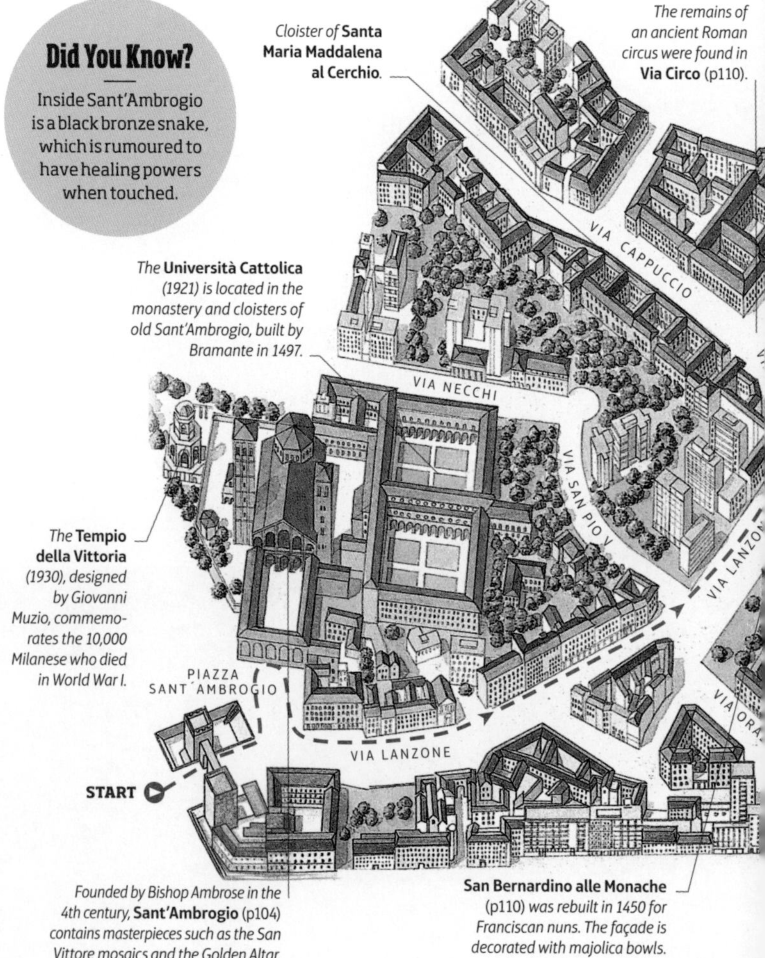

Cloister of ***Santa Maria Maddalena al Cerchio****.*

The remains of an ancient Roman circus were found in **Via Circo** (p110).

The **Università Cattolica** *(1921) is located in the monastery and cloisters of old Sant'Ambrogio, built by Bramante in 1497.*

The **Tempio della Vittoria** *(1930), designed by Giovanni Muzio, commemorates the 10,000 Milanese who died in World War I.*

Founded by Bishop Ambrose in the 4th century, **Sant'Ambrogio** (p104) *contains masterpieces such as the San Vittore mosaics and the Golden Altar.*

San Bernardino alle Monache *(p110) was rebuilt in 1450 for Franciscan nuns. The façade is decorated with majolica bowls.*

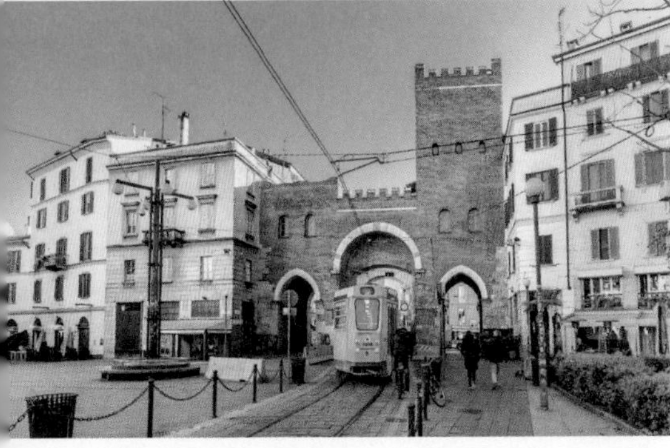

↑ A tram running through the medieval Porta Ticinese

From Sant'ambrogio to San Lorenzo
SOUTHWEST MILAN

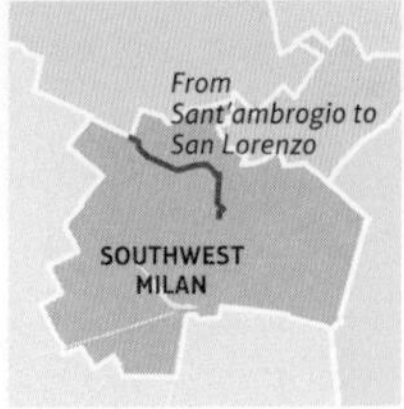

Locator Map
For more details see p100

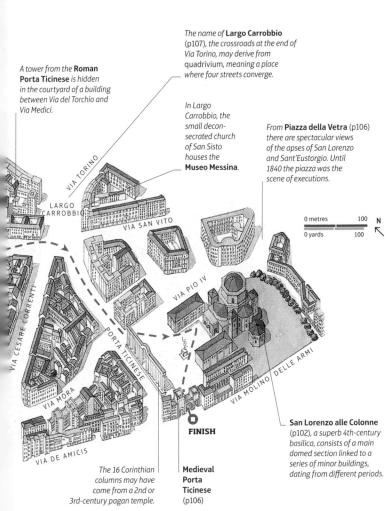

The name of **Largo Carrobbio** (p107), *the crossroads at the end of Via Torino, may derive from* quadrivium, *meaning a place where four streets converge.*

A tower from the **Roman Porta Ticinese** *is hidden in the courtyard of a building between Via del Torchio and Via Medici.*

In Largo Carrobbio, the small deconsecrated church of San Sisto houses the **Museo Messina**.

From **Piazza della Vetra** (p106) *there are spectacular views of the apses of San Lorenzo and Sant'Eustorgio. Until 1840 the piazza was the scene of executions.*

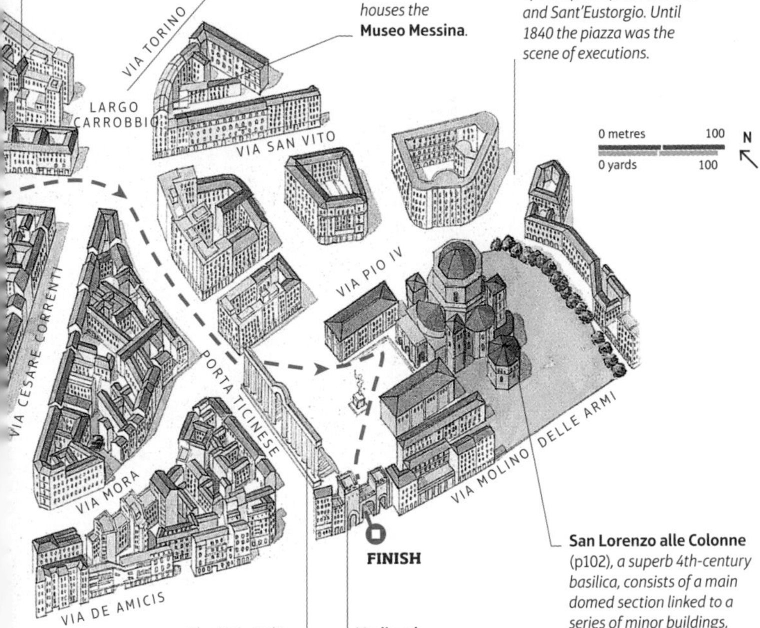

VIA TORINO
LARGO CARROBBIO
VIA SAN VITO
VIA PIO IV
VIA CESARE CORRENTI
PORTA TICINESE
VIA MORA
VIA DE AMICIS
VIA MOLINO DELLE ARMI
FINISH
0 metres 100
0 yards 100
N

San Lorenzo alle Colonne (p102), *a superb 4th-century basilica, consists of a main domed section linked to a series of minor buildings, dating from different periods.*

The 16 Corinthian columns may have come from a 2nd or 3rd-century pagan temple.

Medieval Porta Ticinese (p106)

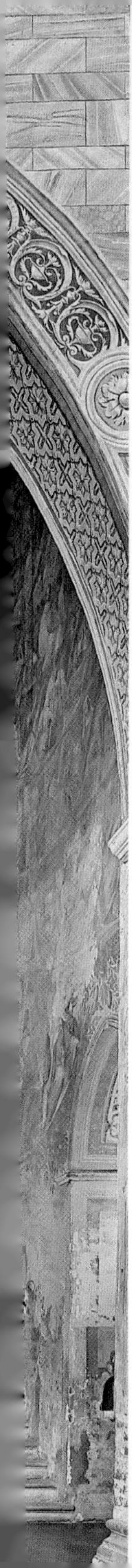

Detailed frescoes in Abbazia di Chiaravalle

SOUTHEAST MILAN

Southeast Milan mostly comprises the district of Guastalla, bordered by the Porta Monforte neighbourhood to the north. Formed of monasteries and bourgeois residences up until the early 19th century, Guastalla is named after the Baroque-style Giardino della Guastalla, one of the city's most delightful green spaces. The district's history can be traced back to the 17th century, perhaps most notably through the beautiful Rotonda della Besana. Used as a cemetery in the 1600s, its function ceased when the Austrians took control of the city in the late 18th century.

Austrian history can also be found in the street names across Southeast Milan. The area stretches as far as Piazza Cinque Giornate, named after the five days of heavy street fighting between Milanese locals and the Austrian army in 1848. The fierce battle pushed General Radetzky and his Austrian forces out of Lombardy, eventually leading to the First Italian War of Independence that same year.

The area experienced heavy airstrikes during World War II, and the latter half of the 20th century became a time of rejuvenation. Architects seized the opportunity to experiment with new heights and styles with the construction of the Brutalist Torre Velasca in 1958. Meanwhile, Ca' Granda, a former hospital, was transformed into a university campus that buzzes with students today.

SOUTHEAST MILAN
Must See
1 Abbazia di Chiaravalle
Experience More
2 San Nazaro Maggiore
3 Torre Velasca
4 Ca' Granda
5 Corso di Porta Romana
6 Giardino della Guastalla
7 Largo Augusto and Via Durini
8 Santo Stefano Maggiore and San Bernardino alle Ossa
9 Palazzo Sormani Andreani
10 San Pietro in Gessate
11 Palazzo di Giustizia
12 Rotonda della Besana
13 Conservatorio di Musica Giuseppe Verdi
14 Santa Maria della Passione
15 Palazzo Isimbardi
16 Fondazione Prada
Eat
① Il Panino
② Incontro Restaurant & Drink
Drink
③ Gecko23
④ Bar Luce
Stay
⑤ Aparthotel Meneghino
⑥ Bloom Hotel
HISTORIC CENTRE
p52
SOUTHWEST MILAN
p98
Palazzo Morando
Museo Poldi Pezzoli
VIA MONTENAPOLEONE
VIA DELLA SPIGA
CORSO G. MATTEOTTI
San Babila
S. Fedele
Pal. Durini
CORSO EUROPA
Duomo
Largo Augusto and Via Durini
Palazzo Reale
Santo Stefano Maggiore and San Bernardino alle Ossa
PIAZZA DIAZ
V. RASTRELLI
VIA LARGA
VIA SAN BERGAMINI
VIA ANDREANI
VIA CHIARAVALLE
VIA S. ANTONIO
Ca'Granda (ex Ospedale Maggiore)
Torre Velasca
Ca' Granda
VIA FRANCESCO SFORZA
Giardino Della Guastalla
San Nazaro Maggiore
Ospedale Maggiore di Milano (Policlinico)
CORSO DI PORTA ROMANA
V. SANTA SOFIA
Teatro Carcano
S. Calimero
LARGO D. CROCETTA
Crocetta
VIA A. LAMARMORA
PIAZZA CARD. FERRARI
Istituto Ortopedico G. Pini
VIA G. PINI
VIA QUADRONNO
CORSA DI PORTA VIGENTINA
S. Pietro dei Pellegrini
VIA CASSOLO
Sant' Eustorgio
PIAZZA XXIV MAGGIO
VIALE GIAN GALEAZZO
VIA BIANCA DI SAVOIA
VIA L. MANELLI
VIA CARLO CRIVELLI
VIA B. ORIANI
VIALE BEATRICE D'ESTE
PIAZZA A. MONDADORI
VIA PIETRO CUSTODI
VIA PIETRO TEULIÈ
VIALE SABOTINO
VIA SALASCO
CORSO S. GOTTARDO
VIA GIOVENALE
Università Comm. Bocconi
VIA F. BOCCONI
VIA VIGNOLA
VIA CARLO VITTADINI
VIALE J. S. BACH
VIA G. BELLEZZA
VIA R. SARFATTI
VIA ODOARDO TABACCHI
VIA GIAMBOLOGNA
VIA G. CASTELBARCO
Parco Ravizza
VIA F. SOAVE
VIA A. BOSELLI
VIALE TOSCANA
VIA GIUSEPPE RIPAMONTI
VIA GIUSEPPE MEDA
Provveditorato agli Studi
VIALE TIBALDI
G
H
J
K
6
7
8
9
10

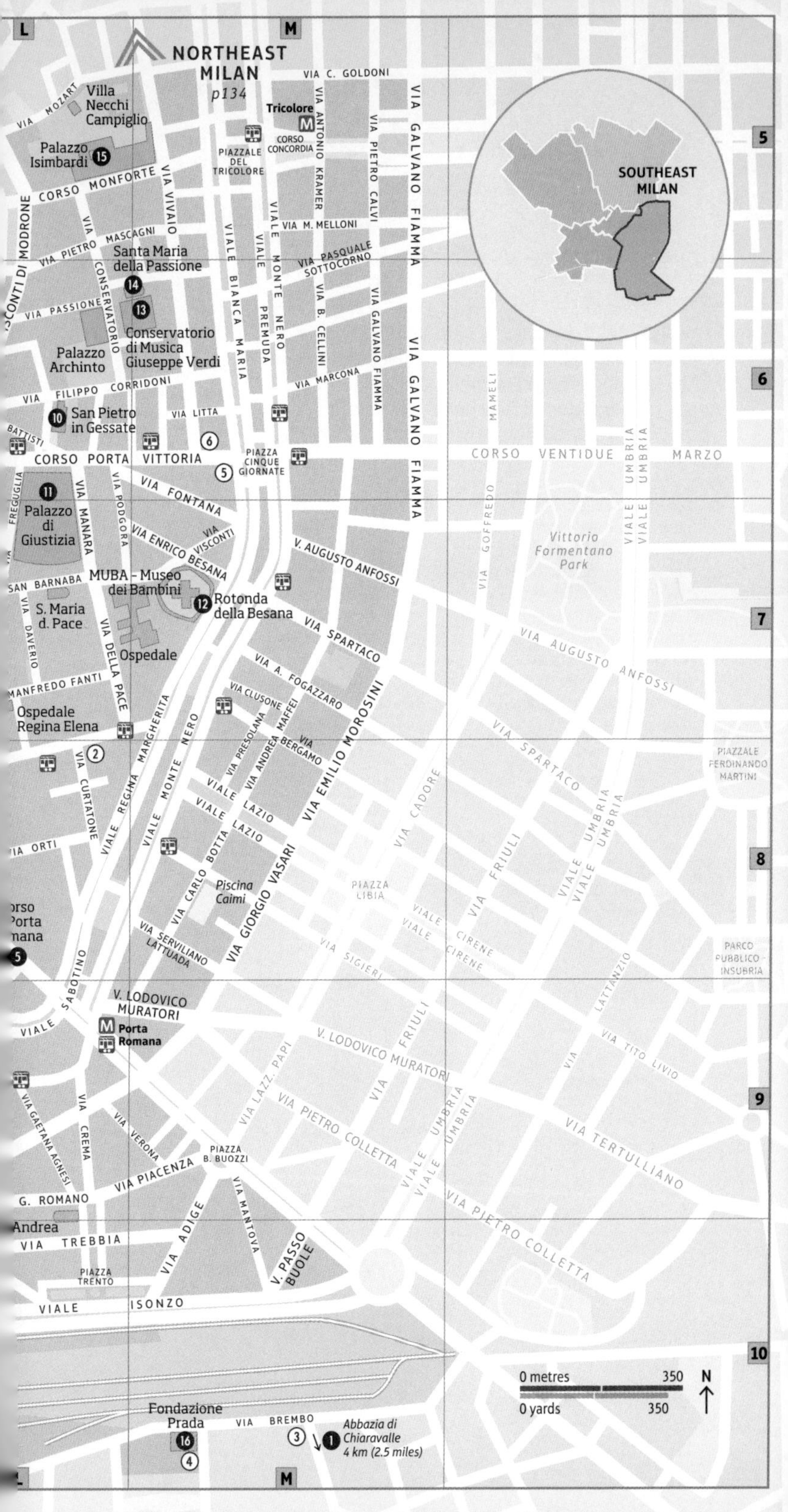

NORTHEAST MILAN
p134
SOUTHEAST MILAN
Villa Necchi Campiglio
Palazzo Isimbardi
Santa Maria della Passione
Conservatorio di Musica Giuseppe Verdi
Palazzo Archinto
San Pietro in Gessate
Palazzo di Giustizia
MUBA - Museo dei Bambini
Rotonda della Besana
S. Maria d. Pace
Ospedale
Ospedale Regina Elena
Vittoria Formentano Park
Piscina Caimi
Tricolore
Porta Romana
Fondazione Prada
Abbazia di Chiaravalle 4 km (2.5 miles)
CORSO MONFORTE
CORSO PORTA VITTORIA
CORSO VENTIDUE MARZO
VIA GALVANO FIAMMA
VIA SPARTACO
VIA AUGUSTO ANFOSSI
VIA EMILIO MOROSINI
VIA GIORGIO VASARI
V. LODOVICO MURATORI
VIA PIETRO COLLETTA
VIA TERTULLIANO
VIALE ISONZO
VIA BREMBO
PIAZZA CINQUE GIORNATE
PIAZZALE DEL TRICOLORE
PIAZZA LIBIA
PIAZZA B. BUOZZI
PIAZZALE FERDINANDO MARTINI
PARCO PUBBLICO INSUBRIA
0 metres 350
0 yards 350

1

ABBAZIA DI CHIARAVALLE

M10 Via Sant'Arialdo 102, Chiaravalle Milanese
9am-noon & 2:30-5:30pm Tue-Sat, 2:30-5pm Sun
monasterochiaravalle.it

Embellished with frescoes by Renaissance greats, this beautiful monastery is an important place of devotion for the local Cistercian community. Outside, the manicured grounds include a fully functional water mill and a peaceful medicinal herb garden.

French Cistercian monks began constructing this church in 1150–60, and it was dedicated to the Virgin Mary in 1221. The complex is a combination of French Gothic and Lombard Romanesque, resulting in a delightful example of Cistercian architecture. The bell tower was added in 1349. The entrance is in the 16th-century tower flanked by two small churches. In 1798, Napoleon suppressed the monastic order, the monks were forced to leave and the abbey deteriorated so much that in 1861 Bramante's 15th-century cloister was demolished to make room for a railway line. Restored and returned to the monks, the abbey has regained its former splendour and is again an oasis of peace.

THE MONKS' LAND RECLAMATION

The Cistercian monasteries were based on the rule of *ora et labora* - prayer and labour - and played a crucial role in transforming the marshy Milanese terrain. They used the new water meadow technique, which consisted of flooding the meadows with water from an adjoining stream (kept at a constant temperature of 12° C/54° F) so that the grass would grow quickly and could be harvested even in winter.

Did You Know?

The tower houses the oldest Ambrosian system bell still in operation, dating back to 1453.

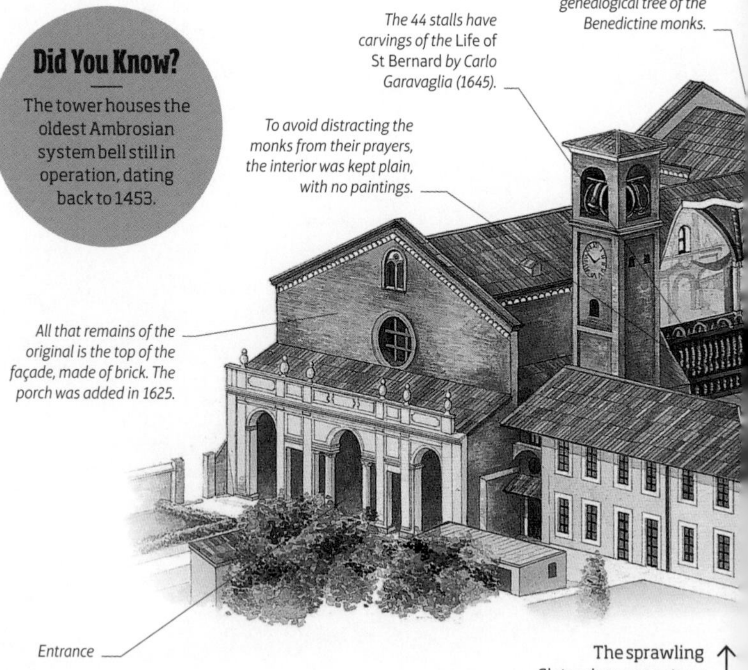

On the dome are 14th-century frescoes telling The Legend of the Virgin. Those in the transept represent the genealogical tree of the Benedictine monks.
The 44 stalls have carvings of the Life of St Bernard by Carlo Garavaglia (1645).
To avoid distracting the monks from their prayers, the interior was kept plain, with no paintings.
All that remains of the original is the top of the façade, made of brick. The porch was added in 1625.
Entrance

The sprawling Cistercian monastery of Chiaravalle

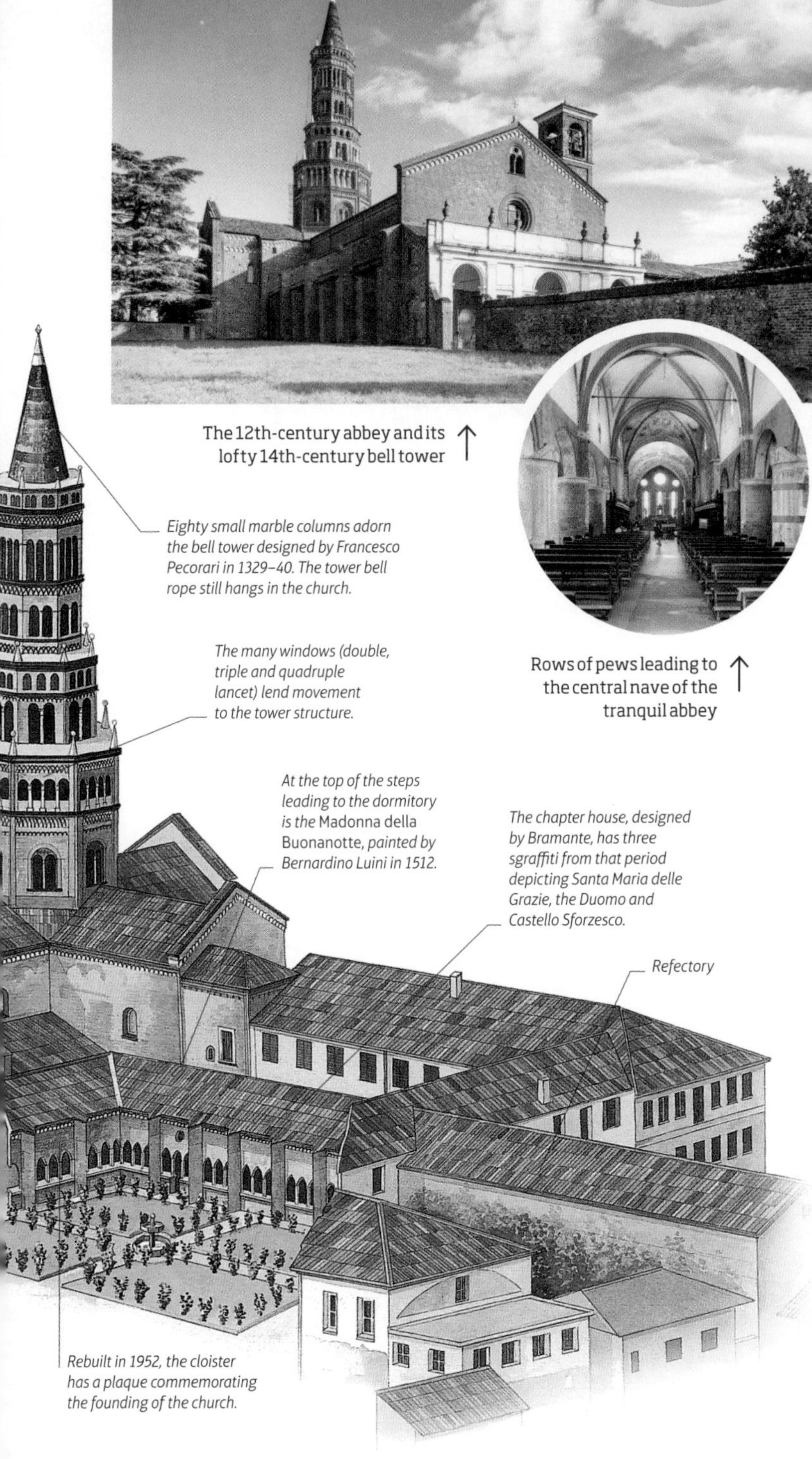

Eighty small marble columns adorn the bell tower designed by Francesco Pecorari in 1329–40. The tower bell rope still hangs in the church.
The many windows (double, triple and quadruple lancet) lend movement to the tower structure.
At the top of the steps leading to the dormitory is the Madonna della Buonanotte, painted by Bernardino Luini in 1512.
The chapter house, designed by Bramante, has three sgraffiti from that period depicting Santa Maria delle Grazie, the Duomo and Castello Sforzesco.
Refectory
Rebuilt in 1952, the cloister has a plaque commemorating the founding of the church.

The 12th-century abbey and its lofty 14th-century bell tower ↑

Rows of pews leading to the central nave of the tranquil abbey ↑

The iconic Torre Velasca skyscraper, dominating Milan's skyline

EXPERIENCE MORE

San Nazaro Maggiore

K7 Piazza San Nazaro 02-5830 7719 M3 Missori, Crocetta 16, 24 77, 94 7am-noon & 3:30-6:30pm Mon-Fri; 8am-12:30pm & 4-6:30pm Sat & Sun

The original basilica was built by Sant'Ambrogio in 382–6 CE to house the remains of the Apostles Andrew, John and Thomas, which is why it was known as the *Basilica Apostolorum*. It was dedicated to San Nazaro when his remains – found by Sant'Ambrogio near the basilica – were buried here in 396. The church was built outside the walls in an early Christian burial ground – as can be seen by the sarcophagi outside and the epitaph in the right-hand transept – and looked onto an ancient Roman porticoed street. It was rebuilt after a fire in 1075, reusing much original material.

In front of the façade is the octagonal Trivulzio Chapel, begun in Renaissance style in 1512 by Bramantino and continued by Cristoforo Lombardo. It houses the tomb of Gian Giacomo Trivulzio.

The nave of the church has a cross vault. Either side of the entrance are the remains of the Romanesque doorway covered by the Trivulzio Chapel. On the walls, among fresco fragments, are parts of the original masonry. In the crossing, the dome is supported by the 4th-century piers; two choir altars contain the remains of the Apostles and San Nazaro. Left of the altar is the cruciform chapel of San Lino, featuring traces of 10th- to 15th-century frescoes. In the transepts are a fine *Last Supper* by Bernardino Lanino and *Passion of Jesus* by Luini. The Chapel of St Catherine (1540) has Lanino's *Martyrdom of St Catherine* and a stained-glass window depicting the *Life of St Catherine*.

Torre Velasca

J7 Piazza Velasca 5 M3 Missori 12, 15, 16, 24, 27 94

This tower, built in the late 1950s by architects Belgioioso, Nathan Rogers and Peressutti, is one of the best-known monuments in modern-day Milan. The overhang of the upper part of the building and its red colour are reminiscent of Italian medieval towers, but the shape actually grew out of the need to create more office space in a limited area.

Ca' Granda

K7 Via Festa del Perdono 5 02-5032 5032 M Missori 12, 15, 16, 24, 27 54, 77, 94 7:30am-7:30pm Mon-Fri (first 3 wks of Aug: to 3:30pm), 8am-noon Sat Sun & public hols

The "Casa Grande", or Ospedale Maggiore, was built for Francesco Sforza from 1456 with the aim of uniting the city's 30 hospitals. The "large house" was designed by Filarete, who built only part of it, and was finished in stages in the 17th and 18th centuries. In 1939, the hospital moved to a new site, and since 1952 the Ca' Granda has housed the liberal arts faculties of the Università Statale, Milan's university. The hospital was modern for its

PICTURE PERFECT

Ca' Granda

The impressive Renaissance cloister inside the Università Statale's faculties housed in Ca' Grande is a great backdrop for group photos. Play with the perspectives and angles for extra depth.

time: there were separate wings for men and women – each with a central infirmary – and a large courtyard between them. Known as the Cortile Maggiore, this courtyard housed a Renaissance arcade and Baroque loggia. Also of note here is the church of the Santa Maria Annunciata (17th century), which contains a 1639 canvas by Guercino.

Corso di Porta Romana

L8 M3 Missori, Crocetta 12, 15, 16, 24, 27 77, 94

This avenue was laid out over a porticoed stretch of the ancient Roman road outside the city walls (2nd–3rd century CE) that led to Rome. It ran from Porta Romana to a triumphal arch (near the widening in the road known as Crocetta), transformed by Barbarossa into a fortified gate in the walls in 1162. The new gate (1171) was demolished in 1793.

The Corso is lined with many noble palazzi, such as Palazzo Annoni at No 6, designed by Francesco Maria Richini (1631), famous for its art collection, which houses works by Rubens and Van Dyck. Via Santa Sofia crosses the Corso, and goes over the Naviglio canal close to the Crocetta.

Opposite is the Teatro Carcano (1803), where the great Italian actress Eleonora Duse performed. The Corso ends at the Porta Romana (in Piazzale Medaglie d'Oro), built in 1598. To the right are remains of the Spanish walls built by Ferrante Gonzaga (1545), which were demolished in 1889.

EAT

Il Panino

Head to Il Panino for gourmet sandwiches on the go. Try the panino with deer salami, goat's cheese and marmalade.

K6 Via del Laghetto 7 339 3838 785 Sun

Incontro Restaurant and Drink

This spot serves local dishes with creative twists. Order the lamb with smoked carrot cream and honey-glazed carrot or the risotto with shellfish and scampi tartare.

L8 Via Lamarmora 36 Mon incontro.restaurant

Ca' Granda's ornate 15th-century brick façade and *(inset)* Cortile Maggiore

STAY

Aparthotel Meneghino
This hotel offers comfortable studio apartments with private kitchenettes and microwaves. The rooms feature wall-sized modern photos of Milan.

M6 Corso di Porta Vittoria 58 aparthotel meneghino.com

Bloom Hotel
The rooms at Bloom Hotel are spacious and tastefully decorated with contemporary furnishings. Some rooms have balconies with great city views.

M6 Corso di Porta Vittoria 51 bloomhotelmilano.it

Giardino della Guastalla

K7 Via Francesco Sforza, Via S Barnaba, Via Guastalla 12, 23, 27 60, 73, 77, 84, 94 7am-7pm daily (Mar: to 8pm; Apr & Oct: to 9pm; May-Sep: to 10pm)

This pretty garden – Milan's oldest – was laid out in 1555 by Countess Ludovica Torelli della Guastalla, next to the college of the same name for the daughters of impoverished aristocrats. In the early 1600s, it was transformed into an Italian-style garden, and a goldfish pond on two communicating terraces was added. There is also a 17th-century shrine representing Mary Magdalen attended by angels, and a Neo-Classical temple by Luigi Cagnola. In 1939, the garden was separated from the adjacent Sormani park and opened to the public. At the Via Guastalla exit (No 19) you can visit the Synagogue, designed by Luca Beltrami (1890–92) and, at the corner of Via San Barnaba, the church of Santi Barnaba e Paolo, which is part of the nearby Chierici Regolari di San Paolo college. It is a prototype of 16th-century Lombard churches, founded in 1558 and then modified by Galeazzo Alessi. Inside are paintings by Aurelio Luini, son of Bernardino, Camillo Procaccini and Moncalvo.

Largo Augusto and Via Durini

K6 M1, 3 Duomo 12, 15, 23, 27 54, 60, 61, 73, 77, 84, 94

The Verziere Column, commissioned by Carlo Borromeo to celebrate the end of the 1576 plague, has stood in Largo Augusto since 1580. It is one of the few votive columns to survive the late 18th century. Many were lost after the suppression of the monastic orders that owned them, or sacrificed to make room for new buildings. This square marks the start of Via Durini, which is dominated by the concave façade of Santa Maria della Sanità (1708). No 20 is Casa Toscanini, the conductor's house, and No 24 is Palazzo Durini, built in 1648

←

The Baroque fish pond in the Italian-style Giardino della Guastalla

by Francesco Maria Richini, and now an office building. Nearby, on Corso Europa, is 16th-century Palazzo Litta Modignani, where a Roman mosaic was found.

8

Santo Stefano Maggiore and San Bernardino alle Ossa

K6 Piazza Santo Stefano 02-5849 9801 M1, 3 Duomo 12, 23, 27 54, 60, 73, 77 8am-noon & 4-6:30pm Mon-Sat, 8am-12:30pm & 3-7:30pm Sun

Santo Stefano dates back to the 5th century. It was rebuilt in 1075 after being destroyed by a fire and rebuilt again in its present form in 1584 by Giuseppe Meda. The Baroque bell tower was built in 1643–74 by Carlo Buzzi: the pilaster at the base is all that remains of the quadriporticus that once faced the medieval basilica.

The church was used as the Diocesan Archive, which has now moved. Next door are San Bernardino alle Ossa, originally medieval but since rebuilt many times, and the ossuary chapel (with a concave façade) built in 1210 and altered in 1695. The latter is small and covered with human bones and skulls. The dim light and dark walls contrast with the bright colours of the fresco on the vault by Sebastiano Ricci (1695): *The Triumph of Souls Among Angels.*

SPOOKY MILAN

Decorated from floor to ceiling with human skulls and bones from abolished cemeteries, San Bernardino alle Ossa makes for a haunting visit but it's not the only site in Milan with a spooky history. Duchess Lucrezia Borgia's ghost is said to haunt the Pinacoteca Ambrosiana *(p62)*, while according to folklore, the two holes in a Roman column at Sant'Ambrogio's basilica *(p104)* were made by the devil's horns in a fight with St Ambrose, the patron saint of Milan.

Palazzo Sormani Andreani

L7 Corso di Porta Vittoria 6 800-88 00 66 12, 23, 27 54, 60, 73, 77, 84, 94 9am-7:30pm Mon-Sat Public hols, Aug

The palazzo, constructed in the 18th century, was enlarged in 1736 by Francesco Croce, who made it into one of the most lavish residences to exist at that time. Croce also designed the characteristic late Baroque curved façade. Reconstructed after World War II, the palazzo became the home of the Municipal (or Sormani Andreani) Library, the largest in Milan. It features over 580,000 works, including Stendhal's private library, a newspaper library with about 19,500 Italian and foreign publications, and a record and CD collection. An expansive catalogue of all the Milan libraries is also located here, as is the regional periodicals catalogue.

The Neo-Classical back opens onto a garden, part of the larger original one, which is used for small, temporary exhibitions. Nearby, at No 2 Via Visconti di Modrone, is one of Milan's excellent traditional *pasticcerie*, the Taveggia 1909 pastry shop.

→

San Bernardino's ossuary and its ceiling fresco by Sebastiano Ricci

San Pietro in Gessate

L6 Piazza San Pietro in Gessate 02-5410 7424 12, 23, 27 60, 73, 77, 84 8am-5:30pm Mon-Fri; 8:30-noon & 3:30-5:30pm Sat, 9:30am-1:15pm & 5-8pm Sun

This church was built in 1447–75 by the Solari school and financed by the banker Pigello Portinari, whose emblem is on the outer wall of the apse. In the middle of the façade, rebuilt in 1912, is a portal with an effigy of St Peter, which was added in the 1600s. The Gothic interior has a three-aisle nave with ribbed vaulting and pointed arches, and has preserved some original painting. The church was damaged during World War II, in particular the right-hand chapels, where there are traces of frescoes by Antonio Campi, Moncalvo and Bergognone (whose *Funeral of St Martin* is in the fifth chapel). The third and fifth chapels on the left have fine frescoes by Montorfano: *Life of St John the Baptist* (1484) and *The Legend of St Anthony Abbot*. The eight choir stalls were rebuilt with the remains of the 1640 ones by Carlo Garavaglia, damaged in 1943 and partly used as firewood during the war. The left-hand transept has frescoes of the *Life of Sant'Ambrogio* (1490) commissioned by the Sforza senator Ambrogio Grifi from Bernardino Butinone and Bernardino Zenale. In the lunettes under the vault, next to *Sant'Ambrogio on Horseback*, you can see the figure of a hanged man whose rope "drops" into the scene below, down to the hangman. These frescoes were discovered in 1862.

Palazzo di Giustizia

L6 Corso di Porta Vittoria 12, 23, 27 60, 73, 77, 84

The centre of attention in the early 1990s because of the Mani Pulite (Clean Hands) corruption inquests and trials that changed much of the face of Italian politics, the Milan Law Courts were designed in typical Fascist style (1932–40) by Marcello Piacentini. The building also houses the Notarial Acts Archive, formerly in the Palazzo della Ragione *(p68)*. The Palazzo has 1,200 rooms and 65 law courts with works by contemporary artists, including Mario Sironi's fresco in the Assize Court.

12   

Rotonda della Besana

M7 Via San Barnaba, corner of Via Besana 9, 12, 16, 19, 27 60, 73, 84 For exhibitions and summer cultural events only; Museo dei Bambini (MUBA): 7am-8pm Tue-Sun (Apr & Oct: to 9pm; May-Sep: to 10pm) muba.it

The Rotonda was the cemetery of the nearby Ca' Granda Hospital *(p124)*, designed in 1695 by Francesco Raffagno on present-day Viale Regina Margherita. When it was closed in 1783, viceroy

Façade of the Romanesque San Pietro in Gessate

↑ The church within the Rotonda di Via Besana complex and *(inset)* its octagonal bell tower

Eugène de Beauharnais tried to change it into the Pantheon of the Regno Italico (1809), but the project fell through and the round brick building first housed patients with infectious diseases and then, up to 1940, was the hospital laundry. It is now used for temporary exhibitions and as an outdoor cinema in summer.

The Rotonda is also home to the Museo dei Bambini, an educational museum for kids that holds specially conceptualised laboratory activities and several interactive exhibits.

In the middle is the deconsecrated San Michele ai Nuovi Sepolcri, built in 1713. It has a Greek cross plan with a central altar, visible from all sides. The small skulls sculpted on the capitals are a reminder of the original function of this complex.

On Via San Barnaba is Santa Maria della Pace, designed by Pietro Antonio Solari in 1466, the property of the Order of Knights of the Holy Sepulchre. In 1805, the church was suppressed and the paintings removed (some are now in the Brera), but some 17th-century frescoes by Tanzio da Varallo remain.

The nearby monastery is the home of the Società Umanitaria, founded in 1893 to educate and aid the poor. It has a library devoted to labour problems. The only remaining part of the monastery is the refectory, with a *Crucifixion* by Marco d'Oggiono. Returning to Corso di Porta Vittoria, you come to Piazza Cinque Giornate, with a monument by Giuseppe Grandi (1895) commemorating the anti-Austrian insurrection of 1848 *(p47)*. The female figures symbolize the Five Days, whose dead are buried in the crypt below.

13

Conservatorio di Musica Giuseppe Verdi

M6 Via Conservatorio 12 02-762 1101 12, 23, 27 54, 61, 77 For concerts only; Library: 9am-6pm Mon-Fri

Milan's Conservatory was founded by viceroy Eugène de Beauharnais in 1808. Although the Milan Conservatoire was named after Giuseppe Verdi, the composer was refused admission to that very school in 1832. The conservatory has trained some of the most important musicians and conductors in Italian history. Among those who have studied here are prominent artists such as Alberto Mozzati, Giacomo Puccini, Riccardo Muti and Ludovico Einaudi.

The building houses a chamber music hall and a large auditorium for symphonic music. The library contains over 35,000 books and 460,000 pieces of written music and scores, including works by Mozart, Rossini, Donizetti, Bellini and Verdi. A small museum showcases several precious stringed instruments.

Did You Know?

Verdi was refused admission to the conservatory for his incorrect hand posture on the piano.

The nave of Santa Maria della Passione and its impressive vault

14

Santa Maria della Passione

L/M6 Via Conservatorio 14 02-7602 1370 12, 23, 27 54, 61, 77, 94 7am-noon and 3-6:15pm daily

The second-largest church in Milan, after the Duomo, was built under the patronage of the prelate Daniele Birago, who had donated the land to the Lateran Canons. Work began in 1486 to a design by Giovanni Battagio. Originally the church had a Greek cross plan but it was lengthened with a nave and six semi-circular chapels on each side in 1573 by Martino Bassi. The façade of the church – and the nearby convent, now the home of the Conservatory – was added in 1692 by Giuseppe Rusnati, who kept it low so that visitors could appreciate the majestic octagonal covering of the dome designed by Cristoforo Lombardo (1530). To enhance this view and link the church with the Naviglio, Abbot Gadio had the Via della Passione laid out in front of the entrance in 1540.

The interior, with a frescoed barrel vault, is very atmospheric. Fourteen early 17th-century portraits of the saints of the Lateran Order, attributed to Daniele Crespi and his school, are on the piers. In the right-hand chapels, two works worth seeing are *Christ at the Pillar* by Giulio Cesare Procaccini, on the altar of the third chapel, and the *Madonna di Caravaggio*, a fresco attributed to Bramantino, in the sixth chapel. The presbytery still has its original Greek cross structure. The paintings hanging from the piers, mostly the work of Crespi, narrate the Passion and include *Christ Nailed to the Cross*. Behind the Baroque high altar is a wooden choir (16th-century) with mother-of-pearl inlay.

The church became a place of intense musical activity throughout the 16th and 17th centuries, when two organs were built opposite each other, on either side of the choir. The instrument on the right was created by the famous Antegnati, and the one on the left by Cristoforo Valvassori, who was involved in building the organ in the Duomo. The doors of the latter instrument have scenes from the Passion painted by Crespi. Frequent classical music concerts for organs pieces composed for four hands are still held here.

There are remarkable Cinquecento paintings in the transepts: the artwork on the right-hand side has a *Deposition* altarpiece by Bernardino Ferrari (after 1514) with the *Legend of the Cross* in the predella; and on the altar to the left is Gaudenzio Ferrari's *Last Supper* (1543), with a *Crucifixion* by Giulio Campi (1560) alongside.

The chapels on the left side of the nave contain fine works by Camillo Procaccini, Vermiglio and Duchino. The first chapel is noteworthy because of the impressive realism of Crespi's *St Charles Fasting*, and the vault frescoed by Giulio Campi (1558) is also impressive. The 15th-century Chapter House was designed and painted by Bergognone: saints and doctors are in a false peristyle.

On the right-hand wall is *Christ with the Apostles*. In Via Bellini you can see the left side of the church and the dome. At No 11 is the Art Nouveau Casa Campanini (1904), with wrought iron work by Alessandro Mazzucotelli.

DRINK

Gecko23

A chic yet informal café, Gecko24 has an outdoor patio and is known for serving great cocktails and large aperitivos.

M10 Via Brembo 23 02-364 530

Bar Luce

This cinematic café was designed by director Wes Anderson for the Fondazione Prada. Take in the Italian 1950s aesthetics and arched ceilings while sipping on one of the delicious cocktails they have to offer.

M10 Fondazione Prada, Via Isarco 2 fondazioneprada.org/barluce

Palazzo Isimbardi

L5 Corso Monforte 35 02-8845 5555 (Tourist information and reception desk) M1 San Babila 9, 23 54, 61, 94 Several days in the year, by appointment only

The seat of the Milan provincial government since 1935, this palazzo dates from the 15th century but was enlarged by the noble families who lived in it, among whom were the Isimbardi, who purchased it in 1775. The 18th-century façade on Corso Monforte leads to the porticoed court of honour (16th century), which still has its original herringbone pattern paving. The garden behind this has an admirable Neo-Classical façade designed by Giacomo Tazzini (1826).

The palazzo is open to the public twice a month. Inside there are many interestingly decorated rooms and fine works of art, such as the wooden 17th-century globe by Giovanni Jacopo de Rossi. The most important room is the Giunta (Council Chamber), which in 1954 became the home of Tiepolo's masterful *Triumph of Doge Morosini*, which came from Palazzo Morosini in Venice. The Sala dell'Antegiunta has a lovely 18th-century Murano glass chandelier, while the Sala degli Affreschi features 17th-century frescoes taken from the villa of Cardinal Monti at Vaprio d'Adda. The Studio del Presidente is decorated with a Neo-Classical ceiling, partly in fine gold. In 1940, the Province of Milan enlarged the palazzo. The new façade on Via Vivaio was decorated with bas-reliefs sculpted by Salvatore Saponaro depicting the activities of the Milanese. At No 31 Corso Monforte is the Palazzo della Prefettura, rebuilt in its present state in 1782. It has frescoes by Andrea Appiani. It is not open to the public.

Fondazione Prada

M10 Largo Isarco 2 02-5666 2611 M3 Lodi TIBB 65 10am-7pm Wed-Mon 1 Jan, 25 Dec fondazioneprada.org

The brainchild of fashion designer Miuccia Prada and her husband Patrizio Bertelli, the Fondazione Prada is an institution dedicated to contemporary art, cinema and culture. Among the exhibits is the Milan Atlas project, a group exhibition spread across six levels, containing works by ten artists, including Carla Accardi and Jeff Koons.

As well as organizing exhibitions by international artists, the Fondazione promotes activities such as film festivals, multidisciplinary and philosophical conferences and events related to architecture and design.

The venue itself, an early 20th-century distillery attractively redesigned by the Dutch architect Rem Koolhaas, is worth the visit alone.

PRADA'S HISTORY

It was 1910 when Milanese brothers Mario and Martino Prada opened a fashion store in Via Vittorio Emanuele. They went on to become the royal family's official suppliers of leather accessories in 1919. When they retired in the 1950s, the shop went to Luisa, Mario's daughter, and later to her daughter Miuccia, who, with her husband Patrizio Bertelli, turned the brand into one of the world's most famous fashion names.

The glass-and-concrete Fondazione Prada, designed by Rem Koolhaas ↓

A SHORT WALK

SAN NAZARO TO LARGO AUGUSTO

San Nazaro to Largo Augusto

SOUTHEAST MILAN

Locator Map

For more details see p120

Distance 1 km (0.5 miles) **Time** 15 minutes
Nearest metro 3 Missori

There are many interesting old buildings to view while walking in this area, including the university quarter, with cafés and specialist bookshops, as well as crafts shops on Via Festa del Perdono. Architectural styles in this district range from the 4th-century San Nazaro, founded by St Ambrose, to the Ca' Granda, the old hospital, a marvellous sight when viewed from Largo Richini because of its sheer size and the beauty of its 15th-century arcade. More changes of style come with the palazzi in Corso di Porta Romana and Via Sant'Antonio, and the modern Torre Velasca. The quarter's hospital tradition can be seen in the votive columns at the crossroads, where mass for the sick took place, and the San Bernardino alle Ossa chapel, decorated with the bones of former hospital patients.

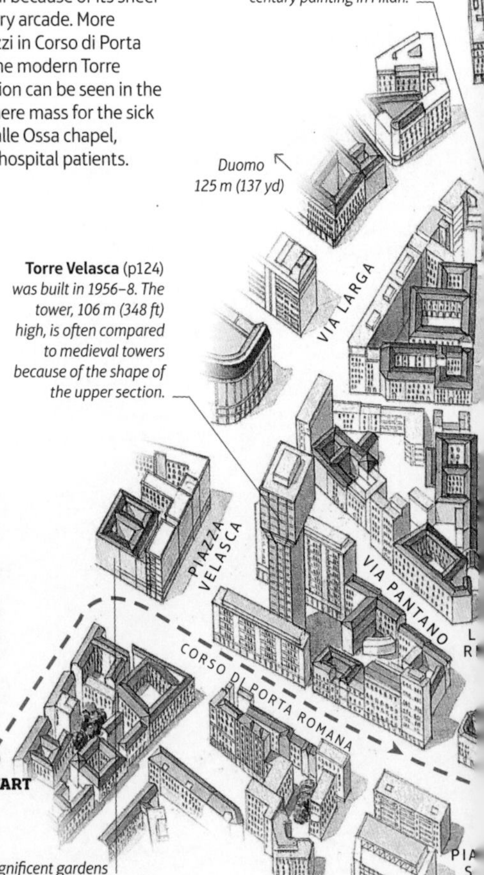

Sant'Antonio Abate was rebuilt in 1582. It houses paintings by Bernardino Campi and Moncalvo, and is a gallery of early 17th-century painting in Milan.

Torre Velasca (p124) *was built in 1956–8. The tower, 106 m (348 ft) high, is often compared to medieval towers because of the shape of the upper section.*

Palazzi with magnificent gardens line **Corso di Porta Romana** (p125). *It follows the route of the ancient Roman road that led from Porta Romana all the way to Rome.*

↑ The iconic Torre Velasca, a symbol of modern Milan

←

Cycling past Santo Stefano Maggiore and San Bernardino alle Ossa

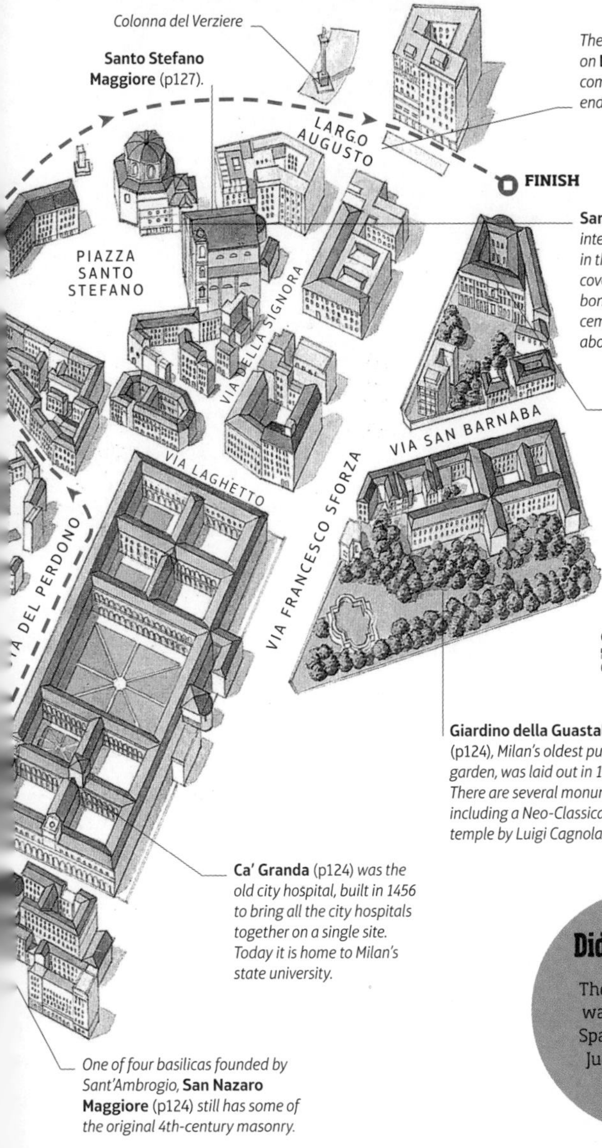

Colonna del Verziere

Santo Stefano Maggiore (p127).

The Colonna del Verziere on **Largo Augusto** (p126) *commemorates the end of the 1576 plague.*

LARGO AUGUSTO

FINISH

PIAZZA SANTO STEFANO

VIA DELLA SIGNORA

San Bernardino alle Ossa's *interior chapel* (p127), *rebuilt in the 17th century, is entirely covered with human bones and skulls from the cemeteries that were abolished in the 1600s.*

VIA SAN BARNABA

The Biblioteca Civica di Milano, housed in **Palazzo Sormani Andreani** (p127), *is the largest library in Milan. It has the private library of novelist Stendhal.*

VIA LAGHETTO

VIA FRANCESCO SFORZA

VIA DEL PERDONO

0 metres 100

0 yards 100

N

Giardino della Guastalla (p124), *Milan's oldest public garden, was laid out in 1555. There are several monuments, including a Neo-Classical temple by Luigi Cagnola.*

Ca' Granda (p124) *was the old city hospital, built in 1456 to bring all the city hospitals together on a single site. Today it is home to Milan's state university.*

One of four basilicas founded by Sant'Ambrogio, **San Nazaro Maggiore** (p124) *still has some of the original 4th-century masonry.*

Did You Know?

The Torre Velasca was named after Spanish governor Juan Fernàndez de Velasco.

The intricate archways of Cimitero Monumentale.

NORTHEAST MILAN

Loosely stretching from the Brera quarter to Via Montenapoleone and Corso Venezia, northeast Milan has long been a hub of creativity, recognized by many of the eponymous street names in the area. The Brera Academy, a famous art school, was established here in 1776 and Via Brera, which runs north, is named for the academy. The building was a popular meeting place for artists including writer Alessandro Manzoni and composer Giuseppe Verdi. In the 19th century, parts of the area were rebuilt in a Neo-Classical style, attracting wealthy aristocractic families and later luxury fashion houses, which transformed the neighbourhood into a prestigious fashion district known as the Quadrilatero della Moda. Many of Milan's creatives are buried in Cimitero Monumentale, further northeast, including the painter Francesco Hayez.

The city's main railway station, Stazione Centrale, was built in the early 20th century near the cemetery, transforming northeast Milan into a hub for transport and business. It is still functional today, transporting locals, visitors and keen shoppers to and from the bustling city.

NORTHWEST MILAN
p74
HISTORIC CENTRE
p52
NORTHEAST MILAN
ISOLA
Milano Lancetti
Pirelli Hangar Biocca 4 km (2.5 miles)
Cimitero Monumentale
Sacro Volto
Bosco Verticale
Stazione Porta Garibaldi F.S.
Garibaldi
Isola
Gioia
S. Antonio di Padova
Santa Maria Incoronata
Ospedale Fatebenefratelli
Moscova
Chiesa Anglicana
Sant' Angelo
Turati
Arena Civica
Arco della Pace
Acquario Civico
San Simpliciano
San Marco
Questura
Torre Branca
Parco Sempione
Triennale
Palazzo dell'Arte
Lanza
Pinacoteca di Brera
Palazzo Cusani
Orto Botanico
Santa Maria del Carmine
Montenapoleone
Museo Bagatti Valsecchi
Castello Sforzesco
Cairoli
Poldi Pezzoli
Via Manzoni
Teatro Dal Verme
Cordusio
Posta Telegr e Telefoni
Piazza del Duomo
Duomo
S. Sebastiano
Palazzo Reale
Pal. Arcivescovile
Via Alserio
Via Carlo Farini
Via Valtellina
Via Lario
Via Torquato Taramelli
Via Ugo Bassi
Via Cola Montano
Via Luigi Porro Lambertenghi
Via Jacopo Dal Verme
Via Sassetti
Via G. Pepe
Via F. Confalonieri
Via Gaetano de Castillia
Via Giuseppe Ferrari
Cavalcavia E. Bussa
Via Luigi Nono
Via Messina
Piazzale Cimitero Monumentale
Via Ceresio
Via C. Farini
Via P. Maroncelli
Viale Luigi Sturzo
Via del Nord
Via Melchiorre Gioia
Viale della Liberazione
Via Paolo Lomazzo
Via Bramante
Viale Pasubio
Corso Como
Viale Francesco Crispi
Viale Monte Grappa
V. Joe Colombo
Viale Montello
Via A. Volta
Via Varese
Bastioni di P.ta Nuova
Via Marsala
Via Solferino
Via Castelfidardo
V. Pinamonte da Vimercate
Via L. Canonica
Via Bertani
Viale Elvezia
Piazzale Lega Lombarda
Via Tenaglia
Via della Moscova
V. Giuseppe Parini
Via Appiani
Via Legnano
Corso Garibaldi
Via Statuto
Corso di Porta Nuova
Via L. Mantegazza
Via Palermo
Via San Marco
Piazza Mirabello
Via Montebello
Via Filippo Turati
Viale Cervantes
Viale Malta
Via Cernia
V. de Marchi
Via Gadio
Piazzale Marengo
Via Cav. D.S. Sepolcro
Via Pontaccio
Via dell' Annunciata
Piazza Castello
Foro Buonaparte
Via Mercato
Via Fiori Chiari
V. Brera
Via Monte di Pietà
Via Manzoni
Via Montenapoleone
Via Lauro
Via Verdi
Via Bochetto
Via Mengoni
1
2
3
4
5
6
F
G
H
J
K

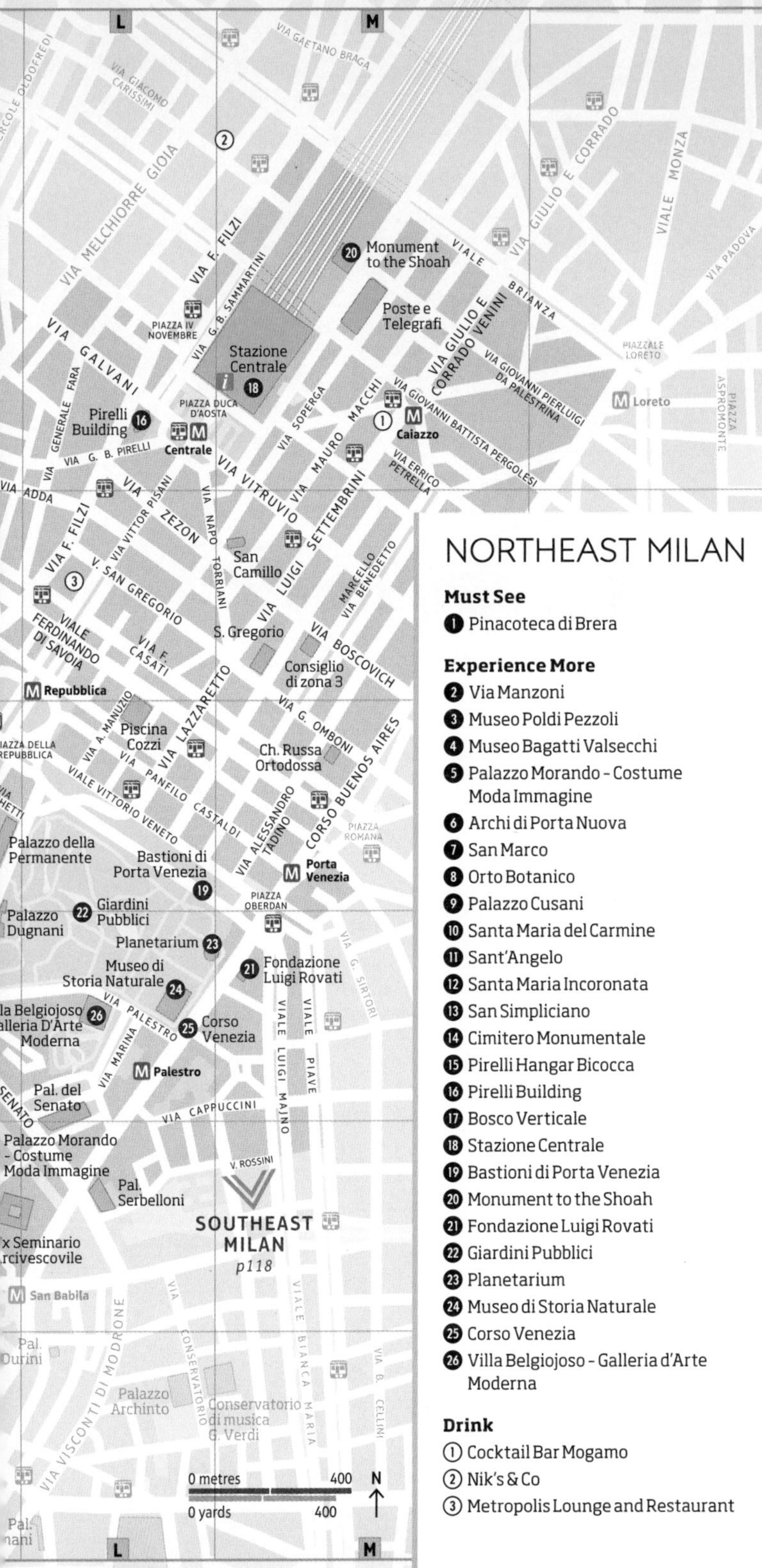

NORTHEAST MILAN

Must See

1 Pinacoteca di Brera

Experience More

2 Via Manzoni
3 Museo Poldi Pezzoli
4 Museo Bagatti Valsecchi
5 Palazzo Morando - Costume Moda Immagine
6 Archi di Porta Nuova
7 San Marco
8 Orto Botanico
9 Palazzo Cusani
10 Santa Maria del Carmine
11 Sant'Angelo
12 Santa Maria Incoronata
13 San Simpliciano
14 Cimitero Monumentale
15 Pirelli Hangar Bicocca
16 Pirelli Building
17 Bosco Verticale
18 Stazione Centrale
19 Bastioni di Porta Venezia
20 Monument to the Shoah
21 Fondazione Luigi Rovati
22 Giardini Pubblici
23 Planetarium
24 Museo di Storia Naturale
25 Corso Venezia
26 Villa Belgiojoso - Galleria d'Arte Moderna

Drink

① Cocktail Bar Mogamo
② Nik's & Co
③ Metropolis Lounge and Restaurant

Admiring Venetian masterpieces from the early 1500s

PINACOTECA DI BRERA

J4 Via Brera 28 M1, 3 Duomo, 2 Lanza 1, 4, 12, 14, 27 61 8:30am-7:15pm Tue-Sun (last adm 6pm) 1 Jan, 25 Dec pinacotecabrera.org

The Pinacoteca di Brera art gallery holds one of Italy's most important art collections, featuring masterpieces by leading Italian artists from the 13th to the 20th centuries, including Raphael, Mantegna, Ambrogio Lorenzetti, Piero della Francesca and Caravaggio.

The Pinacoteca is housed in the 17th-century Palazzo di Brera, a grand palace built as a Jesuit college and later used as an art academy. In the early 19th century, Napoleon augmented the academy's collection with works stolen from churches across the region, opening a picture gallery here in 1809. Over the next two centuries, the collection grew, spanning 38 rooms, with some of the finest Italian Renaissance and Baroque paintings.

13th-15th-Century Italian Painting

Rooms 2–4 feature frescoes from the *Oratory at Mocchirolo*, painted by an unknown Lombard master in around 1365–70. Other highlights include Ambrogio Lorenzetti's *Madonna and Child* (1320–3) and *Christ the Judge* by Giovanni da Milano (1365–9).

Inner courtyard of Pinacoteca di Brera, overlooked by a bronze statue of Napoleon

FRANCESCO HAYEZ

Born in Venice, Hayez (1791-1881) moved to Rome on a scholarship to study art before relocating to Milan in 1823. His earlier paintings explored many themes, including religious and political themes. Hayez's famous painting, *The Kiss* (1859), also captured his keen interest in Italian history. The artwork is intended to be an allegory of the passionate struggle for independence during the *Risorgimento*.

2,000

The number of artworks in the gallery's collection.

↑ Francesco Hayez's patriotic and sentimental painting *The Kiss*

15th-16th-Century Italian Painting

The Venetian section (Rooms 5–9, 14 and 19) features works by 15th- and 16th-century artists active in the Veneto, including Gentile and Giovanni Bellini, Carpaccio, Titian and Veronese. Mantegna's *Dead Christ* (c 1480), a piece known for its intense light and bold foreshortening, is a star attraction.

A collection of 15th–16th-century Lombard paintings is exhibited in Rooms 10–12, 14–16 and 19, including works by Bergognone, Luini, Bramantino and Vincenzo Foppa.

Rooms 20–23 illustrate artistic movements in the regions of Emilia and Marche. The Ferrara school is represented by its leading artists, Cosmè Tura, Francesco del Cossa and Ercole de' Roberti. In Room 24 is Raphael's altarpiece *The Marriage of the Virgin* (1504). Some scholars say the young man breaking the staff in the background to this painting is a self-portrait of the artist. Piero della Francesco's *Montefeltro Altarpiece* (c 1475) is in the same room. The egg suspended from its shell is a symbol of the Creation and of the Immaculate Conception.

17th-18th-Century Italian, Flemish and Dutch Painting

Among the non-Italian artists featured in Rooms 31–2 are Rubens, Van Dyck, Rembrandt, El Greco and Brueghel the Elder. In Room 38 is Italian artist Francesco Hayez's *The Kiss* (1859), a frequently reproduced work epitomizing the optimism that prevailed after Italy's unification.

Jesi Collection

The 72 works donated by Emilio and Maria Jesi in 1976 and 1984 are on show in Room 10. The collection, mostly by Italian artists, covers the 1910–40 period.

EXPERIENCE MORE

Via Manzoni

J5 M3 Montenapoleone, 1 Duomo 1 61, 94 Palazzi To the public

Once known as "Corsia del Giardino" (Garden Lane) because of its many parks, this street acquired its present name in 1865, when the great Italian novelist Manzoni died. Its aristocratic appearance is created by the patrician palazzi and Teatro alla Scala *(p60)*, which stimulated the opening of chic cafés in the area.

At No 6 is the 19th-century Palazzo Brentani, decorated with medallions with busts of illustrious persons, and No 10 is the Palazzo Anguissola (1775–8), which now houses the historic archive of the Banca Commerciale Italiana.

HIDDEN GEM

Palazzo Olivazzi

This palazzo at Via Manzoni 18 was a famous artist hangout in the late 1800s, frequented by the likes of Giuseppe Verdi and Francesco Hayez. Albert Einstein also lived here from 1894 to 1900.

No 12, another 19th-century building, is the home of the famous Museo Poldi Pezzoli, and No 29 is the Grand Hotel et de Milan (1865), where Giuseppe Verdi died in 1901.

Near the end of Via Montenapoleone stands Aldo Rossi's monument to former Italian President Sandro Pertini (1990) and, next to this, Palazzo Gallarati Scotti (No 30), built in the early 1700s. Opposite, Via Pisoni takes you to the remains of the 15th-century cloister of the Umiliate di Sant'Erasmo monastery, now part of a modern building. In the last stretch is 18th-century Palazzo Borromeo d'Adda, which was a haunt for literati and artists.

3 Museo Poldi Pezzoli

K5 Via Manzoni 12 M3 Montenapoleone 1 61, 94 10am-6pm Wed-Mon (last adm: 5:30pm) Most public hols museopoldipezzoli.it

This private museum was established by nobleman Gian Giacomo Poldi Pezzoli and opened to the public in 1881. A singular example of a late 19th-century aristocratic Milanese residence, it contains Pezzoli's collection of paintings, sculpture, rugs, armour, glass, and textiles.

The ground floor houses arms and armour from the 14th to the 19th centuries in a setting designed by artist Arnaldo Pomodoro. The Fresco Room, named after *The Apotheosis of Bartolomeo Colleoni* frescoed by Carlo Innocenzo Carloni, features a Tabriz carpet with hunting scenes (Persia, 1542–3). In the adjoining room is the museum's collection of lace.

The staircase, decorated with landscapes by Magnasco, leads to the first floor. In the Lombard Rooms is 15th- to 16th-century Lombard painting, with works by Bergognone, Luini, the Leonardoesque painters, a *Polyptych* by Cristoforo Moretti, and Vincenzo Foppa's *Portrait of Giovanni Francesco Brivio*. The portraits of Martin Luther and his wife by Lucas Cranach (1529) are in the Foreign Artists Room. A showcase of precious porcelain separates

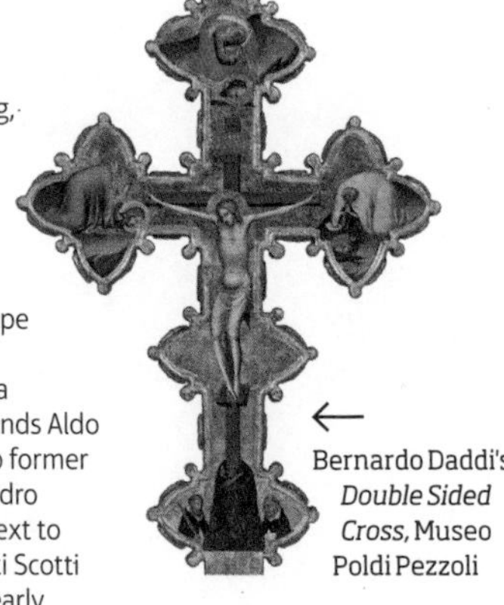

← Bernardo Daddi's *Double Sided Cross*, Museo Poldi Pezzoli

The 19th-century Grand Hotel de Milan, off Via Manzoni

↑ Guiseppe Bagatti Valsecchi's bedroom, the "Red Room", in Museo Bagatti Valsecchi

the next room from the Golden Room, where more master-pieces are on display. These include *St Nicholas of Tolentino* by Piero della Francesca, Botticelli's *Madonna and Child* and *Lamentation*, a *Madonna and Child* by Andrea Mantegna, Giovanni Bellini's *Pietà* and the *Portrait of a Young Woman* attributed to Piero del Pollaiolo. Three small rooms house the Visconti Venosta collection, the portraits by Fra Galgario, including *The Gentleman with the Tricorn*, and a very important collection of clocks from the 16th to the 19th centuries. The Murano Glass Room has fine specimens of Venetian glasswork, and the Dante Study features two stained-glass windows celebrating Dante's life. The last rooms house paintings by Tiepolo, Guardia and Canaletto, and 14th-century panels. Lastly, the Jewellery Room hosts a collection of precious jewellery and goldsmithery from antiquity up until the 19th century.

On some Wednesdays the museum organizes a "happy hour" between 6 and 9pm. The fee includes admission to the museum and a drink to enjoy while taking in the exhibits. Check the museum website for further details.

4   

Museo Bagatti Valsecchi

K5 Via Gesù 5 M3 Montenapoleone 1 61, 94 1-5:45pm Wed-Sun (tours by appt only, check website) Most public hols museobagattivalsecchi.org

Opened in 1994 in the prestigious late 19th-century residence of the two Bagatti Valsecchi brothers, Fausto and Giuseppe, this museum is an important record of art collectors' taste in that period. The building was designed in Neo-Renaissance style, with an elegant façade and two well-proportioned courtyards, and was furnished with works of art and imitation Renaissance furniture. It was seen as a private house and not a museum, and was furnished with every possible comfort. The rooms feature tapestries, ivory work, ceramics and arms, as well as important paintings such as the elegant *Santa Giustina* by Giovanni Bellini (c 1475; kept in what was Giuseppe Bagatti Valsecchi's bedroom), Bernardo Zenale's panels and a *Polyptych* by Giampietrino. The library, with its valuable 15th-century parchments and a series of 16th- to 17th-century porcelain pharmacy vases, is also worth a look.

The intriguing Valtellinese bedroom has a magnificent 16th-century bed with Christ ascending Calvary and scenes from the Old Testament carved in the bedstead. The Sala della Stufa Valtellinese is also interesting, with its marvellous 16th-century wood panelling with an elegant sculpted frieze and a piece of furniture ingeniously concealing a piano. The Camera Rossa (Red Room) contains a delightful small collection of 15th- to 17th-century furniture for children that includes a high chair, a baby walker and a cradle. The dining room has a collection of kitchenware, tapestries and sideboards.

Museo Bagatti Valsecchi's Valtellinese bedroom has a 16th-century bed with Christ ascending Calvary and scenes from the Old Testament carved in the bedstead.

DRINK

Cocktail Bar Mogamo
This relaxed bar, serving refreshing mojitos and other classic cocktails, is ideal for unwinding on the weekend. Sample their large sharing platters and finger food alongside your drinks.

M1 Viale Andrea Doria 12 Sun mogamo.it

Nik's & Co
A curated selection of cocktails inspired by bar cultures around the world are served at this unique and atmospheric bar.

M1 Via Giovanni Schiaparelli 14 niksandco.it

Metropolis Lounge and Restaurant
This Italian-style bar offers an extensive list of creative cocktails to enjoy at aperitivo hour. There is ample seating for larger groups, too.

L2 Via Vittor Pisani 5 cafe metropolis.it

↑ Archi di Porta Nuova, the gate which once led to Milan's old city centre

Palazzo Morando - Costume Moda Immagine

K5 Via Sant'Andrea 6 M3 Montenapoleone, 1 San Babila 1, 2 94 9am-1pm & 2-5:30pm Tue-Sun 1 Jan, 1 May, 25 Dec cos tumemodaimmagine.it

Appropriately located in the Fashion District (Quadrilatero della Moda), Milan's Museum of Costume can be found in an 18th-century aristocratic townhouse that displays the elegant style of the time with its original furnishings.

The collection illustrates the history of Milanese fashion from the 18th to the 20th centuries, combining the costumes and accessories of the Municipal Collections of Applied Arts (which used to be stored at the Castello Sforzesco) with the contents of the former Museum of Milan. The paintings and artifacts displayed alongside the costumes on the first floor reveal the extensive heritage of the city's art.

On the ground floor are temporary exhibits connected with the history of Milan's fashion. Documentaries are screened at the museum, and concerts are also held here.

6

Archi di Porta Nuova

K4 M3 Montenapoleone 1 61, 94

This city gate, restored in 1861, is one of two that survive from the medieval wall system. Construction began in 1171, and the gate was probably modelled on the corresponding Porta Romana, some of whose building mat-erials it used. The inner side on Via Manzoni is decorated with copies of 1st-century CE Roman tombstones, while the outside facing Piazza Cavour bears a tabernacle decorated with a *Madonna and Child with Saints Ambrose, Gervase and Protasius* (1330–39).

Facing the piazza is Palazzo dei Giornali (No 2), built in 1942 as the main office of the popular newspaper *Il Popolo d'Italia* and decorated beautifully with bas-reliefs by Mario Sironi. The square is framed by the Giardini Pubblici, in front of which is a monument to Cavour, a figure linked with the unification of Italy, by Odoardo Tabacchi (1865).

San Marco

J4 Piazza San Marco 2 43, 61, 94 7am-noon & 4-7pm daily

This church was begun in 1254 by the Augustine monk Lanfranco Settala. It was built on the site of an older church, dedicated by the Milanese to St Mark, patron saint of Venice, to thank the Venetians for help in the struggle against Emperor Frederick Barbarossa. In 1871, Carlo Maciachini built a Neo-Gothic façade around the Campionese school ogival portal and tabernacle.

The church has a Latin cross plan and nine patrician chapels, which were added to the right-hand aisle in the 14th–19th centuries. They contain 16th- to 17th-century paintings, including some by Paolo Lomazzo. In the right-hand transept is the lovely *Foundation of the Augustine Order* by the Fiammenghino brothers, Settala's sarcophagus by Giovanni Balduccio (1317–49), and fragments of late Gothic frescoes found during the 1956 restoration.

The presbytery is decorated with large canvases by Camillo Procaccini and Cerano, which depict the life and teachings of St Augustine. Also on display is the *Genealogical Tree of the Order* by Genovesino (17th century), who also painted the *Angels' Backs* on the cupola.

The left-hand transept leads to the Chapel of the Pietà, with *The Ascent to Calvary* by Ercole Procaccini. The left-hand aisle has canvases, by Camillo and Giulio Cesare Procaccini and Palma il Giovane. There's also a Leonardo-esque fresco that was found in 1975. From outside the Romanesque transept the 13th-century bell tower is visible.

Orto Botanico

J4 Via Brera 28 and Via Fratelli Gabba 10 M1, 3 Duomo, 2 Lanza 1, 4, 12, 14, 27 61 Apr-Oct: 10am-6pm Mon-Sat; Nov-Mar: 9:30am-4:30pm Mon-Sat 1 Jan, 1 May, 2 Jun, 25 & 26 Dec ortibotanici.unimi.it

Spanning a mere 5,000 sq m (53,820 sq ft), the Orto Botanico di Brera is probably one of the tiniest botanical gardens on earth. It forms part of a large cultural compound housed in the nearby Brera Palace, which includes the Pinacoteca di Brera art gallery *(p138)*, the Astronomical Observatory, the Biblioteca Braidense library and the Academy of Fine Arts. The secluded and peaceful gardens make a welcome change from the hustle and bustle of the city.

Once a place of meditation for Humiliati priests, and later the Jesuits, the garden was officially founded in 1774 under the Austrian Empress Maria Theresa. Today, it houses medicinal plants, salvias, peonies and decorative trees.

RARE PLANTS IN ORTO BOTANICO

Ginkgo biloba
The symbol of this botanical garden is the gingko biloba tree and there are two species here. In autumn, the leaves on these giant trees turn gold.

Salvia sclarea
An unusual species of sage, this herb also has medicinal properties.

Marsilea quadrifolia
A protected four-leaf clover-shaped fern.

Hieracium australe
This Italian perennial is the only endemic plant in Milan. It was originally sourced from the walls of the Castello Sforzesco.

Palazzo Cusani

J4 Via Brera 15 M2 Lanza 2, 12, 14 61 To the public

Originally built in the 1500s, this palazzo was rebuilt in 1719 by Giovanni Ruggeri, who designed the Baroque façade with its ornate windows and balconies, while the Neo-Classical façade facing the garden was designed by Piermarini. Tradition has it that the Cusani brothers ordered twin entrances so that each could have independent yet equal access. In the drawing room is an allegorical Tiepolo-like fresco (1740). The palazzo was the seat of the Ministry of War in the 19th century.

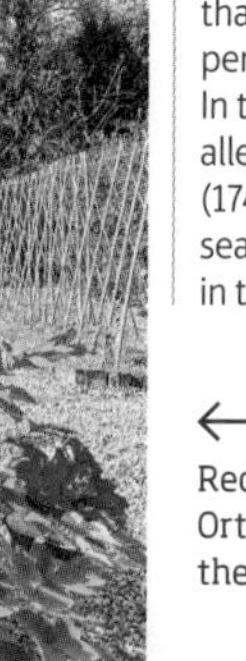

← Red peonies flowering in Orto Botanico, part of the Brera Palace compound

Santa Maria del Carmine

J4 Piazza del Carmine 2 02-8646 3365 2, 4, 12, 14 61 7:15am-7:15pm daily

Santa Maria del Carmine was built in Gothic style in 1447 over a Romanesque church and was then rebuilt in the Baroque period, while the present-day façade was designed by Carlo Maciachini in 1880. The spacious interior has a three-aisle nave covered by cross vaulting. The inclination of the first piers is due to the absence of a façade for a long period and the subsequent gradual settling of the building.

The right-hand transept contains part of the tomb of the ducal councillor Angelo Simonetta, above which are two paintings by Carlo Francesco Nuvolone and Fiammenghino. The opposite transept is decorated with an exquisite painting by Camillo Landriani. The statues in the wooden choir (1579–85) are the original plaster models created for the spires of the Duomo by 19th-century artists. The Cappella del Rosario, built on the right of the choir (1673) by Gerolamo Quadrio, has marble dressing and is decorated with canvases by Camillo Procaccini depicting *The Legend of Mary*.

On the left-hand side of the church is the monastery cloister, with remains of noble tombs and ancient tombstones, and a Baroque sacristy, with furniture made by Quadrio in 1692.

Sant'Angelo

K3 Piazza Sant'Angelo 2 02-6347 0547 43, 94 6:30am-8pm Mon-Sat, 9am-8pm Sun

Built in 1552 by Domenico Giunti to replace the older Franciscan church outside the Porta Nuova, which had been demolished to make room for the Spanish ramparts, Sant'Angelo is an important example of 16th-century Milanese architecture. The nave is separated from the presbytery by a triumphal arch with the *Assumption of Mary* by Legnanino (17th century). There are many 16th- and 17th-century paintings in the chapels. The first one on the right has canvases by Antonio Campi (1584) and a copy of the *Martyrdom of St Catherine of Alexandria* by Gaudenzio Ferrari (the original is in the Brera); the second has Morazzone's *St Charles in Glory*.

Santa Maria Incoronata

J2 Corso Garibaldi 116 02-65 48 55 M 2, 5 Garibaldi 43, 70, 94 7am-noon & 4-7pm daily

This church consists of two buildings designed by Guiniforte Solari, which were merged in 1468. The left one

The 19th-century façade of the Santa Maria del Carmine and *(inset)* its central nave, featuring a cross-vaulted ceiling

was built for Francesco Sforza in 1451 and the other was built soon afterwards for his wife. The brick façade is double, as is the nave, which has two apses with 15th- and 17th-century frescoes. In the right-hand chapels are plaques in memory of Sforzesco court personages. The chapels opposite have frescoes by Montalto and Bernardino Zenale (the fresco in the first chapel is attributed to Zenale).

13

San Simpliciano

H4 Piazza San Simpliciano 7 02-862 274 M2 Lanza 2, 4, 12, 14 43, 57, 61, 94 7:30am-noon & 3-7pm Mon-Sat; 8am-12:30pm & 4-7pm Sun

The church was founded by Sant'Ambrogio in the 4th century as the Basilica Virginum and completed in 401. It is preceded by a porch and once had open galleries on either side where penitents and new converts could take part in Mass. The façade, decorated with beautiful glazed plates, was added in 1870 by Maciachini, who retained the main portal. The capitals have 12th-century carvings of the processions of the Wise and Foolish Virgins. Fourteenth-century frescoes have been discovered in the first chapel on the right, and in the fourth is Enea Salmeggia's *Miracle of St Benedict* (1619). The apse is frescoed with the *Coronation of the Virgin* by Bergognone (1508). The Neo-Classical altar covers the wooden choir (1588), and on either side are two organ pedestals frescoed by Aurelio Luini in the 1500s. The transept leads to the early Christian Sacellum of San Simpliciano (closed), built to house the remains of San Simpliciano and of martyrs.

Coronation of the Virgin by Bergognone in San Simpliciano

SAN SIMPLICIANO, THE THREE MARTYRS AND THE CARROCCIO

St Ambrose asked the young Sisinius, Martirius and Alexander to go to Anaunia (today Val di Non) in northern Italy to spread Christianity. In 397, they were martyred and the bodies were given to Bishop Simpliciano, who buried them in the Basilica Virginum. According to legend, the martyrs were decisive in leading the Milanese to victory in the battle of Legnano against Barbarossa (1176). On that occasion three white doves flew out of the basilica and landed on the Carroccio (cart), the symbol of Milan, waiting to be blessed before the battle. On 29 May, the city commemorates this event with a solemn ceremony.

14

Cimitero Monumentale

G1 Piazzale Cimitero Monumentale 02-8846 5600 M5 Monumentale 2, 4, 12, 14 37 8am-5:30pm Tue-Sun

Extending over an area of 25 ha (62 acres), the Cimitero Monumentale was begun by Carlo Maciachini in 1866. The eclectic taste of the time dictated the use of various styles for the cemetery, from mock-Lombard Romanesque to Neo-Gothic, with touches of Tuscan thrown in.

The main entrance is via the Famedio *(Famae Aedes)*, or House of Fame, a sort of pantheon of illustrious Milanese and non-Milanese buried here. Author Alessandro Manzoni, Luca Beltrami, the architect who oversaw restoration of the Castello Sforzesco, the patriot Carlo Cattaneo and the Nobel Prize-winning poet Salvatore Quasimodo all have tombs in this cemetery. There are also busts of Garibaldi, Verdi and Cavour. The Romantic painter Hayez lies in the crypt.

A visit to the Cimitero Monumentale, which is a kind of open-air museum of art from the late 19th century to the present, begins at the large square inside, which contains the tombs of important Milanese figures. Around the square are monumental shrines and the Civico Mausoleo Palanti, an enormous mausoleum with a crypt, used as an air-raid shelter in 1943. Among its tombs are those of comic actor Walter Chiari and Hermann Einstein, Albert's father. On the terraces, to the left are the Elisi (sculpted by Francesco Penna, 1916) and Morgagni tombs, and an epigraph by Benito Mussolini commemorating a disastrous aeroplane crash. In the central avenue are two tombs designed and sculpted by Enrico Butti: that of Isabella Casati, *Young Woman Enraptured by a Dream*, a typical Lombard realist work (1890), and the Besenzanica shrine with *Work* (1912). On the right is the Toscanini tomb (Bistolfi, 1909–11), built for the conductor's son.

Among other monumental tombs for major figures in Milanese life are those of Carlo Erba, Bocconi, Campari and Falck. Many famous sculptors made pieces for this place: Leonardo Bistolfi, Giacomo Manzù, Odoardo Tabacchi, Adolfo Wildt and Lucio

The final resting place of Alessandro Manzoni in the Cimitero Monumentale and *(inset)* the Famedio ↓

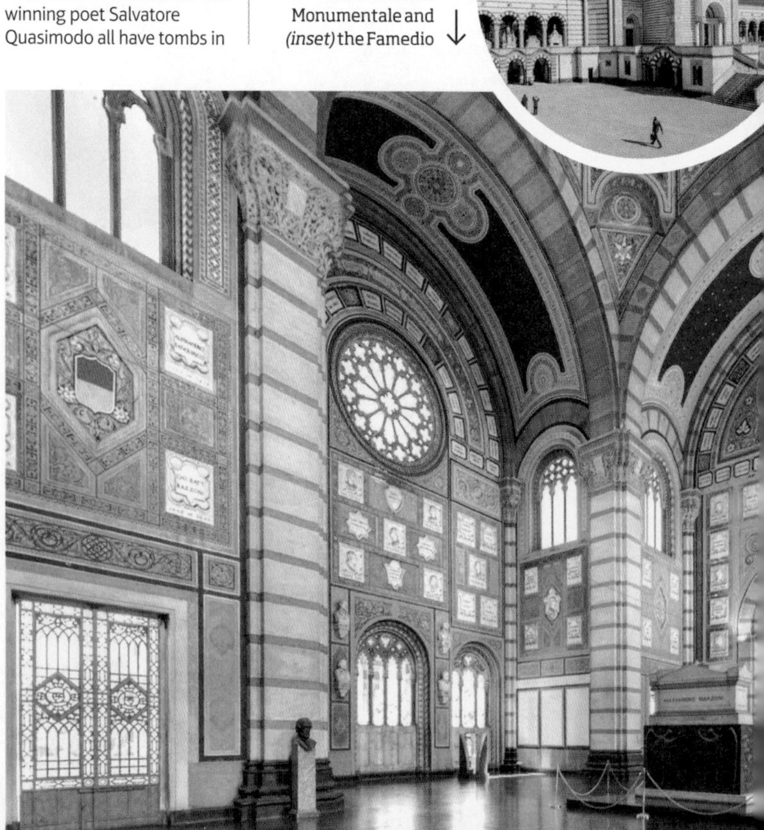

Fontana. The two enclosures beside the Famedio are for Jews and non-Catholics, with the remains of sculptor Medardo Rosso, publishers Arnoldo Mondadori and Ulrico Hoepli, and Jules Richard, founder of the Richard-Ginori ceramics industry.

Pirelli Hangar Bicocca

J1 Via Chiese 2 02-6611 1573 M1 Sesto Marelli 51, 87 10:30am-8:30pm Thu-Sun 1 Jan, 1 May, 2 Jun, 25 & 26 Dec pirellihangarbicocca.org

Housed in a former factory building (part of an industrial complex owned by Ansaldo-Breda-Pirelli), Pirelli Hangar Bicocca is the result of a renovation project to redevelop the area. A space devoted to the production, exhibition and promotion of contemporary art, it offers some of the best cultural programmes in Milan, including activities for kids.

Beyond the entrance, visitors are welcomed by Fausto Melotti's *La sequenza* (1981), an installation made of steel floating in a bed of ornamental grasses and wild flowers designed by the Milan-based architect Marco Bay. Inside there is another site-specific masterpiece: Anselm Kiefer's *The Seven Heavenly Palaces*. Created in 2004, it is considered one of the most important works by this German artist.

16

Pirelli Building

L1 Piazzale Duca d'Aosta-Via Pirelli M2, 3 Centrale 2, 9, 33 60, 82 To the public

The symbol of postwar reconstruction in Milan, the Pirelli Building, affectionately called "Pirellone" (big Pirelli) by the Milanese, was built in 1955–60. It was designed by a group of leading architects and engineers: Giò Ponti, Antonio Fornaroli, Alberto Rosselli, Giuseppe Valtolina, Egidio Dell'Orto, Pier Luigi Nervi and Arturo Danusso. At 127 m (417 ft) high, it was the largest reinforced concrete skyscraper in the world until the 1960s. The elegant edifice occupies only 1,000 sq m (11,000 sq ft) and stands on the site where, in 1872, Giovan Battista Pirelli built his first tyre factory.

The skyscraper was constructed as the company's main offices. Among the many records claimed by the Pirellone was that it was the first building in Milan taller than the Madonnina on the Duomo (108.50 m/356 ft). As a token of respect, a small statue of the Virgin Mary was placed on the Pirelli roof. Since 1979 the building has been the headquarters of the regional government of Lombardy. Next door is the luxurious Excelsior Hotel Gallia, opened in the 1930s.

↑ Bosco Verticale's iconic verdant apartment buildings

Bosco Verticale

J1 Via Gaetano de Castillia 11 M2, 5 Garibaldi 60, 81, 90, 166 To the public

The Bosco Verticale (Vertical Forest) residential buildings were designed as an urban reforestation project and an attempt to restore biodiversity to the city. Inaugurated in 2014, the two tall apartment buildings are home to around 20 different species of bird. There are terraces and outdoor spaces with vegetation equivalent to 30,000 sq m (320,000 sq ft) of woodland, featuring 800 trees, 15,000 perennials and 5,000 shrubs. This building creates an ideal microclimate for the apartment residents, as the plants regulate both temperature and humidity.

Did You Know?

Bosco Verticale is watered from the outside by a team of climbers called the Flying Gardeners.

Gae Aulenti Square, fronted by the green Bosco Verticale

18 Stazione Centrale

M1 Piazzale Duca d'Aosta M 2, 3 Centrale 5, 9 42, 60, 81, 87, 90, 91, 92

Milan's main railway station is one of the largest in Europe. Ulisse Stacchini's project design was ready in 1912, but construction work proved so slow that the building was not opened until 1931. The new railway station replaced one located in present-day Piazza della Repubblica.

The building, made with Aurisina stone, was inspired by the late Art Nouveau style, in marked contrast to the austere 1930s architecture of the surrounding buildings.

The façade is 207 m (679 ft) wide and 36 m (118 ft) tall. The arcades link up with the Galleria dei Transiti, a gallery decorated with four medallions by Giannino Castiglioni. In the ticket office hall, flights of steps lead up to the departures and arrivals lobby, with tile panels representing the cities of Milan, Rome, Turin and Florence.

The massive building is a landmark in Milan and second only to the cathedral in size. There are numerous shops inside, and some are open 24 hours a day.

HIDDEN GEM
Underground Clubbing

Housed in the tunnel of a former railway station near Stazione Centrale, club Tunnel *(www.tunnelclub.it)* offers a glimpse into Milanese nightlife right in the centre of town.

19 Bastioni di Porta Venezia

L3 M 1 Porta Venezia, 3 Repubblica 5, 9, 33

What is today a major road was once part of the walls built to defend the city in 1549–61 by the Spanish governor Ferrante Gonzaga. In 1789, the walls became a tree-lined avenue for walking and coach parking. The Porta Venezia ramparts, flanked by the Giardini Pubblici, link Piazza della Repubblica and Piazza Oberdan. The former was laid out in 1931 when the 19th-century railway station was demolished and rebuilt 800 m (875 yds) away and greatly enlarged to cope with increasing traffic resulting from the opening of the St Gotthard (1882) and Simplon (1906) passes through the Alps.

Not far from the piazza, in Via Turati, is the Palazzo della Permanente, designed by Luca Beltrami in 1885, as the home of the Permanent Fine Arts Exhibition. It is now used to hold temporary exhibitions.

Wide Piazza Oberdan is dominated by Porta Venezia, the city gate rebuilt in 1828 on the site of the Spanish gate of the same name and used

The monumental Stazione Centrale, constructed with Aurisina stone

Stazione Centrale was inspired by the late Art Nouveau style, in marked contrast to the austere 1930s architecture of the surrounding buildings.

as a customs toll station. The two buildings are decorated with statues and reliefs concerning the history of Milan. Porta Venezia separates Corso Venezia and Corso Buenos Aires, a major commercial thoroughfare.

In 1488–1513, Lazzaro Palazzi chose a site beyond the gate to build the *lazzaretto*, a hospital for plague victims commissioned by Ludovico il Moro. The few remains from the 1880 demolition can be seen in Via San Gregorio. A slight detour from Piazza Oberdan towards Viale Piave will take you past some interesting Art Nouveau-style buildings: Casa Galimberti, designed by Giovan Battista Bossi in 1903–4, decorated with wrought iron and panels of ceramic tiles, and the Hotel Diana Majestic.

20  

Monument to the Shoah

M1 Piazza Edmond Jacob Safra, 1 M2, 3 Centrale 42, 53, 81, 90, 91, 92 10am-4pm Thu, Sat-Mon memorialeshoah.it

Dedicated to the victims of the Shoah, Milan's Shoah Memorial is an exhibition commemorating the Nazi deportation of around 1,200 Italian Jews between 1943 and 1945 from Stazione Centrale. The foundation includes first-person accounts, video interviews with survivors, and a wall of names, listing all those who were deported. There's also a library and an educational space where visitors can conduct their own research.

21   

Fondazione Luigi Rovati

M4 Corso Venezia, 52 M1, 4 42, 61, 75, 94 10am-8pm Wed-Sun fondazioneluigirovati.org

Ancient artifacts and contemporary art coexist at this museum, which opened in 2022 in the remodelled 19th-century Palazzo Bocconi Rizzoli. The underground galleries have curved walls and domed ceilings made of layered stone. The lower level also hosts the foundation's extensive Etruscan collection, with urns, vases, statues and the famous Cernuschi Warrior displayed alongside works by Warhol and Picasso. The ground floor extends to an elegant courtyard designed by landscape architect Marilena Baggio, while the first and second floors display collections of contemporary art and temporary exhibitions. The restaurant is on the third floor.

INSIDER TIP
Pink Flamingoes

Peek through the fence of Villa Invernizzi *(Via dei Cappuccini 7)* near Giardini Pubblici and you'll spot a colony of pink flamingoes. The birds were first brought here in 1970 by "cheese king" Romeo Invernizzi.

Giardini Pubblici

L3/4 Corso Venezia, Via Palestro, Via Manin, Bastioni di Porta Venezia M 1 Porta Venezia, Palestro, 3 Repubblica, Turati 1, 9, 33 94 6:30am-sunset daily

Forming the largest city park in Milan, the public gardens extend for about 16 ha (40 acres). They were designed by Piermarini in 1786 and enlarged in 1857 by Giuseppe Balzaretto. Further changes were made by Emilio Alemagna in 1871–81.

The gardens are home to many tree species, including fir, elm and an ancient plane tree. Every May/June, the gardens host Orticola, a plant and flower market.

Inside the park is the Padiglione del Caffè (1863), now a nursery school, the Museo di Storia Naturale and the Planetarium. Also set in the park is the popular Bar Bianco. This Milan institution has plenty of outside seating and is open daily from 9am to 9pm.

Planetarium

L4 Corso Venezia 57 M 1 Porta Venezia, Palestro 9 Show times vary, check website for details W lofficina.eu

Donated to the city by the publisher Ulrico Hoepli, the Planetarium was built in 1930 in Classical style by Piero Portaluppi. The projection hall features a large hemispherical dome (20 m/65 ft) in diameter), with the skyline outlined just as it was when the Planetarium first opened, and 300 swivelling seats to gaze at the movements of the stars in absolute comfort. The multimedia projection system reproduces the stars as seen from any point on Earth, whether in the past, present or future.

In addition to the shows, the Planetarium offers guided tours suitable for all ages, including tours for students of the subject, and a lively programme of scientific and popular-level lectures on astronomy. There are also special events for students on Sundays.

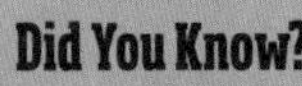

Did You Know?

The Planetarium is the largest and oldest in Italy.

Museo di Storia Naturale

L4 Corso Venezia 55 02-8846 3337 M 1 Porta Venezia, Palestro 9 10am-5:30pm Tue-Sun (last adm: 4:30pm) Most public hols

The Museum of Natural History was founded in 1838 with the donation of the Giuseppe de Cristoforis and Giorgio Jan collections. The building was constructed in Neo-Romanesque style in 1893 by Giovanni Ceruti. It has a specialist library with more than 30,000 volumes. On the ground floor are the mineralogy and entomology collections, and part of the Museo Settala, which was created by a canon named Manfredo. In the palaeontology halls there are reconstructions of dinosaurs, including a Triceratops and a large Allosaurus skeleton. The upper floor displays reptiles, cetaceans and mammals. There are also reconstructions of animal habitats and an area dedicated specifically to illustrating the ecological diversity of Italy and its conservation efforts.

Tyrannosaurus at the Museo di Storia Naturale and *(inset)* the bright building exterior

Corso Venezia

L4 Piazza San Babila 02-7600 2877 M1 Porta Venezia, Palestro, San Babila 9 54, 61, 94 8:30am-noon & 2:30-5:30pm daily

Framing the Fashion District to the west and connecting Piazza San Babila to Corso Buenos Aires, Corso Venezia is one of the city's most elegant and historic avenues. During the 1770s, enhancements were made to the Spanish city walls and new public gardens were created at Porta Venezia to commemorate the arrival of Archduke Ferdinand, the son of Maria Theresa of Austria, who assumed the role of governor of the Duchy of Milan in 1765. Many noble families built palazzi along Corso Venezia, including the Palazzo Serbelloni.

Villa Belgiojoso - Galleria d'Arte Moderna (GAM)

L4 Via Palestro 16 02-8844 5957 M1 Palestro 1 61, 94 9am-5:30pm Tue-Sun (last adm: 5pm); Giardini di Villa Belgiojoso Bonaparte: Apr-Oct: 9am-7pm; Nov-Mar: 9am-4pm 1 Jan, Easter, 15 Aug, 25 Dec gam-milano.com

Milan's modern art gallery is housed in a Neo-Classical villa built by the Austrian architect Leopold Pollack in 1790 for Count Ludovico Barbiano di Belgioioso. It was lived in by Napoleon in 1802 and later by Marshal Radetzky. Frescoes decorate the main floor; the top attraction here is the dining room, with a *Parnassus* by Appiani. The gallery is devoted to 19th-century art movements in Italy, from the Romanticism of Francesco Hayez and Il Piccio to Scapigliatura, and from Divisionism to Macchiaioli, with artists like Fattori and Lega.

The Padiglione di Arte Contemporanea (PAC) is located next to Villa Belgiojoso and is its contemporary art extension. It is one of the first examples of architecture in Italy designed specifically for modern art, similar to the European Kunsthalle, which opened in 1954. Designed by the architect Ignazio Gardella, it is built around a central volume on three levels.

GALLERY HIGHLIGHTS AT THE GAM

The Fourth Estate
This painting by Giuseppe Pelizza da Volpedo depicts a workers' protest.

The Battle of the Centaurs
An expressive drawing by Pablo Picasso of a fight between mythological creatures.

Breton Women
Vincent Van Gogh's interpretation of his friend Émile Bernard's painting *Breton Women at a Wall*.

The ground-floor level has large windows that face the beautiful garden of Villa Reale. Temporary exhibitions are held throughout the year.

→

Genius of the Hunt by Pompeo Marchesi on display at the Galleria d'Arte Moderna

A SHORT WALK
THE FASHION DISTRICT

Distance 1 km (0.5 miles) **Time** 15 minutes
Nearest metro 3 Montenapoleone

Via Montenapoleone represents the elegant heart of Milan and is one of the four sides of the so-called *quadrilatero* or fashion district (the other three sides are Via Manzoni, Via Sant'Andrea and Via della Spiga). When strolling through this district, besides the shops of some of the top Italian and international fashion designers, you will see grand Neo-Classical aristocratic residences such as Palazzo Melzi di Cusano, at No 18 Via Montenapoleone, built in 1830. Via Bigli, on the other hand, is lined with 16th- and 17th-century palazzi with porticoed courtyards.

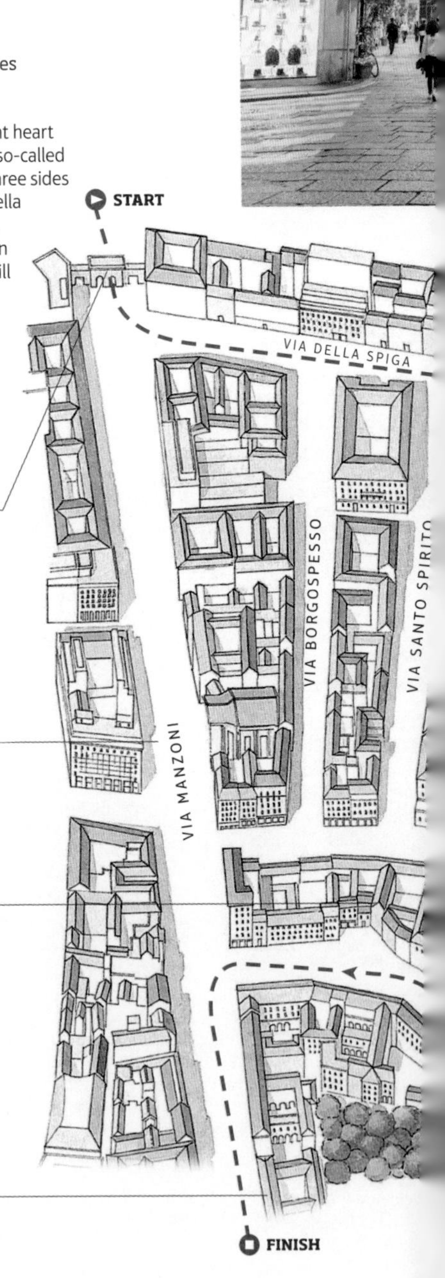

Archi di Porta Nuova (p142), *the city gate, once part of the medieval walls, is decorated with copies of 1st-century CE Roman tombstones.*

0 metres 50
0 yards 50
N

Via Manzoni (p140) *is a broad street lined with aristocratic palazzi.*

Under the **Portico del Lattèe** *(milkman's arcade) is the wall of the demolished church of San Donnino alla Mazza.*

Museo Poldi Pezzoli (p140) *was created by Gian Giacomo Poldi Pezzoli. Besides paintings by Mantegna, Piero della Francesca and Giovanni Bellini, it has rugs, armour and ceramics.*

Locator Map

For more details see p136

←

Designer stores along Via della Spiga and Via Borgospesso

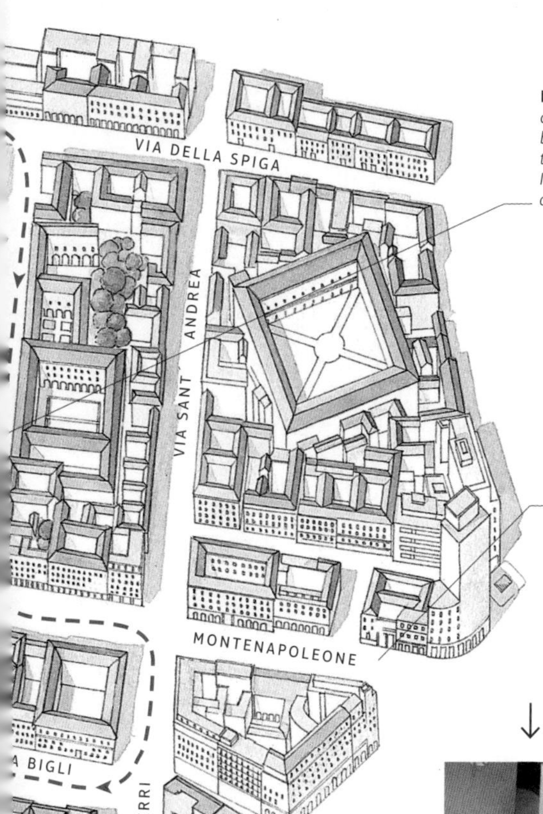

Museo Bagatti Valsecchi, (p141) *a Neo-Renaissance palazzo, was built as the family residence by the Bagatti Valsecchi brothers. It still has 16 rooms with their original 19th-century furnishings.*

Following the course of the ancient Roman walls, **Via Montenapoleone** *gets its name from a bank that once stood here called "Monte Napoleone". Designer shops line the street.*

A Renaissance portal with a bas-relief Annunciation *leads to the courtyard of* **Palazzo Bigli***, decorated with frescoes by the school of Luini.*

Marni's flagship store on a courtyard off Via Montenapoleone

↓

A SHORT WALK
THE BRERA QUARTER

Distance 1 km (0.5 miles) **Time** 15 minutes **Nearest metro** 2 Lanza

The name of Milan's traditional Bohemian quarter derives from the Germanic word *braida*, which denoted a grassy area. The presence of art students at the Accademia di Belle Arti and the world-famous Brera art gallery has contributed to the lively feel of this quarter, which can be further soaked up when walking around the area's many cafés, galleries and antique shops. In summer, weave through the narrow streets, which come alive with street stalls and fortune tellers. An antiques market is held on the third Saturday of each month in Via Brera.

The **Museo Minguzzi** *has 100 pieces by the Bolognese sculptor.*

San Simpliciano (p145) *was one of the four basilicas founded by Sant'Ambrogio and has preserved most of its original early Christian architecture.*

← The striking red brick façade of San Simpliciano

Locator Map
For more details see page 136

↑ Entrance to the Botanical Gardens off Via Brera

The façade of **San Marco** (p142), *founded in 1254, was rebuilt in 1871 in Neo-Gothic style. The only remaining part of the original is the stone doorway, which has a relief of Christ between two saints.*

Pinacoteca di Brera (p138), *one of Italy's top art galleries, contains works from churches that were suppressed in the late 1700s. The Brera has works by Renaissance masters like Raphael and Titian.*

The **Civico Museo del Risorgimento**, *opened in 1896, is in Neo-Classical Palazzo Moriggia.*

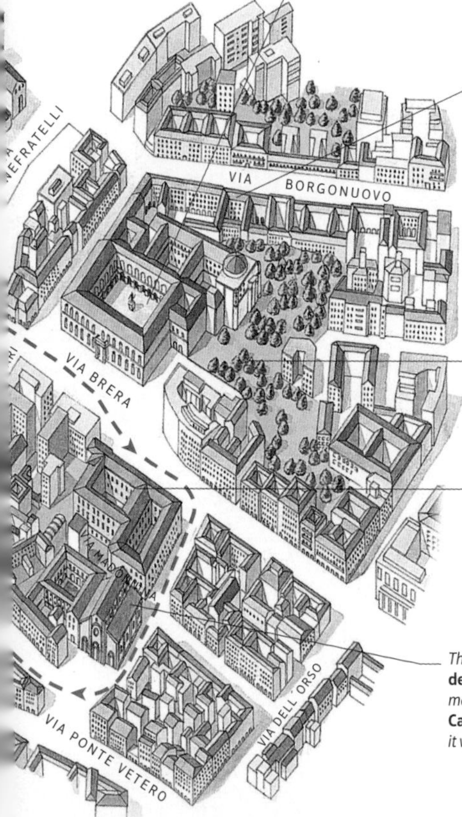

Orto Botanico (p143) *has been part of the Brera Astronomical Museum since 1774. Founded under Empress Maria Theresa of Austria, it has two ginkgo biloba trees, among the oldest in Europe.*

Palazzo Cusani (p143) *has a late Baroque façade (1719) and is the headquarters of the Third Army Corps. On the first floor is the Officers' Club.*

The 15th-century **Santa Maria del Carmine** (p144) *was built with material taken from the nearby* **Castello Sforzesco** (p78) *when it was partly demolished.*

FOOD & WINE
PAIRING
WINE SHOP
WINE
TASTING

The cobbled streets of Bellagio, on Lake Como

THE LAKES

Spread out across four regions – Lombardy, Piedmont, Veneto and Trentino Alto Adige – the Lakes of northern Italy offer a sublime slice of the Mediterranean at the foot of the Alps. Their charming vistas have long inspired writers and artists, including Goethe and Shelley.

Bounded by the snowy mountains to the north, these glacial bodies of water are all oriented north–south, with Lake Maggiore stretching across the border into Switzerland. Lake Maggiore was once a favourite stage on the Grand Tour, the trip around Europe taken by young men of affluent standing between the 17th and 19th centuries. The belle époque buildings lining Stresa's lakefront are a reminder of its past as a glamorous lakeside resort.

During the 20th century, the Lakes played an interesting role. A prime hiking area, its trails, which snake through the mountains, provided a route for Jews, soldiers and partisans seeking to evade German capture throughout World War II. In 1943, after Italy switched sides to the Allies, Mussolini led the short-lived Republic of Salò, a puppet state established by Nazi Germany on Lake Garda.

Today, the Lakes are a popular holiday destination. They enjoy a relatively mild climate, with olive groves and grape vines allowing for the production of olive oil and wine, most notably along the eastern shore of Lake Garda. Franciacorta, south of Lago d'Iseo, also produces some of Italy's finest sparkling wine.

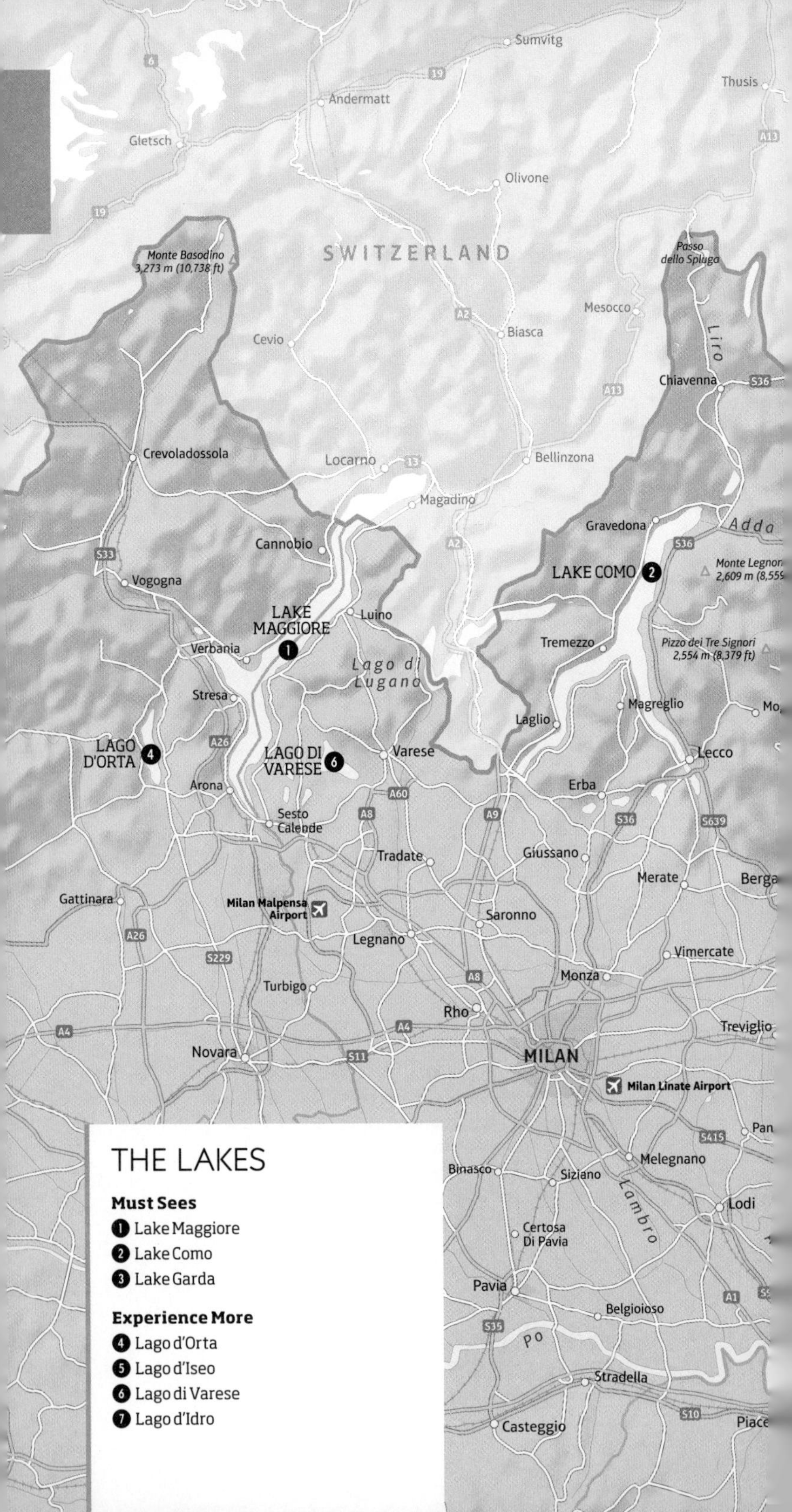

THE LAKES

Must Sees

1. Lake Maggiore
2. Lake Como
3. Lake Garda

Experience More

4. Lago d'Orta
5. Lago d'Iseo
6. Lago di Varese
7. Lago d'Idro

Graun im Vinschgau
Susch
Wiesen
Vernago
Inn
Prad am Stilfser Joch
Livigno
St. Moritz
Bormio
Santa Gertrude
Pizzo Bernina 4,049 m (13,284 ft)
Sondalo
Pizzo Badile 3,308 m (10,853 ft)
Pizzo Scalino 3,323 m (10,902 ft)
Dimaro
Ponte di Legno
Valtellina
Tirano
Sondrio
Edolo
Adamello 3,554 m (11,660 ft)
Madonna di Campiglio
Alpi Orobie
Valbondione
Parco Nazionale delle Incisioni Rupestri
Ponte Arche
Roncobello
Pizzo Arera 2,512 m (8,241 ft)
Val Camonica
Monte Colombine 2,215 m (7,267ft)
Riva del Garda
Gandino
Lovere
Alzano Lombardo
LAGO D'ISEO
5
Marone
LAGO D'IDRO
7
Magasa
Malcesine
Carró
Sarnico
Iseo
Barghe
Gargnano
Salò
VENETO
Rovato
Brescia
3
LAKE GARDA
Antegnate
LOMBARDY
Desenzano del Garda
Ghedi
Montichiari
Verona
Verona Villafranca Airport
Solferino
Castelleone
Chiese
Pontevico
Goito
Roverbella
Ostiano
Cremona
Piadena
San Daniele Po
Po
0 kilometres
20
0 miles
20
N
S42
S38
S510
S11
A4
S236
S415
S45b
A21
A22
S12
27

Landscaped Isola Bella, the most famous of the Borromean Islands

1

LAKE MAGGIORE

FS Stazione Centrale (89 20 21); Trenord (02-7249 4949) SAFduemila (0323-55 21 72); Autolinee Varesine (0332-731 110) Navigazione Lago Maggiore (800-551 801) navlaghi.it

Once an important stopover for European aristocracy on the Grand Tour, Lake Maggiore is home to some of the Italian Lakes' most spectacular gardens, notably the terraced Italian-style gardens of Isola Bella.

With borders in Piedmont, Lombardy and the Ticino canton in Switzerland, Lake Maggiore, or Verbano, is the second-largest lake in Italy (212 sq km, 82 sq miles) after Lake Garda and has a maximum depth of 372 m (1,220 ft). For the most part, it is fed and drained by the Ticino river, and is also fed by the Toce. The towns around the shore were embellished with churches and paintings from 1449 onwards, thanks to the wealthy Borromeo family, and with villas and gardens in the 18th–19th centuries. The opening of the Simplon Pass and the introduction of ferry services (1826) helped trade to develop in the area.

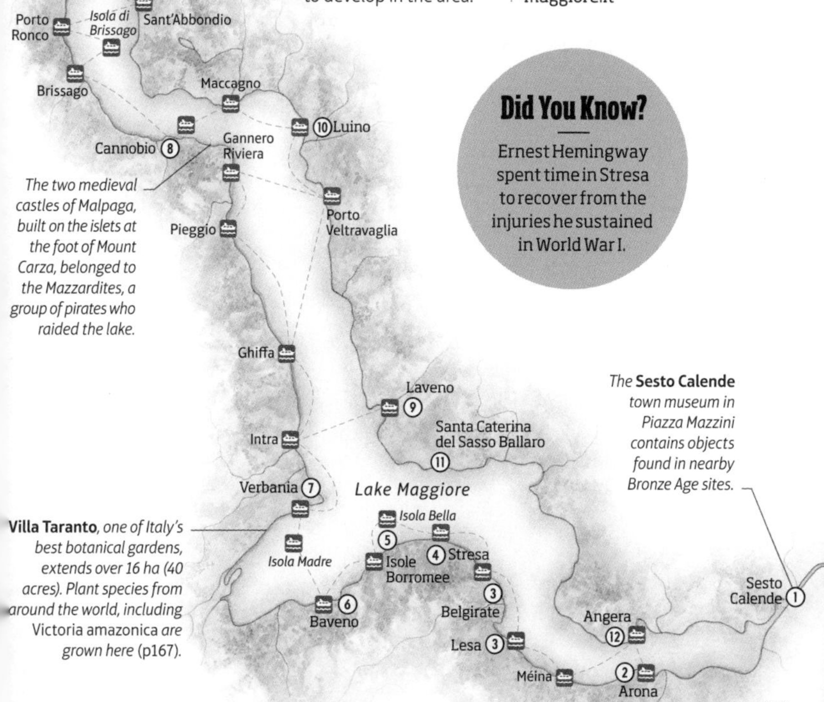

The two medieval castles of Malpaga, built on the islets at the foot of Mount Carza, belonged to the Mazzardites, a group of pirates who raided the lake.

Villa Taranto, *one of Italy's best botanical gardens, extends over 16 ha (40 acres). Plant species from around the world, including Victoria amazonica are grown here (p167).*

The **Sesto Calende** *town museum in Piazza Mazzini contains objects found in nearby Bronze Age sites.*

①

Sesto Calende

Varese IAT, Viale Italia 3; www.prosestocalende.it

The town at the southern tip of Lake Maggiore marks the end of two motorways leading to Verbano. The road to Arona leads to **Abbazia San Donato**, a 9th-century basilica with frescoes from the 15th and 16th centuries in the nave and from the 18th century in the crypt. South of Sesto is the Golasecca Iron Age site. State road 33 to Arona will take you to the **Lagoni di Mercurago Regional Park**, with varied bird species and the remains of ancient villages.

Abbazia San Donato

Via San Donato 6 0331-924 271 8am–7pm daily

Lagoni di Mercurago Regional Park

Via Gattico 6, Mercurago parcoticinolago maggiore.it

Did You Know?

Ernest Hemingway spent time in Stresa to recover from the injuries he sustained in World War I.

The imposing Rocca sitting above Arona, protecting the shore of Lake Maggiore

Arona

Novara Largo Duca d'Aosta; 0322-243 601)

Arona once occupied an important trading position between Milan and the lake and mountain regions of northern Italy. Because of its strategic location, a Rocca, or fortress (the twin of the one at Angera; *p169*), was built here; it was later enlarged by the Borromei and dismantled by Napoleon. Corso Marconi has a view of the Rocca at Angera, and leads to Piazza del Popolo. Here are the 15th-century Casa del Podestà, with an arched portico, and the 16th-century Madonna di Piazza church. Santi Martiri has 15th-century paintings by Bergognone, and Santa Maria Nascente has an altarpiece by Gaudenzio Ferrari (1511).

Just north of the centre is a massive **statue of San Carlo**, a saint and former archbishop of Milan, who was born and raised in Arona. The statue , which can be climbed from within via a staircase, was designed by Cerano in 1614 and finished in 1697. (Children under six are not permitted; children aged six–ten years must be accompanied by an adult.) In the nearby church of San Carlo there is a reconstruction of the room where the saint was born.

Villa Ponti is a lavish mid-18th-century villa with Baroque and Art Deco frescoes and decoration. It stands in a flower garden with a nymphaeum and a marble fountain. There's also a large internal courtyard.

Statue of San Carlo

Piazza San Carlo Hours vary, check website Jan, Feb statuasancarlo.it

Villa Ponti

Via San Carlo 63 0322-446 29 To the public

Lesa and Belgirate

Lesa (Novara); Belgirate (Verbania) IAT, Via Portici, Lesa; 0322-772 078

Lesa lies on a particularly charming stretch of the lake between Arona and Stresa, and has been popular as a resort for noble Lombard families since the 18th century.

The **Museo Manzoniano di Villa Stampa** has mementos of Milanese author Alessandro Manzoni *(p66)*, who was a guest here. The hamlet of Villa has the Romanesque church of San Sebastiano.

Once past Lesa, continue to Belgirate and its charming historic centre, whose houses have porticoes and porches.

Lesa lies on a particularly charming stretch of the lake between Arona and Stresa, and has been popular as a resort for noble Lombard families since the 18th century.

Enjoying an evening at Stresa's picturesque pavement café

This village also commands a panoramic view of the lake. It was a haunt of philosopher Antonio Rosmini and poet Guido Gozzano.

On the hills 4 km (2 miles) from Belgirate is the **Castello Visconteo**, built in the 13th century and decorated with frescoes of the period. Nearby is the Romanesque church of San Michele, with a leaning bell tower.

Museo Manzoniano di Villa Stampa

Via alla Fontana 18, Lesa
0322-764 21 Aug: 10am-noon Thu, 5-9pm Sat & Sun (by appt only, call ahead)

Castello Visconteo

Via Visconti 2, Massino Visconti 032-221 9713
By appt only, call ahead

④

Stresa

Verbania IAT, Piazza Marconi 16; www.stresa turismo.it

The origins of medieval Strixia, dating from before the 1st millennium CE, are partially hidden by the palazzi and villas built for the aristocracy in the late 19th–early 20th centuries, partly because of the opening of an electric rack-railway (the first in Italy), which goes to the top of Mount Mottarone. The town is now a centre for conferences and tour groups, attracted by the easy access to the Borromean islands. On the lakefront are 19th-century villas, the 18th-century Sant'Ambrogio and the **Villa Ducale** (1770), with mementos of 19th-century philosopher Antonio Rosmini, who died here (the villa is now the Rosmini Study Centre). Mount Mottarone (1,491 m/4,890 ft), a ski resort, has a view from the Alps to the plain.

The **Parco di Villa Pallavicino** near Stresa is famous for its gardens. The English garden has centuries-old plants as well as animals from around the world, such as llamas and pelicans.

Villa Ducale Centro di Studi Rosminiani

Corso Umberto I 15
0323-300 91 9-11:45am & 3-5:45pm Mon-Fri

Parco di Villa Pallavicino

State road 33
0323-324 07 10am-5:30pm daily

INSIDER TIP
Stresa Festival

Each summer, Stresa hosts the Stresa Festival, with live jazz and classical concerts performed in scenic locations around town. Book tickets well in advance *(www.stresafestival.eu)*.

5 Isole Borromee

Verbania Isola Madre and Isola Bella (0322-233 200; 800-551 801) Late Mar-mid-Oct: 9am-5:30pm daily; guided tours by appt only, check website isoleborromee.it

These three islands– Isola Bella, Isola Madre and Isola dei Pescatori – can be reached easily from Stresa. They became famous thanks to the Borromeo family, who built elegant palazzi and gardens there. The most popular is Isola Bella, an old fishing village transformed from 1632 to 1671 by the Borromeo family into a lovely complex consisting of a Baroque palazzo and a terraced Italian-style garden with rare plants. Inside are a music room (where Mussolini met British and French officials in 1935); the Sala di Napoleone, where Napoleon stayed in 1797; a ballroom; and a bedroom with paintings by Carracci. The six grottoes are decorated with shells and pebbles.

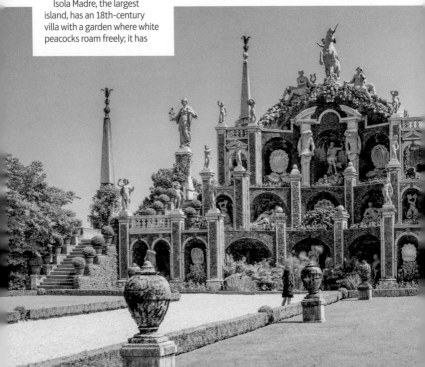

Isola Madre, the largest island, has an 18th-century villa with a garden where white peacocks roam freely; it has rare plants and beautiful flowers. The villa has period furnishings and 18th- and 19th-century puppet theatres.

Tiny Isola dei Pescatori, once the leading fishing village, has retained its quaint atmosphere and architecture.

6 Baveno

Verbania IAT, Piazza della Chiesa 8; 0323-924 632

Baveno was made famous by its pink granite quarries, which supplied the stone for the Galleria Vittorio Emanuele II *(p64)*. It became a fashionable resort in the 19th century, with guests such as Queen Victoria, who stayed in the Villa Clara (now Villa Branca) in 1879. A major attraction is Santi Gervasio e Protasio, with its 12th-century façade and 15th-century octagonal baptistery with Renaissance frescoes.

Going towards Verbania, the turn-off at Montorfano leads to San Giovanni, one of the area's loveliest churches.

TOP 3 WATER ACTIVITIES AT THE LAKE

Sailing
A popular pastime, sailing is suitable all year round and lessons are available for beginners in most major towns of the area.

Kayaking
Kayaking is the perfect way to get a closer view of the lakeside villas.

Stand Up Paddleboarding (SUP)
Test your balancing skills while taking in panoramic views.

7 Verbania

Inside the Maggiore theatre, Via San Bernardino 49; 0323-503 249

Pallanza and Intra were merged in 1939 to create

the town of Verbania (capital of the Verbano-Cusio-Ossola province established in 1992). The former, facing the Borromeo gulf, is the seat of the municipal government and has retained its medieval aspect. The latter dominates the promontory of Castagnola and has a Baroque and Neo-Classical flavour.

Intra, the main port of call on the lake and a major industrial centre, was the regional leader in textile manufacturing in the 18th century.

Pallanza was the only town on Lake Maggiore not under Borromeo dominion, and it has some of the most important monuments. These include Romanesque Santo Stefano, the parish church of San Leonardo and the 18th-century Palazzo Viani Dugnani, home to the **Museo del Paesaggio**. The last of these has an exhibit of 16th- to 20th-century landscape paintings, sculpture by Arturo Martini and Giulio Branca and a plaster-cast gallery. Isolino di San Giovanni was the refuge of Arturo Toscanini.

In the environs is 16th-century Madonna di Campagna, with a small Romanesque campanile and frescoes by Gerolamo Lanino and Camillo Procaccini (16th–17th centuries).

In 1931, Neil McEacharn, a Scottish captain, created one of the outstanding botanical gardens in Europe on the Castagnola promontory, using the lake water for irrigation. McEacharn exploited the valley terrain, creating terraced gardens, a winter garden and a marsh garden among small falls and water lily ponds. He donated the **Villa Taranto garden** to the Italian state and it was opened to the public in 1952. He was buried in the small park church onsite in 1964. Today, it has a range of rare plants, including *Victoria amazonica* in the glasshouses. Azaleas, dahlias and rhododendrons (over 300 varieties) look wonderful in full flower.

Museo del Paesaggio
Via Ruga 44 0323-557 116 10am-6pm Wed-Mon

Giardini di Villa Taranto
Via Vittorio Veneto, Pallanza Mid-Mar-Sep: 9am-6pm daily; Oct: 9am-5pm daily villataranto.it

←
The sculpture garden of the Baroque palazzo on *(inset)* the Isola Bella

Cannobio

Verbania IAT, Largo alla Chiesa 3; www.procannobio.it

This pleasant tourist resort is the last Italian town on the Piedmontese side of the lake. It still retains its old medieval character, exemplified in the Palazzo della Ragione (or Palazzo Parrasio), with a 12th-century Commune Tower. The building now serves as the town hall. Also of note is the Santuario della Pietà, which was rebuilt by San Carlo Borromeo in 1583 and contains a fine altarpiece by Gaudenzio Ferrari.

In nearby Val Cannobina, the Orrido di Sant'Anna is worth a visit. This deep gorge was carved out of the rock by the Cannobino river.

STAY

Hotel Belvedere
This modern lakeside hotel serves delicious local food from its on-site restaurant.

Via di Mezzo, Isola dei Pescatori
belvedere-isolapescatori.it

Boutique Hotel Elvezia
At this hotel, stay in bright and cosy rooms overlooking the Borromean Gulf.

Lungolago Vittorio Emanuele 18, Isola Bella
boutiquehotelelvezia.it

The quaint town of Laveno, known for its flourishing ceramics industry

Laveno

Varese IAT, Piazza Italia 2; 0332-668 785

The name of this town goes back to Titus Labienus, the Roman general who was Caesar's legate in Cisalpine Gaul. Laveno was important strategically because of its port, the only natural harbour on Lake Maggiore. During their period of rule, the Austrians moored the gun-boats controlling the lake here. Today, the town is the main ferry point for the Piedmontese shores. The Ferrovie Nord railway linked Laveno to Varese and Milan, fostering commercial development, especially in the field of ceramics, with the founding of well-known Società Ceramica Italiana Richard-Ginori, in 1856. In the town centre, the garden in the Villa Frua (18th century) is worth visiting. A cable car goes up to Sasso del Ferro, at 1,062 m (3,483 ft), behind Laveno with fine views of the lake, Monte Mottarone and Monte Rosa.

A cable car goes up to Sasso del Ferro, at 1,062 m (3,483 ft), behind Laveno with fine views of the lake, Monte Mottarone and Monte Rosa.

Luino

Varese IAT, Via Chiara 1; 0332-530 019

Luino, which occupies a cove on the eastern side of the lake, is a town dating from ancient Roman times. Its name may have derived from the Luina torrent or perhaps from the local term *luina* (landslide). In the Middle Ages, it was contested by the leading Como and Milanese families and became famous when Garibaldi landed here in 1848 with a group of volunteers and routed an entire Austrian detachment. The large railway station (1882) shows how important the town was when it linked Italy with Central Europe, a position that declined when railway traffic shifted to Chiasso. Luino's market was founded by an edict of Charles V in 1541 and is still a tourist attraction. San Pietro in Campagna has frescoes by Bernardino Luini and a lovely Romanesque bell tower; the oratory of the Chiesa del Carmine dates back to 1477. A must is a visit to the town's symbol, the 17th-century oratory of San Giuseppe.

Santa Caterina del Sasso Ballaro

Via Santa Caterina 13, Leggiuno Hours vary, check website santacaterina-delsasso.com

To get to this small monastery perched on a steep rock 18 m (59 ft) above the lake, you can either climb the 240 steps near Leggiuno or take a boat, while enjoying the lovely views on the way. This small monastery was founded during the 12th century by a local merchant. The Dominicans arrived in 1230 and, after numerous

The spectacular setting of Santa Caterina del Sasso Ballaro

changes in fortune, have since returned. Over the centuries the original building was enlarged and rebuilt, as can be seen by the different architectural styles. The chapter at the entrance has important 14th- to 15th-century frescoes, including a *Crucifixion with Armigers*. In the second portico the 17th-century fresco, only partly preserved, represents a *Dance of Death*. The frescoes inside the church were executed in the 16th century, and the *Madonna and Child with Saints* on the high altar dates from 1612. By the entrance porticoes, there is a large wine press made in 1759.

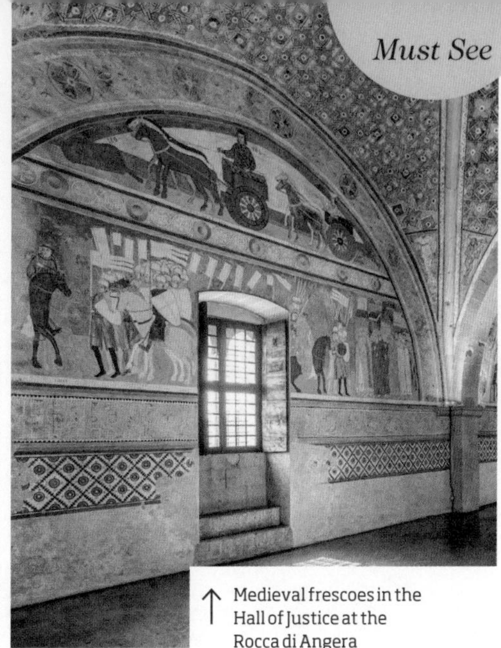

↑ Medieval frescoes in the Hall of Justice at the Rocca di Angera

12   

Rocca di Angera

Via Rocca, Angera
0331-931 300 Apr-Sep: 10am-5:30pm daily; Oct & Nov: 10am-sunset daily

A majestic fortress, probably built over the ruins of an ancient Roman fortification, the Rocca once belonged to the archbishops of Milan. It was taken over by the Visconti family in the 13th century and in 1449 was granted as a fief to the Borromeo family, who still own it.

The Visconti building has single and double lancet windows. The frescoes in the halls are well worth a look, notably those in the Salone Gotico, with a cycle of the *Battles of Ottone Visconti against the Torriani* (14th century). The vaults in this hall are decorated with the Visconti coat of arms, while those in the other rooms have geometric patterns and signs of the Zodiac. The Borromeo wing has frescoes removed from Palazzo Borromeo in Milan in 1946, with *Aesop's Fables* by the school of Michelino da Besozzo (15th century).

The Rocca is used for art shows and is also home to the Museo della Bambola (Doll Museum) in the Visconti wing, one of the best of its kind in Europe, created with the collection of Princess Bona Borromeo. Besides dolls and doll's houses, it contains books, games and children's clothing.

 INSIDER TIP

Bring Water

Stay hydrated on the 30-minute uphill walk from the Angera lakefront to Rocca di Angera by packing a reusable bottle of water. It will come in handy when you climb the fortress stairs, too.

Winter sunrise at Santa Caterina del Sasso Ballaro, Lake Maggiore

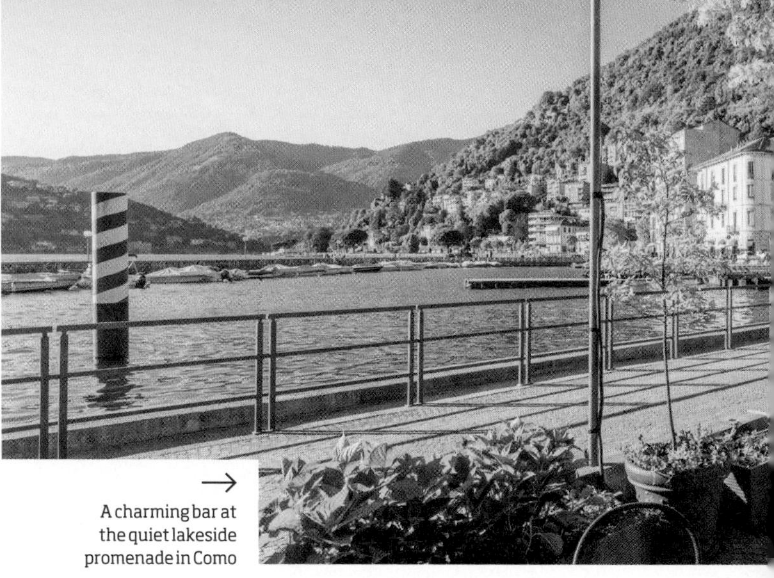

→ A charming bar at the quiet lakeside promenade in Como

2

LAKE COMO

FS: Milan-Chiasso line: 89 20 21; Trenord : 02-72 49 49 49 ASF Autolinee, Piazza Matteotti, Como: 031-24 72 47 Navigazione Lago di Como: 800-55 18 01 (freefone) or 031-57 92 11 Local information bureaux; www.navlaghi.it

Set in an idyllic landscape of mountains and rugged hillsides, Lake Como is ideal for boating and hiking, and is a great place to escape to from the city. The long and narrow lake offers fine views up to the Alps and down to the towns.

This lake, which is also known as Lario, is the third largest in Italy and the deepest (410 m, 1,345 ft). The Como shore features numerous restaurants and hotels, as well as a scenic road that follows the ancient Strada Regina, lined with elegant villas and aristocratic gardens. The Lecco area has more stark scenery and small coves. You may spot the typical "Lucia" boats, named after the heroine in Manzoni's *The Betrothed*, which was partly set here.

①

Como

Via Albertolli 7; www.lakecomo.org

The town that gave its name to the lake is home to a fine **Duomo** that is dominated by Filippo Juvarra's Baroque dome. Its Gothic façade and door were executed by Tommaso and Jacopo Rodari. The nave and side altars are decorated with tapestries and canvases by Ferrari and Luini.

Also of note is the **Tempio Voltiano** (1927), which contains relics of the Como physicist Alessandro Volta, who gave his name to "voltage", and the frescoed **Villa Olmo**, designed by Simone Cantoni in 1797.

Duomo

Piazza Duomo 031-265 244 Hours vary, call ahead

Tempio Voltiano

Viale Marconi 031-574 705 10am-6pm Tue-Sun

Villa Olmo

Via Cantoni 1 031-252 553 10am-6pm Tue-Sun Pub hols

GREAT VIEW
Funicular Fun

Take a scenic funicular ride from Como to Brunate, which passes the town's villas and gardens. Plan your arrival at dusk for marvellous views of the illuminated lake, the mountains and the twinkling city below.

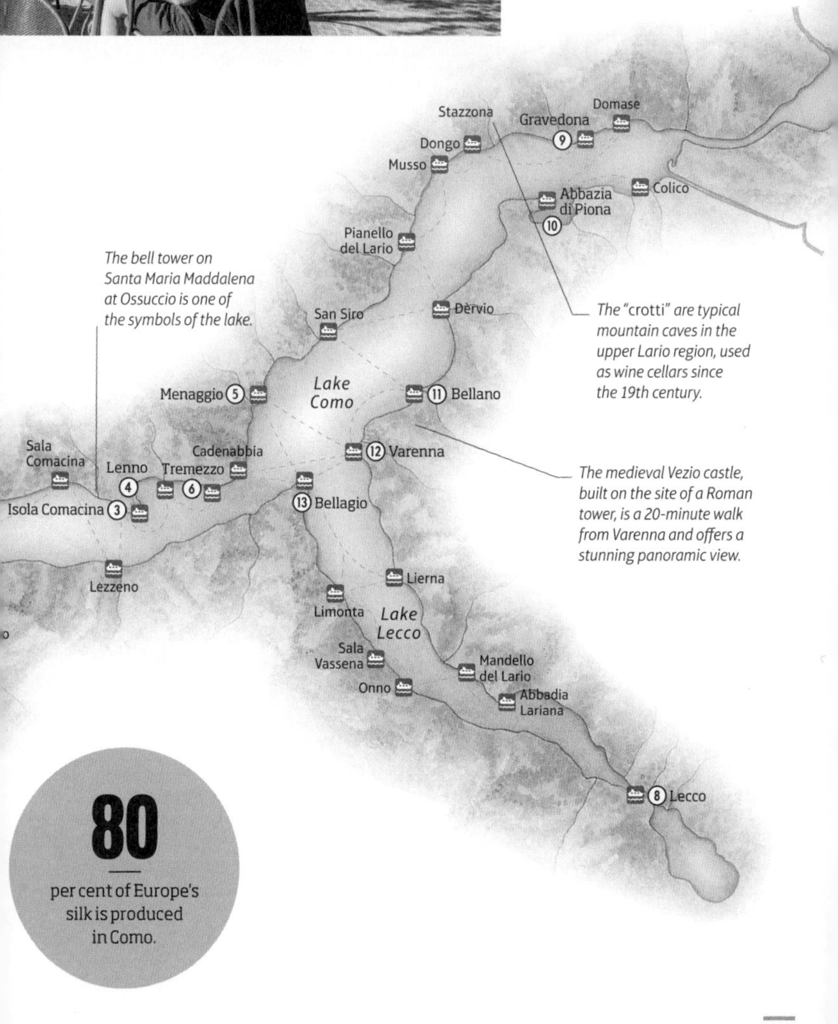

Stazzona
Domase
Gravedona
9
Dongo
Musso
Abbazia di Piona
10
Colico
Pianello del Lario
San Siro
Dèrvio
Lake Como
Menaggio 5
11 Bellano
Sala Comacina
Cadenabbia
Lenno
Tremezzo
4
6
12 Varenna
Isola Comacina 3
13 Bellagio
Lezzeno
Lierna
Limonta
Lake Lecco
Sala Vassena
Onno
Mandello del Lario
Abbadia Lariana
8 Lecco

The bell tower on Santa Maria Maddalena at Ossuccio is one of the symbols of the lake.

The "crotti" are typical mountain caves in the upper Lario region, used as wine cellars since the 19th century.

The medieval Vezio castle, built on the site of a Roman tower, is a 20-minute walk from Varenna and offers a stunning panoramic view.

80

per cent of Europe's silk is produced in Como.

②

Cernobbio

6 km (4 miles) from Como Largo Campanini 1, 031-444 6483; Via Albertolli 7, Como, 031-449 3068

Cernobbio marks the beginning of a series of splendid villas that have made the western side of the lake famous. **Villa d'Este**, built by Pellegrino Tibaldi in 1570 for the Gallio family, became a luxury hotel in 1873, frequented by famous personalities. The rooms have period furnishings and are used for conferences. The villa stands in an Italianate garden with a nymphaeum. The 18th-century **Villa Erba** (now a wedding venue) is known for its interior (visits by request): the Salone da Ballo, chapel and Sala delle Nozze, decorated by architect Giocondo Albertolli, are lovely.

Villa d'Este

Via Regina 40 031-3481 Garden: on request Nov–Mar

Villa Erba

Largo Visconti 4 031-3491 To the public (the Luchino Visconti rooms can be booked for group visits)

TOP 3 **LAKE COMO CYCLING ROUTES**

Valsassina Bike Route
Cycle along the picturesque Pioverna river for 12 km (7 miles).

Como to Bellagio
This 50-km (31-mile) cycling route offers marvellous lake and mountain views.

Around Lago di Como
At 140 km (86-miles), this loop is the ultimate test for hardy cyclists accustomed to challenging inclines.

The scenic loggia of the lakeside Villa del Balbianello, near Lenno

Isola Comacina

26 km (16 miles) from Como To Sala Comacina, then by boat Via Albertolli 7, Como; www.isola-comacina.it

The only island in Lake Como has been inhabited since Roman times. It was fortified by the Byzantines and enjoyed a period of splendour in the Middle Ages. Today, it is home to seven church ruins, along with those of a mosaic-decorated baptistery, which were found after World War II and are now being studied.

Sala Comacina, where boats depart for the island, has an 18th-century church with a fresco by Carlo Carloni.

Lenno

28 km (17 miles) from Como Via Albertolli 7, Como; 03-14 49 30 68

This town is famous for the **Villa del Balbianello**, built by Cardinal Durini in the 17th century onto a 16th-century building attributed to Pellegrini. The magnificent garden has a loggia with views of Isola Comacina and Tremezzina bay. Access to the villa is by boat from Sala Comacina.

Also worth a visit are the octagonal baptistery and church of Santo Stefano, built in the 11th century over a Roman building and decorated with frescoes by Luini. Above the town is the Cistercian abbey of Acquafredda, rebuilt in the 17th century, with frescoes by Fiammenghino.

Villa del Balbianello

Via Comoedia 5, Lenno 034-456 110 (FAI) Villa: by appt only; Garden: mid-Mar–mid-Nov: 10am–6pm Tue, Thu–Sun

Menaggio

35 km (22 miles) from Como IAT, Piazza Garibaldi 8; www.menaggio.com

The name Menaggio supposedly derives from two Indo-European words: *men* (mountain) and *uigg* (water), referring to the mouth of the Sanagra river on which the town lies. Menaggio is the leading commercial centre in the upper Lario region and a popular tourist resort. It is dominated by the ruins of a castle and has preserved some of its medieval layout. Of note are the parish church of Santo Stefano, the Baroque architecture of which conceals its

Romanesque origin and 17th-century San Carlo, with a fine painting by Giuseppe Vermiglio. The lakeside promenade, with arcaded houses and villas, is a must-see. Past Menaggio, at Loveno, is the Neo-Classical Milyus-Vigoni villa with family portraits by Francesco Hayez. Around it is a lovely park, designed by Balzaretto in 1840.

Tremezzo

31 km (19 miles) from Como Via Provinciale Regina, 034-44 04 93; Via Albertolli 7, Como, 03-1449 3068

This lakeside town is famous for the 18th-century **Villa Carlotta**. It houses paintings by Hayez, furniture by Maggiolini and sculpture pieces by Canova, including a copy of *Cupid and Psyche* and *Terpsichore*. Among the rooms decorated with stuccowork is one with Appiani's frescoes taken from the Palazzo Reale in Milan. The residence is surrounded by a terraced garden with landscaped staircases, featuring over 150 species of rhododendron and azalea.

Villa Carlotta
Via Regina 2b
Hours vary, check website villacarlotta.it

Torno

9 km (5 miles) from Como
Pro loco: Via Roma 25

The village of Torno houses the churches of Santa Tecla, which has a beautiful marble portal, and the 14th-century San Giovanni, with its remarkable Renaissance door. However, Torno is best known for the 16th-century Villa Pliniana (attributed to Tibaldi), which was built for Count Anguissola, the governor of Como. The writers Foscolo, Stendhal and Byron, and composer Rossini, have all been guests here.

DRINK

Terrazza 241

Sip on classic cocktails, crisp Italian wines or bubbling champagne at this trendy rooftop lounge.

Via Borgo Vico 241, Como terrazza241.it

Alle Terrazze

This quiet terrace by the lake offers casual aperitivos and drinks.

Viale Geno, Como
031-303 458

Bar Italia

At this bar, gaze across Lake Como with a morning cappuccino or an evening cocktail.

Via Plinio 11, Torno
031-417 023

↑ The town of Tremezzo with snow-capped mountains in the background

↑ The picturesque city of Lecco, illuminated at dusk

Lecco

32 km (20 miles) from Como · Via XX Settembre 23; www.leccotourism.it

Lecco lies on the southern tip of Lake Como. It was inhabited in prehistoric times and fortified in the 6th century CE. In the 1300s, it was taken over by Azzone Visconti, who built the Ponte Vecchio. This city is the birthplace of author Alessandro Manzoni. Mementos of his life can be found in his childhood home, the **Casa Natale di Manzoni**. Sites described by Manzoni in his novel, *The Betrothed*, have been identified, including the castle of the Unnamed at Vercurago, and Lucia's home at Olate. Near Civate is Romanesque San Pietro al Monte (12th century), with frescoes and reliefs depicting the Passion.

In the city centre are the Teatro della Società and San Nicolò, whose baptistery chapel has 14th- to 15th-century frescoes. The **Museo di Storia Naturale** in the 18th-century Palazzo Belgioioso is also of interest, with rooms exhibiting local fauna. There is also a room dedicated to the Lake Como monster, known as the Lariosauro.

Casa Natale di Manzoni

Via Guanella 1 · 034-148 1247 · 10am–6pm Tue–Fri, 2–6pm Sat & Sun

Museo di Storia Naturale

Corso Matteotti 32 · 034-148 1248 · 10am–2pm Tue–Fri, 10am–6pm Sat & Sun · Most public hols

EAT

Ristorante Filet

This cosy Italian restaurant serves traditional Lombard dishes using quality ingredients from local producers.

Corso Giacomo Matteotti 71 · Mon D, Sun & August · salumeriafilet.it

INSIDER TIP

Lake Literature

Alessandro Manzoni's masterpiece, *The Betrothed*, is considered the first Italian historical novel. Largely set in Lecco during the 1600s, this tormented love story touches on themes of politics and religion.

Gravedona

53 km (33 miles) from Como · Piazza Trieste 034-485 005; Via Albertolli 7, Como, 031-1449 3068

A fortified town, Gravedona is known for the 12th-century church of **Santa Maria del Tiglio**. Its main features are the black-and-white striped stone walls and the unusual octagonal bell tower set into its façade. Inside, the aisled nave with tall galleries houses 12th–14th-century frescoes.

Santa Maria del Tiglio

Piazza XI Febbraio · 034-485 291 · 8:30am–5pm (summer: to 7pm)

Abbazia di Piona

Via Santa Maria di Piona 1, Colico 034-194 0331 8:30am-noon & 2-6pm daily

At the tip of the Ogliasca Peninsula sits this Benedictine abbey. Founded in the 9th century, the abbey features some lovely Romanesque carvings. The monks distil and sell potent liqueur, too.

Bellano

26 km (16 miles) from Lecco Via Vittorio Veneto, 23; 034-1157 0370

In the Middle Ages, Bellano was the summer residence of Milanese bishops, and it has preserved its medieval character. Among houses with wrought-iron coats of arms is the church of Santi Nazaro, Celso e Giorgio, the work of Campionese masters. Santa Marta houses a *Pietà* executed in 1518. However, the main appeal of Bellano is the **Orrido**, a deep gorge created by the Pioverna torrent.

Orrido

034-182 1124
Hours vary, call ahead

Varenna

22 km (14 miles) from Lecco Pro Loco, Via IV Novembre 3 (034-183 0367)

This splendid village of Roman origin, with a perfectly intact medieval layout, is famous for two spectacular villas, **Villa Cipressi**, with its terraced garden, and **Villa Monastero**, built over a Cistercian monastery. All around the town were quarries for the black Varenna marble used in the Milan Duomo *(p56)*. Since 1921, Mandello del Lario has housed the Moto Guzzi factory and the motorcycle museum, **Museo Moto Guzzi della Motocicletta**, which exhibits more than 80 bikes with details on their history and production.

Villa Cipressi

Via IV Novembre 18
034-183 0113 Garden: Mar-Oct: 9am-7pm daily

Villa Monastero

Via Polvani 2
034-129 5450 Villa: Mar-Oct: hours vary, check website villamonastero.eu

Museo Moto Guzzi della Motocicletta

Via Parodi 57, Mandello del Lario 034-170 9237
3-4:30pm Mon-Thu, 10am-6pm Fri & Sat Nov-Feb; public hols motoguzzi.com

Bellagio

31 km (19 miles) from Como Piazza della Chiesa 14; www.bellagiolake como.com

Known since antiquity for its fine climate and scenery, Bellagio still has its medieval layout, with stepped alleyways. It became the site of noble villas in the 1700s and, later, a famous resort town in the 19th century. Among the attractive residences, the loveliest are **Villa Serbelloni** and **Villa Melzi d'Eril**. In 1870, the former became a hotel that numbered Winston Churchill among its guests. The Neo-Classical Villa Melzi was built in 1810 by Giocondo Albertolli. Its interior is not open to the public, but the Museo Archeologico, chapel and gardens are accessible. Near the town are the 18th-century Trivulzio and Trotti villas.

Villa Serbelloni

Piazza della Chiesa
031-95 15 55 For guided visits only: mid-Mar-mid-Nov: 11am & 3:30pm Tue-Sun

Villa Melzi d'Eril

Lungolario Marconi
333-487 7427 End Mar-Oct: 10am-7pm daily

One of the many stepped alleyways in the medieval town of Bellagio

↑ Gargnano's pretty harbour, flanked by colourful buildings

3

LAKE GARDA

FS Milan-Venice line (89-2021) Azienda Provinciale Trasporti di Verona (045-805 7811) Navigazione Lago di Garda; www.navlaghi.it

The magnificent Lake Garda is a veritable outdoor playground, offering a variety of water- and land-based activities, from windsurfing and canyoning to trekking and rock climbing. It's rich in history and culture too, making this the most multifaceted of the Italian lakes.

Italy's largest lake was created by glaciation. The scenery is varied, with steep, rugged cliffs at the northern end and softer hills southwards, where the basin widens and Mediterranean flora prevails. Over the centuries praises of pristine Lake Garda have been sung by such greats as Roman poet Catullus, Dante and Goethe. Today, it is a popular tourist attraction, catering to luxury holidays and tour groups alike. Garda is an ideal spot for sailing, and it hosts famous regattas such as the Centomiglia.

①

Sirmione

Brescia Viale Marconi 8; www.visitsirmione.com

Roman Sirmio lay in the hinterland and only the villa quarter faced the lake. In the 13th century, the Scaligeri lords of Verona turned it into a fortress to defend Lake Garda. In 1405, Sirmione was taken over by Venice, which then ruled until the 18th century. The main focus of the town is the **Rocca Scaligera**, a castle built by Mastino I della Scala (13th century), the inner basin of which served as shelter for the Veronese boats. Roman and medieval plaques are in the entrance arcade.

Fifteenth-century Santa Maria Maggiore has a Roman column in its porch, while the campanile was a Scaligera tower. The interior has 15th- and 16th-century frescoes and a 15th-century Madonna.

The spas, such as **Terme Catullo**, use the water from the Boiola spring, known since 1546. San Pietro in Mavino, rebuilt in 1320, features fine 13th- to 16th-century frescoes.

Sirmione is also famous for the so-called **Grotte di Catullo**, a huge Roman residence built in the 1st centuries BCE–CE. The most evocative rooms here are the Grotta del Cavallo, the Cryptoporticus and the pool. The Sala della Trifora del Paradiso and Sala dei Giganti overlook the lake.

HIDDEN GEM

Jamaica Beach

With smooth white rocks and crystal-clear waters, Sirmione's Jamaica Beach looks like a tropical resort. Look for a gate before the entrance of Grotte di Catullo and follow the path to reach the beach.

Did You Know?

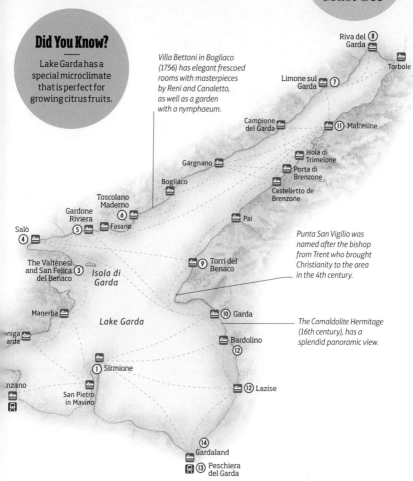

Lake Garda has a special microclimate that is perfect for growing citrus fruits.

Villa Bettoni in Bogliaco (1756) has elegant frescoed rooms with masterpieces by Reni and Canaletto, as well as a garden with a nymphaeum.

Punta San Vigilio was named after the bishop from Trent who brought Christianity to the area in the 4th century.

The Camaldolite Hermitage (16th century), has a splendid panoramic view.

Riva del Garda ⑧
Torbole
Limone sul Garda ⑦
Campione del Garda
⑪ Malcesine
Isola di Trimelone
Gargnano
Porta di Brenzone
Castelletto de Brenzone
Bogliaco
Toscolano Maderno ⑥
Gardone Riviera ⑤
Fasano
Pai
Salò ④
The Valtènesi and San Felica del Benaco ③
Isola di Garda
⑨ Torri del Benaco
Manerba
Lake Garda
⑩ Garda
Bardolino ⑫
① Sirmione
San Pietro in Mavino
⑫ Lazise
⑭ Gardaland
⑬ Peschiera del Garda

The Antiquarium has finds from the villa, including a mosaic seascape and a portrait of Catullus (1st century BCE).

Rocca Scaligera
Piazza Castello 030-916 468 8:30am-7:15pm Tue-Sat, 8:30am-1:30pm Sun Public hols

Terme Catullo (Spa)
Piazza Castello By appt only, check website termedisirmione.com

Grotte di Catullo
Via Catullo 030-916 157 Apr-Sep: 9am-1pm Mon, 8:30am-7:30pm Tue-Sat, 9am-7:30pm Sun

↑ The expansive archaeological site of Grotte di Catullo, Sirmione

The town of Desenzano del Garda, hugging Lake Garda's southern shore

Desenzano del Garda

Brescia Via Porto Vecchio 34; 030-374 8726

Likely founded by the Romans on a site inhabited since prehistoric times, Desenzano was taken over by Venice in the 15th century, when it became the leading lakeside town. Since the 19th century it has been a tourist resort. The heart of the town is Piazza Malvezzi, home to an antiques market known for its silverware and prints. The 16th-century town hall and Provveditore Veneto buildings are also here. In the **Duomo** (16th century) is a fine *Last Supper* by Tiepolo. The **Museo Civico Archeologico**, in the cloister of Santa Maria de Senioribus, houses Bronze-Age finds and the oldest known wooden plough (2000 BCE).

The 4th-century **Villa Romana** was rediscovered in 1921. It had been covered by a landslide, which preserved some lovely mosaics with geometric motifs such as the *Good Shepherd* and *Psyche and Cupids*. Finds from the villa are in the Antiquarium.

STAY

Antica Dimora Desenzano

This luxury hotel has five suites featuring antiques and works of art from the owners' family collection.

Vicolo Androna 4, Desenzano anticadimora-desenzano.com

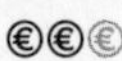

Hotel Ocelle Thermae & Spa

An adult-only hotel with three pools, a private beach and a spa.

Via XXV Aprile 1, Sirmione hotelocellesirmione.it

Duomo

Piazza Duomo 030-914 1849 May-Sep: 8am-noon & 3:30-7pm daily; Oct-Apr: 8am-noon & 3:30-6pm daily

Museo Civico Archeologico

Via Anelli 42 Hours vary, check website museorambotti.it

Villa Romana

Via Crocifisso 2 030-914 3547 Mar-Oct: 9am-7:30pm Tue-Sun; Nov-Feb: 9am-5pm Tue-Sun Mon (Tue if Mon is hol)

The Valtènesi and San Felice del Benaco

Brescia Via Portovecchio 34; 030-374 8726

Valtènesi, the area between Desenzano and Salò, is rich in medieval churches and castles. At Padenghe, the Rocca (9th–10th century) is reached by a drawbridge. Nearby is Sant' Emiliano (12th century) and in Moniga del Garda is Santa Maria della Neve (14th century). On a headland over the lake, lies the Rocca di Manerba del Garda (8th century) Prehistoric finds from this area are at the **Parco Archeologico Naturalistico della Rocca**.

At Solarolo, the 15th-century Santissima Trinità has a fresco cycle with the *Last Judgment*. . The bay between the Punta San Fermo and Punta Belvedere headlands is dominated by San Felice del Benaco. To the south is the Madonna del Carmine sanctuary (1452) with 15th- and 16th-century frescoes. The church in the town centre has a *Madonna and Saints* by Romanino. Opposite Punta San Fermo is the 13th-century monastery Isola di Garda.

Parco Archeologico Naturalistico della Rocca

Via Rocca 20 339-613 7247 Apr-Sep: 10am-6pm Wed-Mon; Oct-Mar: 9am-1pm Wed-Fri, 10am-5pm Sat & Sun 25 & 26 Dec

Salò

Brescia Piazza Sant' Antonio 4; 036-5374 8145

In 1337, Salò became the seat of the Consiglio della Magnifica Patria, the governing body of

42 towns. It met in the palazzo built by Sansovino in 1524 (now the Museo Archeologico).

The town's Centro Culturale Santa Giustina houses **MuSa (Museo di Salò)**, which includes the Museo del Nastro Azzurro, a military museum. Palazzo Terzi-Martinengo at Barbarano was the seat of Mussolini's Salò puppet government.

MuSa (Museo di Salò)
Via Brunati 9
Hours vary, check website
museodisalo.it

Gardone Riviera

Brescia Corso Repubblica 8; 334-282 5186

With the highest winter temperatures in northern Italy, Gardone Riviera became a popular tourist resort in the late 19th century because of its mild dry climate, which is beneficial for those suffering from lung ailments. Two celebrated villas in the area are Villa Alba and Villa Fiordaliso.

Gardone is also famous for the **Vittoriale degli Italiani**, Gabriele D'Annunzio's residence, featuring the art, books and mementos that the poet collected. In the garden are the Prioria, the Auditorium, the Mausoleum and Schifamondo. On display are objects related to his exploits during and after World War I, such as his motor boat and aeroplane.

Another attraction is the **Giardino Botanico Hruska**, a botanical garden with over 2,000 Alpine, Mediterranean and subtropical plants.

Vittoriale degli Italiani
Gardone
Hours vary, check website
vittoriale.it

Vittoriale degli Italiani in Gardone Riviera and (*inset*) its bold interior

Giardino Botanico Hruska
Via Roma 2 336-410 877 15 Mar-15 Oct: 9am-7pm daily

Toscolano Maderno

Brescia Viale Ugo Foscolo; 036-551 5114

This town is made up of the two villages of Toscolano and Maderno. In Maderno are the Romanesque church of Sant' Andrea and the parish church of Sant'Ercolano, with paintings by Veronese and Andrea Celesti. Here the Gonzaga family built the Palazzina del Serraglio (17th century) for Vincenzo I. Toscolano, ancient Benacum, was the largest town on Lake Garda in Roman times.

At Santa Maria del Benaco, archaeologists found Roman and Etruscan objects and the ruins of a villa (1st century CE). In Gargnano are San Giacomo di Calino (11th–12th century) and San Francesco (1289). Another sight is Villa Feltrinelli, Mussolini's residence during the Republic of Salò.

GREAT VIEW
Lake Views

A short distance from Limone Sul Garda, the hilltop lemon museum Limonaia del Castel is the perfect place to enjoy spectacular views of Lake Garda while enjoying a relaxing stroll among the lemon groves.

Limone sul Garda

Brescia Via 4 Novembre 29/L; 036-595 4720

Limone may have been named after the lemon tree terraces (no longer used) typical of this area. Or the name may derive from *limen* (border), since the Austrian frontier was here until 1918. In the town centre is the 15th-century church of San Rocco. Further south, near Tignale, is the **Montecastello Sanctuary** (13th–14th century) with a *Coronation of the Virgin* (14th century) and medal-lions by Palma il Giovane. Towards Tremosine is the panoramic Brasa river gorge.

Montecastello Sanctuary
Via Triboldi, Tignale
036-573 019 Mid-Apr-Oct: 9:30am-6pm daily

Riva del Garda

Trento Largo Medaglie d'Oro; www.gardatrentino.it

Situated on the northern tip of the lake in Trentino, Riva was under Austrian rule until 1918. The Rocca (12th century) and Torre Apponale (13th century) were built to defend the town. In the square opposite are Palazzo Pretorio (1370) and Palazzo del Provveditore (1482). The Rocca houses the **Museo Alto Garda (MAG)**, with 14th- to 20th-century paintings. Santa Maria Assunta has two canvases by Piazzetta, while the Inviolata (1603) has works by Palma il Giovane. Above the towns are the waterfalls of the Varone river, which stand 80 m (262 ft) high.

Museo Alto Garda (MAG)
Piazza Cesare Battisti 3
10am-6pm Tue-Sun
museoaltogarda.it

Torri del Benaco

Verona Via Gardesana 815; 045-629 6162

Roman Castrum Turrium was a major stop between Riva and Garda and has preserved the typical grid plan. Its castle is now a **museum**, with old farm tools and prehistoric finds. Santissima Trinità has some 15th-century frescoes.

Museo del Castello
Via Fratelli Lavanda
045-629 6111 Hours vary, call ahead

Garda

Verona Piazzetta Donatori di Sangue; 045-627 0384

Built around a small bay, Garda was once a major town that controlled the southern basin. Its name, then given to the lake, comes from the German *warten* (fortress), referring to the wall around the historic centre. Its small port is access-ible through the Torre dell'-Orologio tower and gate. Make sure to visit the 15th-century Palazzo del Capitano, the losa, the dock of Palazzo Carlotti and **Santa Maria Assunta**, (18th century) with a painting by Palma il Giovane and a 15th-century cloister. At the new port is Villa Albertini, with an English-style park, while at Punta San Vigilio is Villa Guarienti, where you can see Bronze Age engravings.

Santa Maria Assunta
Piazzale Roma
045-725 6825

Malcesine

Verona Seasonal office: Via Gardesana 238; 045-740 00 44

Malcesine stands on a stretch of impervious rock, hence the name *mala silex*, or inaccessible

Boats docked at the blooming town of Limone sul Garda

rock. The 12th-century Castello was rebuilt by the Scaligeri of Verona in 1277. It houses the Museo di Storia Naturale del Garda e del Monte Baldo, the lake's natural history museum. The parish church contains a 16th-century Deposition. Towering above Malcesine is Monte Baldo (2,218 m, 7,275 ft), accessible by cable car, with nature trails and great views.

Bardolino and Lazise

Verona Bardolino Piazzale Aldo Moro; 045-721 0078

The Cornicello and Mirabello headlands enclosing Bardolino made it a natural harbour. Originally there was a prehistoric settlement here and later a Roman camp.

Bardolino's historic centre has two early medieval churches, San Zeno and San Severo. The first still has its 9th-century Carolingian cruciform structure. Romanesque San Severo was founded in the 9th century but rebuilt in the 12th. It has 12th–13th-century frescoes with battle scenes and biblical episodes, and a 10th-century crypt. Among the civic buildings is the Loggia Rambaldi, in the Rambaldi family palazzo. Bardolino is also famous for its wine.

Lazise also lays claim to having a prehistoric civilization. A castle was built in the 11th century and the lords of Verona erected the town walls in the 1300s. The 16th-century Venetian Customs House is all that remains of the old harbour. Next to it is San Nicolò (12th century), with Giotto school frescoes.

Peschiera del Garda

Verona Piazzale Betteloni 15; www.tourism.verona.it

Peschiera has retained its military image more than any other town on Lake Garda. The old town lies on an island surrounded by a star-shaped wall – "a fortress beautiful and strong", says Dante. The walls were reinforced by the Scaligeri of Verona, rebuilt for the new Venetian rulers by Sanmicheli in 1556, and completed with two forts by the Austrians two centuries later. Besides the 18th-century San Martino, there is the 16th-century Madonna del Frassino sanctuary.

↑ Scenic Malcesine, dominated by the 12th-century Castello

EAT

Inchiostro Restaurant

Sample the Tyrrhenian Sea's "catch of the day".

Via Don Lenotti 9, Peschiera del Garda 045-832 5270 Mon

Hostaria al Buongusto

Enjoy a meal on a terrace with lovely lake views.

Via Fontana 2, Limone sul Garda albuongusto.com

George Fish and Chips

A gourmet fish and chips joint ideal for a quick lunch or a picnic.

Corso Ospedale 13, Lazise 347-173 4604

14

GARDALAND

Peschiera del Garda Hours vary across rides, check website; special openings around Halloween and Christmas gardaland.it

Located in the southeastern corner of Lake Garda, this vast theme park is one of Italy's oldest. It offers a fun day out for all ages, with live entertainment shows scheduled throughout the day and a selection of exhilarating roller-coasters, rides and 4D screenings.

INSIDER TIP
Park App

Download the Gardaland app *(www.gardaland.it/en/useful-information/useful-services/gardaland-app)* for up-to-date show schedules, tickets, park maps and the latest park news.

This theme park was opened in 1975 and is one of the largest in Italy covering 50 ha (124 acres). The 36 attractions include roller-coasters, reconstructions of the pyramids, a jungle, the Gardaland Theatre, the Fantasy Kingdom and even a mini recreation of Milan. The fun park facilities are good, including a wide range of refreshments and theme shops selling souvenirs. There are luxury hotels on-site for visitors seeking an uninterrupted trip here. At busy times queues are kept informed about the length of the wait.

The themed rides and attractions in Gardaland's vast complex

Mammoth

Space Vertigo is designed to look like a space station. Plunge into the void at top speed from its 40-m (131-ft) high tower– a thrilling experience.

Mowgli 4D Jungle Adventure

Lovers of ancient Egypt can enter the temple of Abu Simbel and explore its dark corridors while shooting laser guns at Ramses the Awakening.

Top Spin

Monorail station

Magic Mountain is a popular super-fast roller-coaster, with two hairpin bends and death-defying spins.

The floating tree trunks of the Colorado Boat confront the canyon rapids.

The park's actors take to the stage of Gardaland Theatre every day to perform musicals for both adults and children.

Escape from Atlantis

LEGO® miniland and water park.

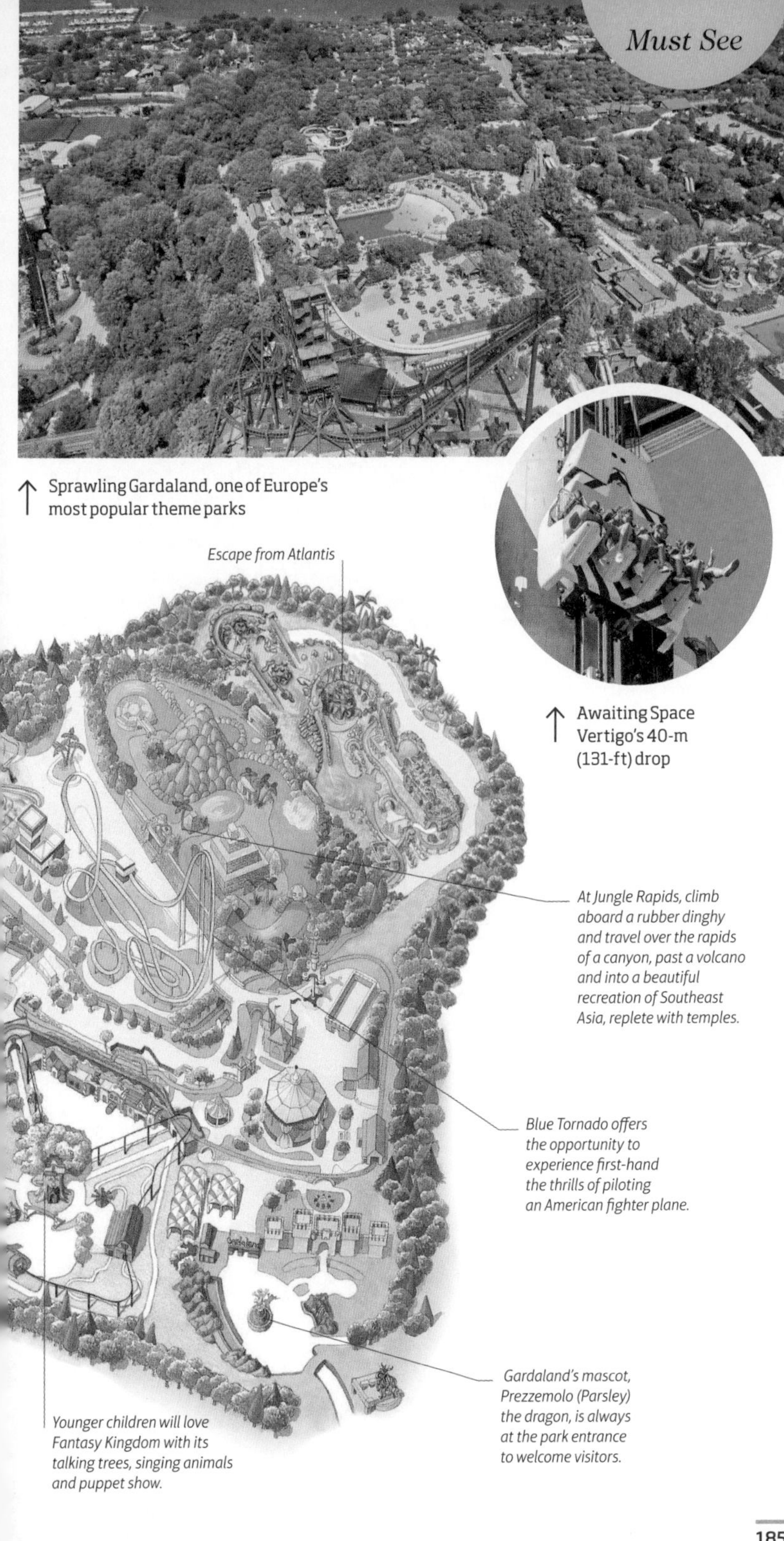

Escape from Atlantis
At Jungle Rapids, climb aboard a rubber dinghy and travel over the rapids of a canyon, past a volcano and into a beautiful recreation of Southeast Asia, replete with temples.
Blue Tornado offers the opportunity to experience first-hand the thrills of piloting an American fighter plane.
Gardaland's mascot, Prezzemolo (Parsley) the dragon, is always at the park entrance to welcome visitors.
Younger children will love Fantasy Kingdom with its talking trees, singing animals and puppet show.

↑ Sprawling Gardaland, one of Europe's most popular theme parks

↑ Awaiting Space Vertigo's 40-m (131-ft) drop

EXPERIENCE MORE

Lago d'Orta

FS Novara-Domodossola line Nav Lago d'Orta APTL, Via Panoramica, Orta-San Giulio; 032-290 5163

Lake Orta, or Cusio, the westernmost lake in the lower Alps region, is surrounded by scenic villages. The Mottarone, a ski resort, and the other mountains around the lake offer attractive hiking trails.

The chief town here is Orta San Giulio. The alleyways wind around Piazza Motta, on which lies the Palazzetto della Comunità (1582) and where the stepped Motta ascent begins. Opposite the square is the island of San Giulio, converted to Christianity by the Greek deacon Julius, who built the 4th-century **Basilica di San Giulio**. The UNESCO World Heritage Site of **Sacro Monte** is a sanctuary built in 1591 on the rise above Orta. Dedicated to St Francis, it consists of 20 chapels with 17th- to 18th-century terracotta statues and frescoes. Opposite, perched over a quarry, is the Madonna del Sasso sanctuary (1748).

North of the lake is Omegna, which has the late Romanesque collegiate church of Sant'Ambrogio.

At Quarna there is the **Museo Etnografico e dello Strumento Musicale a Fiato**, with displays of wind instruments, made in this village for centuries. Other interesting villages are Vacciago di Ameno, with the Calderara Collection of contemporary art, featuring 327 works of the 1950s and 1960s; and San Maurizio d'Opaglio, which has a curious museum about taps.

Basilica di San Giulio
Isola di San Giulio APTL, Ring Road, Orta San Giulio Hours vary, check website benedettineisolasan giulio.org

Sacro Monte
Via Sacro Monte 032-291 1960 Hours vary, call ahead 1 & 6 Jan, 25, 26 & 31 Dec

Museo Etnografico e dello Strumento Musicale a Fiato
Via Roma, Quarna Sotto 033-8562 2191 Jul-Aug: 4-7pm Wed-Fri, 10am-noon & 4-7pm Sat & Sun

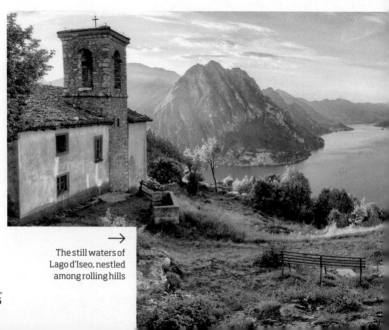

Lago d'Iseo

FS to Brescia, then Trenord Navigazione Lago d'Iseo; www.lago diseo.org IAT, Lungolago Marconi 26, Iseo

Lake Iseo, also known as Sebino, is the sixth-largest lake in Italy. It was created by a glacier descending from the Val Camonica. The chief towns here are Iseo, Sarnico, Lovere and Pisogne. The historic centre of Iseo has kept its medieval character, with the church of Sant'Andrea (1150), which contains a painting by Hayez. On a hill at the entrance to the town is the Castello degli Oldofredi (built in the 14th century), which in 1585 became a Capuchin monastery.

→

The still waters of Lago d'Iseo, nestled among rolling hills

At Provaglio d'Iseo is the San Pietro in Lamosa Cluniac monastery, founded in 1030. Its 11th- to 12th-century church has frescoes by the school of Romanino. Sarnico was an important commercial and industrial town. Among the Art Nouveau houses built here by Giuseppe Sommaruga is Villa Faccanoni (1912), one of the best examples of this style.

The road that follows the western side of the lake has fine views of Monte Isola, the largest lake island in Europe, dominated by the Madonna della Ceriola sanctuary and the 15th-century Rocca Oldofredi. At the northern end of the lake is Lovere, which has medieval tower-houses.

On the lakeside is the **Galleria dell'Accademia Tadini**, featuring works from the 14th–20th centuries by renowned artists, including Jacopo Bellini, Hayez and Canova. The church of Santa Maria in Valvendra (1483) has paintings by Floriano Ferramola and Moretto. At Pisogne is Santa Maria della Neve (15th century), with scenes of the Passion frescoed by Romanino (1534). From here you can access the Val Camonica rock engravings park. The lake is also famous for the Piramidi di Zone, pinnacles protected from erosion by the massif above them, and the Torbiere d'Iseo, a marsh with peat bogs.

Galleria dell'Accademia Tadini
 Via Tadini 40, Lovere
035-962780 Apr-Sep: 3-7pm Tue-Sat, 10am-noon & 3-7pm Sun

6 Lago di Varese

Trenord Milano, Milan-Laveno line to Gavirate
Autolinee Varesine
Via Luigi Sacco 11, Varese (033-228 1913)

Home to the Campo dei Fiori massif, this lake basin, was created by glacial movement during the Quaternary era. In prehistoric times it was inhabited by a civilization the remains of which were found on the island of Isolino Virginia. They are on display at the **Museo Preistorico**, a UNESCO Heritage Site.

Part of the lake shore is now protected as the Brabbia marsh nature reserve. The **Chiostro di Voltorre** at Voltorre di Gavirate is worth a visit. It was part of a 12th-century Cluniac monastery and is now used for exhibitions. On the slopes of Campo dei Fiori you can see the lake and the UNESCO Site **Sacro Monte di Varese**, a sanctuary made up of 14 chapels built in the 17th century.

GLACIAL LAKES

The lakes of northern Italy were formed about 15,000 years ago. They are categorized as glacial lakes, meaning that they were created by glaciers advancing and retreating through the ages, ripping rocks from the surrounding mountains and making large basins that fill up with rainwater. The resulting lakes are deep and lined by hills formed by the debris.

Museo Preistorico
 Isolino Virginia
032-8837 7206 (Musei Civici di Varese) 10am-5:30pm Sun

Chiostro di Voltorre
Voltorre di Gavirate
033-274 8278 3-6pm Tue, 10am-noon Thu

Sacro Monte di Varese
Varese 033-222 9223
7am-noon & 2-6pm daily

7 Lago d'Idro

Via San Michele 56, Idro; www.lagodidro.it

The highest large lake in Lombardy (368 m/1,207 ft above sea level) was turned into an artificial basin in 1932 to provide irrigation and hydroelectricity. It is dominated by the Rocca di Anfo, a fortress with a panoramic view that was built over older fortifications by the Venetians in 1450, and then rebuilt many times. From here you can reach Bagolino, with its stone houses and San Rocco (1478), which contains a fresco cycle by Giovan Pietro da Cemmo.

NEED TO KNOW

High-speed trains at Milan's Central Station

ROMA TERMINI
13
AV 9627
12:00
Biglietti

BEFORE YOU GO

Things change, so plan ahead to make the most of your trip. Be prepared for all eventualities by considering the following points before you travel.

AT A GLANCE
CURRENCY
Euro
AVERAGE DAILY SPEND
SAVE €50
SPEND €100
SPLURGE €200+
BOTTLED WATER €1.10
COFFEE €1.20
BEER €5.00
DINNER FOR TWO €60
ESSENTIAL PHRASES
Hello — Buongiorno / ciao
Goodbye — Arrivederci / ciao
Please — Per favore
Thank you — Grazie
Do you speak English? — Parla inglese?
I don't understand — Non capisco

ELECTRICITY SUPPLY
Power socks are type F and L, fitting two-pronged and three-pronged plugs. Standard voltage is 220-230v.

Passports and visas

For entry requirements, including visas, consult your nearest Italian embassy or check the **Polizia di Stato** website. Citizens of the UK, US, Canada, Australia and New Zealand do not need a visa for stays of up to three months, but in future must apply in advance for the European Travel Information and Authorization System (**ETIAS**); roll-out has continually been postponed so check website for details. EU nationals do not need a visa or an ETIAS.

ETIAS
W travel-europe.europa.eu/etias
Polizia di Stato
W poliziadistato.it

Government Advice

Now more than ever, it is important to consult both your and the Italian government's advice before travelling. The **UK Foreign, Commonwealth and Development Office**, the **US State Department**, the **Australian Department of Foreign Affairs and Trade**, and the Italian **Ministero della Salute** offer the latest information on security, health and local regulations.

Australian Department of Foreign Affairs and Trade
W www.smartraveller.gov.au
Ministero della Salute
W salute.gov.it
UK Foreign, Commonwealth and Development Office
W www.gov.uk/foreign-travel-advice
US State Department
W www.travel.state.gov

Customs Information

You can find information on laws relating to goods and currency taken in or out of Italy on the ENIT (Italy's national tourist board) website *(p196)*.

Insurance

We recommend taking out a comprehensive insurance policy covering medical care, theft,

loss of belongings, cancellations and delays, and reading the small print carefully. UK citizens are eligible for free emergency medical care in Italy provided they have a valid European Health Insurance Card (EHIC) or UK Global Health Insurance Card (**GHIC**). Australia has a reciprocal health care agreement with Italy, and citizens can access essential medical treatment as long as they are registered to **Medicare**.

GHIC
W www.ghic.org.uk
Medicare
W humanservices.gov.au/individuals/medicare

Booking accommodation

Milan and the Lakes offer a wide range of accommodation for all budgets, from hostels and campsites to luxury five-star hotels. Year-round, lodgings fill up quickly and prices can also soar during major events such as Milan Fashion Week. City taxes are common (around €2–€5 per person, per night).

Under Italian law, hotels are required to register guests at police headquarters and issue a receipt of payment *(ricevuta fiscale)*.

Money

Italy's currency is the euro. Major credit and debit cards are accepted by most businesses; prepaid currency cards and American Express are accepted in some. Contactless payments are increasingly common but it's always wise to carry cash for smaller items and local markets, just in case. Cash machines are ubiquitous.

Italy does not have a big tipping culture. Restaurants usually charge a *coperto* (cover charge), Italy's equivalent to service charge. It is customary to round up to the nearest euro when tipping taxi drivers. You're not expected to tip hotel porters, although tips are always appreciated.

Travellers with Specific Needs

Travelling in northern Italy can present challenges for some, due to narrow cobbled streets and historic buildings. Some efforts are being made, however. In Milan, the metro and bus are wheelchair accessible, while **Radiotaxi** has a fleet of wheelchair-friendly taxis. **AIAS** in Milan provides assistance and tourist board site **YesMilano** *(p196)* details accessible attractions.

AIAS
W www.aiasnazionale.it
Radiotaxi
W 026969.it

Language

The official language spoken in Milan and the Lakes is Italian. In urban areas, a modest level of English is spoken. In rural areas, it can be limited. Locals appreciate visitors' efforts to speak Italian, if only a few words.

Opening Hours

Situations can change quickly and unexpectedly. Always check before visiting attractions and hospitality venues for up-to-date opening hours and booking requirements.

Monday Many museums and attractions close.
Sunday Many shops close early or for the day .
Public holidays Schools, post offices and banks are closed.
August Many restaurants in Milan close for up to a month. Some attractions alter opening hours.

PUBLIC HOLIDAYS

1 Jan	New Year
6 Jan	Epiphany
Mar/Apr	Easter Sunday and Monday
25 Apr	Liberation Day
1 May	Labour Day
2 Jun	Republic Day
15 Aug	Ferragosto
1 Nov	All Saints' Day
8 Dec	Feast of the Immaculate Conception
25 Dec	Christmas Day
26 Dec	St Stephen's Day

GETTING AROUND

Forward planning is essential for any successful trip. Prepare yourself for any eventuality by brushing up on the following points before you set off.

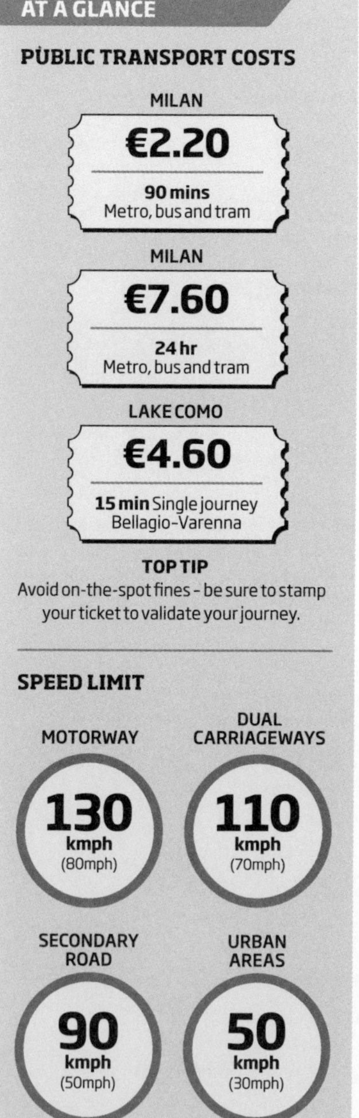

AT A GLANCE
PUBLIC TRANSPORT COSTS
MILAN
€2.20
90 mins
Metro, bus and tram
MILAN
€7.60
24 hr
Metro, bus and tram
LAKE COMO
€4.60
15 min Single journey
Bellagio-Varenna
TOP TIP
Avoid on-the-spot fines - be sure to stamp your ticket to validate your journey.
SPEED LIMIT
MOTORWAY
130 kmph (80mph)
DUAL CARRIAGEWAYS
110 kmph (70mph)
SECONDARY ROAD
90 kmph (50mph)
URBAN AREAS
50 kmph (30mph)

Arriving by Air

Milan is home to three airports: Milan Malpensa lying around 40 km (25 miles) northwest of the city centre and a major hub for national and international flights; the much smaller Linate, which lies east of the city centre; and Bergamo Orio al Serio, approximately 50 km (31 miles) east of Milan.

For Lake Como, Lake Maggiore and Lake Orta, Milan Malpensa is the most convenient. European budget airlines land at Bergamo Orio al Serio, conveniently located to reach Lecco on Lake Como's eastern arm, as well as the smaller Lake Iseo, which lies 38 km (24 miles) east of Bergamo Airport. Verona Airport is the closest airport to Lake Garda, while Torino Caselle Airport is the nearest to Lake Orta and Lake Maggiore.

Train Travel

International Train Travel

High-speed Le Frecce and Intercity trains by **Trenitalia** along with **Italo** services connect several European destinations, such as Vienna, Hamburg, Barcelona and Paris to Milan; **Tilo** connects Lake Como to destinations in Switzerland's Ticino region. For multiple international journeys, take a look at the various types of tickets and passes provided by **Eurail** or **Interrail**; note you may need to pay an additional reservation fee depending on which rail service you travel with. Book in advance for the best fares and always check that your pass is valid before boarding to avoid receiving a hefty fine.

Eurail
W eurail.com
Interrail
W interrail.eu
Italo
W italotreno.it
Trenitalia
W trenitalia.it
Tilo
W tilo.ch

GETTING TO AND FROM THE AIRPORT

Airport	Distance to City	Taxi fare	Public Transport
Malpensa	45 km (28 miles)	€110	Train (40 mins), coach (1.25 hrs)
Linate	7km (4 miles)	€30	Metro (10 minutes), bus (60 minutes)
Bergamo Orio al Serio	50 km (31 miles)	€126	Bus (50 mins)

CAR JOURNEY PLANNER

Plotting the main driving routes according to journey time, this map is a handy reference for travelling between Milan and the Lakes' main towns and cities by car. The times given reflect the fastest and most direct routes available. Tolls may apply.

Milan to Como	1 hr	**Sirmione to Desenzano del Garda**	15 mins
Como to Bellagio	1 hr	**Desenzano del Garda to Salò**	30 mins
Como to Tremezzo	50 mins	**Salò to Limone sul Garda**	45 mins
Tremezzo to Menaggio	10 mins	**Milan to Stresa**	1hr 25mins
Milan to Sirmione	1hr 40mins	**Stresa to Arona**	25 mins
Sirmione to Peschiera del Garda	15 mins	**Arona to Luino**	1hr 10 mins
Peschiera del Garda to Verona	30 mins		

Regional Trains

Trains are run by **Trenitalia** and **Trenord**, with the majority serving Milano Centrale, the city's main station. Lake Como has three key railway stations – Como, Varenna-Esino and Lecco – with services from Milan taking around 40–60 minutes. Lake Garda is served by three railway stations: Peschiera, Desenzano and Rovereto; Lake Maggiore can be accessed via stations at Arona, Stresa, Baveno and Verbania-Pallanza.

Trenitalia
W trenitalia.it
Trenord
W trenord.it

Long-Distance Bus Travel

Long-distance buses are an affordable way to travel between Milan and the Lakes but options are fairly limited. **Safduemila** and Comazzi connect Milan Malpensa to Lake Maggiore, with Safduemila also connecting Lake Maggiore to Lake Orta during the peak summer months. **Flixbus** has long-distance bus services to Peschiera del Garda on Lake Garda from destinations around Europe.

Flixbus
W flixbus.co.uk
Safduemila
W safduemila.com

Public Transport

Milan offers a good public transport network, with metro, buses and trams connecting all points of the city. In the Lakes, travelling by boat or car is the easiest way to get around.

Metro, Tram and Bus

In Milan, public transport, including metro, tram and bus services, is run by **ATM**. Buses and trams are affordable, but can be affected by traffic, so the metro is often the quickest way to travel.

Several bus companies connect the Lakes' towns, including **Safduemila** on Lake Maggiore, **ASF Autolinee** on Lake Como, **Arriva** on the western shore of Lake Garda, **Trentino Trasporti** in the northern basin of Lake Garda and **ATV** on the eastern shore of Lake Garda.

Arriva
W arriva.it
ASF Autolinee
W asfautolinee.it
ATM
W atm.it
ATV
W atv.verona.it
Safduemila
W afduemila.com
Trentino Trasporti
W trentinotrasporti.it

Tickets

Tickets for ATM services in Milan can be bought at metro stations from ticket machines and booths as well as at tobacconists, dedicated cafés and newspaper kiosks throughout the city. You can also buy tickets via the ATM app.

Tickets are valid for 90 minutes from validation and can be used on any ATM service to get to your destination in that time. All tickets must be validated when boarding. On buses and trams, you'll find validation machines on board; to enter the metro, insert your ticket to activate the turnstiles. Alternatively, use your contactless bank card (the same 90-minute rule applies). Card restrictions apply, so check before travelling.

By the Lakes, boat tickets can be purchased from ticket booths at the piers. Bus tickets are sold at kiosks and tobacconist stores. Some bus services accept cash on board, often for a small surcharge, while others offer online payment.

Boats and Ferries

Navigazione Laghi operates boats and ferry services around Lake Garda, Lake Como and Lake Maggiore. There are several types of passenger-only boats, with affordable slower services or fast services with premium prices.

Ferries transport both cars and foot passengers, making them convenient if you need to cross from one shore to the other. Note that services are greatly reduced in late autumn and winter, when most hotels and attractions are closed before they reopen for the new season come Easter. In high season, there can be long queues to board services – make sure to arrive well in advance of your journey.

Navigazione Laghi
W navigazionelaghi.it

Taxis

Taxis in Milan are white and cannot be hailed on the street. They can be booked at a taxi rank, via the Milano in Taxi app or by calling 027-777. Taxis normally charge by the meter, but there are fixed fares for certain destinations such as Malpensa Airport. Uber is also available in Milan.

In the Lakes, taxis can be very costly and difficult to secure in high season, so book well in advance at peak times. There are several taxi companies at the Lakes, including **Radio Taxi Como** on Lake Como, **Stresa Taxi** on Lake Maggiore and **Taxi Desenzano** on Lake Garda.

Radio Taxi Como
W radiotaxicomo.com
Stresa Taxi
W stresataxi.it
Taxi Desenzano
W taxidesenzano.com

Driving

One of the best ways to explore the Lakes and its remote areas is by car. In the city, save time by travelling by public transport.

Driving to Milan and the Lakes

Driving in northern Italy is straightforward, with a good network of motorways and clearly marked exits. Motorways marked with green signs are subject to tolls. Most are payable on motorways throughout Italy; drivers must take a ticket from an automatic machine on entering the motorway and this is used to calculate the toll automatically at the exit. To avoid queuing to leave the motorway, pay by card or invest in a GO by **Telepass**.

Most *tangenziali* (ring roads) around major urban centres tend to be free. A notable exception is the **Pedemontana** ring road of Como and Verese – there are no toll stations for the Pedemontana and tolls must be paid online, which can make it all too easy to miss.

Pedemontana
W apl.pedemontana.com
Telepass
W www.telepass.com

Driving in Milan and the Lakes

Milan's historic centre is part of **Area C**, a low emissions zone. Older vehicles are subject to a €7.50 fee – visit the Area C website to pay in advance.

In smaller towns, several historical areas are protected by Limited Traffic Zones known as ZTL *(zona traffico limitato)*, which limit vehicle entry. If your hotel is located inside a ZTL, register your car via the hotel in advance to avoid incurring a fine. If you're driving from Milan to the Lakes, you may come across toll roads. Road signs for motorways are green; signs for toll-free main roads are blue. The **ACI** (Automobile Club d'Italia) offers helpful advice for visiting drivers.

ACI
W aci.it
Area C
W areac.atm-mi.it

Car Rental

To rent a car in Italy you must be over 18 and have a valid EU driving licence or International Driving Permit. Most rental companies require you to have held a licence for at least one year. Some have a minimum age of 21 and most apply young driver surcharges for under-25s. You also need to have a credit card as a guarantee.

Rules of the Road

Drive on the right, use the left lane only for passing, and give way to traffic from the right. Seatbelts are required for all passengers and using a mobile phone while driving is prohibited, unless it's completely hands-free. The legal drink-drive limit *(p197)* is strictly enforced.

During the day dipped headlights are compulsory when driving on motorways, dual carriageways and on all out-of-town roads. You must carry a red warning triangle and fluorescent vest at all times and winter tyres or snow-chains (not appplicable to motorcycles) between mid-November and mid-April.

In the event of a breakdown, call the ACI freephone emergency line – 803-116 from an Italian phone or 800-116-800 from a non-Italian phone – or the emergency services (112 or 113).

Parking

Parking can be limited in Milan. Spaces marked with yellow stripes are reserved for residents; blue stripes require payment; white stripes are free. There are charging stations for electric vehicles on streets and public parking spaces; the **NEXTCHARGE** app can help locate the nearest charge points.

NEXTCHARGE
W nextcharge.app/map

Cycling

There are over 140 km (86 miles) of cycle paths and lanes in Milan, with bike-sharing schemes available in the city through agencies such as **BIKEMI**. Daily fares start at €4.50 for two hours. The Lakes are a magnet for keen cyclists, with plenty of cycling routes for all levels.

BIKEMI
W bikemi.com

Bicycle Hire

There are plenty of bike rental shops in towns around the Lakes, including **Rental Bike and Scooter Como**, **Stresa Bike Rental** and **Garda Bike Shop**. Several hotels also offer bike hire.

Garda Bike Shop
W gardabikeshop.com
Rental Bike and Scooter Como
W rentalbikecomo.com
Stresa Bike Rental
W stresabikerental.com

Bicycle Safety

Helmets are not compulsory for adults but it's a good idea to wear one, especially on major roads.

Walking

Wandering around Milan is one of the most enjoyable aspects of any trip to the city. Many parts of Milan are easier and quicker to explore by foot, including pedestrianized areas such as Corso Vittorio Emanuele and the Brera quarter. There are also many scenic walks by the Lakes.

PRACTICAL INFORMATION

A little local know-how goes a long way in Milan and the Lakes. Here you can find all the essential advice and information you will need during your stay.

AT A GLANCE

EMERGENCY NUMBERS

GENERAL EMERGENCY	POLICE	FIRE SERVICE	AMBULANCE
112	113	115	118

TIME ZONE

CET/CEST Central European Summer Time runs from the last Sunday in March to the last Sunday in October.

TAP WATER

Unless otherwise stated, tap water in Milan and the Lakes is safe to drink (though most Italians drink and serve bottled water).

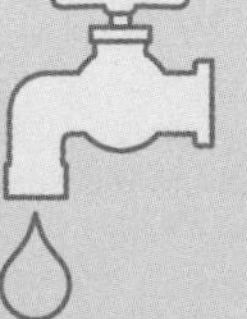

WEBSITES

ENIT
Italy's national tourist board website *(www.italia.it)*

YesMilano
Milan's official tourist board website has plenty of helpful tips *(www.yesmilano.it)*

Lago di Garda Italia
Lake Garda's official tourist board *(www.visitgarda.com)*

Lago di Como
The official tourist board of Lake Como *(www.lakecomo.is)*

Personal Security

Northern Italy is generally safe, but petty crime does take place. Pickpockets work in known tourist areas, busy streets and on public transport. Use your common sense and be alert to your surroundings. If you have anything stolen, report the crime as soon as possible at the nearest police station (*Polizia* or *Carabinieri*). Get a copy of the crime report *(denuncia)* if you need to make an insurance claim. Contact your embassy or consulate immediately if your passport is stolen or in the event of a serious crime or accident.

As a rule, Italians are accepting of all people, regardless of their race, gender or sexuality. Homosexuality was legalized in 1890, and in 1982, Italy became the third country in the world to recognize the right to legally change your gender. Same-sex civil unions were legalized in 2016. Milan in particular is very welcoming and is often viewed as Italy's most LGBTQ+-friendly city, with many hotels, bars and clubs that embrace the community. If you experience discrimination while using a tourist service, **AITGL** (Italian Gay & Lesbian Tourism Association) provides a dedicated legal desk for LGBTQ+ travellers; if you feel unsafe, head to the nearest police station.

AITGL
W www.turismolgbt.org

Health

Italy has a world-class healthcare system. Emergency medical care in Italy is free for all UK, EU and Australian citizens. If you have an EHIC, GHIC *(p191)* or Australian Medicare card, be sure to present this as soon as possible. You may have to pay for treatment and reclaim the money later. For other visitors, payment of hospital and other medical expenses is the patient's responsibility. It is therefore important to arrange comprehensive medical insurance before you travel.

Seek medicinal supplies and advice for minor ailments at pharmacies *(farmacie)*. You can find details of the nearest 24-hour service on pharmacy doors. For a more serious injury

or illness, head to the emergency department. Most hospitals have English-speaking staff that can help with translations.

Smoking, Alcohol and Drugs

Smoking is banned in enclosed public places. Possession of narcotics is prohibited and could result in a prison sentence. Alcohol may not be bought by or sold to minors under the age of 18. Italy has a strict limit of 0.5mg BAC (blood alcohol content) for drivers. This means that you cannot drink more than one small beer or a small glass of wine if you plan to drive. For drivers with less than three years' driving experience, the limit is 0.

ID

By law you must carry identification with you at all times in Italy. A photocopy of your passport photo page (and visa if applicable) should suffice. If you are stopped by the police you may be asked to present the original document within 12 hours.

Local Customs

You can be fined for dropping litter and sitting on steps outside certain monuments, and it is an offence to climb into public fountains. Illegal street traders operate along several streets in Milan; avoid making any purchases from them as you could be fined by the local police.

Visiting Places of Worship

Entrance to many churches in the region is free, but you may be charged a small fee to see a certain area, such as a chapel, cloister or underground ruins. Dress codes can apply: cover your torso and upper arms and wear shoes.

Responsible Travel

The climate crisis is having a big impact on northern Italy, with heatwaves and floods increasingly frequent. Do your bit by taking quick showers and reusing towels if staying in hotel accommodation.

Be careful when disposing of cigarette butts and glass bottles in rural areas; starting a fire, even if accidental, is deemed a criminal offence in Milan and the Lakes.

Mobile Phones and Wi-Fi

Wi-Fi is generally widely available, and cafés, bars, restaurants and some cultural venues will usually allow you to use their Wi-Fi on the condition that you make a purchase. Mobile coverage in Milan and the Lakes is overall very good, although it's wise not to rely entirely on mobile phones or other devices for navigation or emergency communications in remote areas where mobile reception can be intermittent.

Visitors travelling to Italy may be subject to higher rates for data, voice calls and SMS services than they would usually pay at home. Usage and roaming fees within the EU may or may not be included in your phone contract, so be sure to check before you depart.

Post

Stamps *(francobolli)* are sold at tobacconists (*tabacchi* – look for a blue sign with a white T).

Taxes and Refunds

VAT (IVA) is usually 22 per cent. Under certain conditions, non-EU citizens can claim a refund.

Either claim the rebate before you buy (show your passport to the shop assistant and complete a form) or claim it retrospectively by presenting your receipts to a customs officer as you leave. Stamped receipts will be sent back to the vendor to issue a refund.

Discount Cards

In Milan, the app-based **YesMilano City Pass** provides entry to multiple museums and attractions over three days, plus public transport. Outside of the city, Lake Garda offers the **Garda Promotions Card**, a visitor's pass that includes discounts on boat services along with discounted entry to some attractions around the lake. The card is often given for free to hotel guests staying at affiliated hotels.

Garda Promotions Card
W promotioncard.navigazionelaghi.it
YesMilano City Pass
W citypass.yesmilano.it

INDEX

Page numbers in **bold** refer to main entries

N

O

P

PHRASE BOOK

IN EMERGENCY

Help!	**Aiuto!**	eye-yoo-toh
Stop!	**Fermate!**	fair-mah-teh
Call a doctor.	**Chiama un medico**	kee-ah-mah oon meh-dee-koh
Call an ambulance.	**Chiama un' ambulanza**	kee-ah-mah oon am-boo-lan-tsa
Call the police.	**Chiama la polizia**	kee-ah-mah lah pol-ee-tsee-ah
Call the fire brigade.	**Chiama i pompieri**	kee-ah-mah ee pom-pee-air-ee
Where is the telephone?	**Dov'è il telefono?**	dov-eh eel teh-leh-foh-noh?
The nearest hospital?	**L'ospedale più vicino?**	loss-peh-dah-leh pee-oo vee-chee-noh?

COMMUNICATION ESSENTIALS

Yes/No	**Si/No**	see/noh
Please	**Per favore**	pair fah-vor-eh
Thank you	**Grazie**	grah-tsee-eh
Excuse me	**Mi scusi**	mee skoo-zee
Hello	**Buon giorno**	bwon jor-noh
Goodbye	**Arrivederci**	ah-ree-veh-dair-chee
Good evening	**Buona sera**	bwon-ah sair-ah
morning	**la mattina**	lah mah-tee-nah
afternoon	**il pomeriggio**	eel poh-meh-ree-joh
evening	**la sera**	lah sair-ah
yesterday	**ieri**	ee-air-ee
today	**oggi**	oh-jee
tomorrow	**domani**	doh-mah-nee
here	**qui**	kwee
there	**la**	lah
What?	**Quale?**	kwah-leh?
When?	**Quando?**	kwan-doh?
Why?	**Perchè?**	pair-keh?
Where?	**Dove?**	doh-veh?

USEFUL PHRASES

How are you?	**Come sta?**	koh-meh stah?
Very well, thank you.	**Molto bene, grazie.**	moll-toh beh-neh grah-tsee-eh
Pleased to meet you.	**Piacere di conoscerla.**	pee-ah-chair-eh dee coh-noh-shair-lah
See you later.	**A più tardi.**	ah pee-oo tar-dee
That's fine.	**Va bene.**	va beh-neh
Where is/are...?	**Dov'è/Dove sono...?**	dov-eh/doveh soh-noh?
How long does it take to get to...?	**Quanto tempo ci vuole per andare a...?**	kwan-toh tem-poh chee voo-oh-leh pair an-dar-eh ah...?
How do I get to...?	**Come faccio per arrivare a...?**	koh-meh fah-choh pair arri-var-eh ah...?
Do you speak English?	**Parla inglese?**	par-lah een-gleh-zeh?
I don't understand.	**Non capisco.**	non ka-pee-skoh
Could you speak more slowly, please?	**Può parlare più lentamente, per favore?**	pwoh par-lah-reh pee-oo len-ta-men-teh pair fah-vor-eh?
I'm sorry.	**Mi dispiace.**	mee dee-spee-ah-cheh

USEFUL WORDS

big	**grande**	gran-deh
small	**piccolo**	pee-koh-loh
hot	**caldo**	kal-doh
cold	**freddo**	fred-doh
good	**buono**	bwoh-noh
bad	**cattivo**	kat-tee-voh
enough	**basta**	bas-tah
well	**bene**	beh-neh
open	**aperto**	ah-pair-toh
closed	**chiuso**	kee-oo-zoh
left	**a sinistra**	ah see-nee-strah
right	**a destra**	ah dess-trah
straight on	**sempre dritto**	sem-preh dree-toh
near	**vicino**	vee-chee-noh
far	**lontano**	lon-tah-noh
up	**su**	soo
down	**giù**	joo
early	**presto**	press-toh
late	**tardi**	tar-dee
entrance	**entrata**	en-trah-tah
exit	**uscita**	oo-shee-ta
toilet	**il gabinetto**	eel gah-bee-net-toh
free, unoccupied	**libero**	lee-bair-oh
free, no charge	**gratuito**	grah-too-ee-toh

MAKING A TELEPHONE CALL

I'd like to place a long-distance call.	**Vorrei fare una interurbana.**	vor-ray far-eh oona in-tair-oor-bah-nah
I'd like to make a reverse-charge call.	**Vorrei fare una telefonata a carico del destinatario.**	vor-ray far-eh oona teh-leh-fon-ah-tah ah kar-ee-koh dell dess-tee-nah-tar-ree-oh
I'll try again later.	**Ritelefono più tardi.**	ree-teh-leh-foh-noh pee-oo tar-dee
Can I leave a message?	**Posso lasciare un messaggio?**	poss-oh lash-ah-reh oon mess-sah-joh?
Hold on.	**Un attimo, per favore**	oon ah-tee-moh, pair fah-vor-eh
Could you speak up a little please?	**Può parlare più forte, per favore?**	pwoh par-lah-reh pee-oo for-teh, pair fah-vor-eh?
local call	**telefonata locale**	te-leh-fon-ah-tah loh-cah-leh

SHOPPING

How much does this cost?	**Quant'è, per favore?**	kwan-teh pair fah-vor-eh?
I would like...	**Vorrei...**	vor-ray
Do you have...?	**Avete...?**	ah-veh-teh...?
I'm just looking.	**Sto soltanto guardando.**	stoh sol-tan-toh gwar-dan-doh
Do you take credit cards?	**Accettate carte di credito?**	ah-chet-tah-teh kar-teh dee creh-dee-toh?
What time do you open/close?	**A che ora apre/chiude?**	ah keh or-ah ah-preh/kee-oo-deh?
this one	**questo**	kweh-stoh
that one	**quello**	kwell-oh
expensive	**caro**	kar-oh
cheap	**a buon prezzo**	ah bwon pret-soh
size, clothes	**la taglia**	lah tah-lee-ah
size, shoes	**il numero**	eel noo-mair-oh
white	**bianco**	bee-ang-koh
black	**nero**	neh-roh
red	**rosso**	ross-oh
yellow	**giallo**	jal-loh
green	**verde**	vair-deh
blue	**blu**	bloo

TYPES OF SHOP

antique dealer	**l'antiquario**	lan-tee-kwah-ree-oh
bakery	**il forno/ il panificio**	eel forn-oh /eel pan-ee-fee-choh
bank	**la banca**	lah bang-kah
bookshop	**la libreria**	lah lee-breh-ree-ah
butcher	**la macelleria**	lah mah-chell-eh-ree-ah
cake shop	**la pasticceria**	lah pas-tee-chair-ee-ah
chemist	**la farmacia**	lah far-mah-chee-ah
delicatessen	**la salumeria**	lah sah-loo-meh-ree-ah
department store	**il grande magazzino**	eel gran-deh mag-gad-zee-noh
fishmonger	**il pescivendolo**	eel pesh-ee-ven-doh-loh
florist	**il fioraio**	eel fee-or-eye-oh
greengrocer	**il fruttivendolo**	eel froo-tee-ven-doh-loh
grocery	**alimentari**	ah-lee-men-tah-ree
hairdresser	**il parrucchiere**	eel par-oo-kee-air-eh
ice cream parlour	**la gelateria**	lah jel-lah-tair-ree-ah
market	**il mercato**	eel mair-kah-toh
newsstand	**l'edicola**	leh-dee-koh-lah
post office	**l'ufficio postale**	loo-fee-choh pos-tah-leh
shoe shop	**il negozio di scarpe**	eel neh-goh-tsioh dee skar-peh
supermarket	**il supermercato**	eel su-pair-mair-kah-toh
tobacconist	**il tabaccaio**	eel tah-bak-eye-oh
travel agency	**l'agenzia di viaggi**	lah-jen-tsee-ah dee vee-ad-jee

SIGHTSEEING

art gallery	**la pinacoteca**	lah peena-koh-teh-kah
bus stop	**la fermata dell'autobus**	lah fair-mah-tah dell ow-toh-booss
church	**la chiesa**	lah kee-eh-zah
	la basilica	lah bah-seel-i-kah
closed for holidays	**chiuso per le ferie**	kee-oo-zoh pair leh fair-ee-eh
garden	**il giardino**	eel jar-dee-no
library	**la biblioteca**	lah beeb-lee-oh-teh-kah
museum	**il museo**	eel moo-zeh-oh
railway station	**la stazione**	lah stah-tsee-oh-neh
tourist information	**l'ufficio del turismo**	loo-fee-choh del too-ree-smoh

STAYING IN A HOTEL

Do you have any vacant rooms?	**Avete camere libere?**	*ah-***veh***-teh* **kah***-mair-eh* **lee***-bair-eh?*
double room	**una camera doppia**	*oona* **kah***-mair-ah* **doh***-pee-ah*
with double bed	**con letto matrimoniale**	*kon* **let***-toh mah-tree-moh-nee-***ah***-leh*
twin room	**una camera con due letti**	*oona* **kah***-mair-ah kon* **doo***-eh* **let***-tee*
single room	**una camera singola**	*oona* **kah***-mair-ah* **sing***-goh-lah*
room with a bath, shower	**una camera con bagno, con doccia**	*oona* **kah***-mair-ah kon ban-yoh, kon* **dot***-chah*
porter	**il facchino**	*eel fah-***kee***-noh*
key	**la chiave**	*lah kee-***ah***-veh*
I have a reservation.	**Ho fatto una prenotazione.**	*oh* **fat***-toh oona preh-noh-tah-tsee-***oh***-neh*

EATING OUT

Have you got a table for...?	**Avete un tavolo per...?**	*ah-***veh***-teh oon* **tah***-voh-loh pair...?*
I'd like to reserve a table.	**Vorrei riservare un tavolo.**	*vor-***ray** *ree-sair-***vah***-reh oon* **tah***-voh-loh*
breakfast	**colazione**	*koh-lah-tsee-***oh***-neh*
lunch	**pranzo**	**pran***-tsoh*
dinner	**cena**	**cheh***-nah*
The bill, please.	**Il conto, per favore.**	*eel* **kon***-toh pair fah-***vor***-eh*
I am a vegetarian.	**Sono vegetariano/a.**	**soh***-noh* **veh***-jeh-tar- ee-***ah***-noh/nah*
waitress	**cameriera**	*kah-mair-ee-***air***-ah*
waiter	**cameriere**	*kah-mair-ee-***air***-eh*
fixed price menu	**il menù a prezzo fisso**	*eel meh-***noo** *ah* **pret***-soh* **fee***-soh*
dish of the day	**piatto del giorno**	*pee-***ah***-toh dell* **jor***-no*
starter	**antipasto**	*an-tee-***pass***-toh*
first course	**il primo**	*eel* **pree***-moh*
main course	**il secondo**	*eel seh-***kon***-doh*
vegetables	**il contorno**	*eel kon-***tor***-noh*
dessert	**il dolce**	*eel* **doll***-cheh*
cover charge	**il coperto**	*eel koh-***pair***-toh*
wine list	**la lista dei vini**	*lah* **lee***-stah day* **vee***-nee*
rare	**al sangue**	*al* **sang***-gweh*
medium	**al puntino**	*al poon-***tee***-noh*
well done	**ben cotto**	*ben* **kot***-toh*
glass	**il bicchiere**	*eel bee-kee-***air***-eh*
bottle	**la bottiglia**	*lah bot-***teel***-yah*
knife	**il coltello**	*eel kol-***tell***-oh*
fork	**la forchetta**	*lah for-***ket***-tah*
spoon	**il cucchiaio**	*eel koo-kee-***eye***-oh*

MENU DECODER

l'acqua minerale gassata/naturale	**lah***-kwah mee-nair-***ah***-leh gah-***zah***-tah/ nah-too-rah-leh*	mineral water fizzy/still
l'agnello	*lah-***niell***-oh*	lamb
l'aceto	*lah-***cheh***-toh*	vinegar
l'aglio	*l***al***-ee-oh*	garlic
al forno	*al* **for***-noh*	baked
alla griglia	*ah-lah* **greel***-yah*	grilled
l'aragosta	*lah-rah-***goss***-tah*	lobster
l'arrosto	*lar-***ross***-toh*	roast
la birra	*lah* **beer***-rah*	beer
la bistecca	*lah bee-***stek***-kah*	steak
il brodo	*eel* **broh***-doh*	broth
il burro	*eel* **boor***-oh*	butter
il caffè	*eel kah-***feh**	coffee
i calamari	*ee kah-lah-***mah***-ree*	squid
i carciofi	*ee kar-***choff***-ee*	artichokes
la carne	*la* **kar***-neh*	meat
carne di maiale	**kar***-neh dee mah-***yah***-leh*	pork
la cipolla	*la chip-***oh***-lah*	onion
i contorni	*ee kon-***tor***-nee*	vegetables
i fagioli	*ee fah-***joh***-lee*	beans
il fegato	*eel* **fay***-gah-toh*	liver
il finocchio	*eel fee-***nok***-ee-oh*	fennel
il formaggio	*eel for-***mad***-joh*	cheese
le fragole	*leh* **frah***-goh-leh*	strawberries
il fritto misto	*eel free-toh* **mees***-toh*	mixed fried dish
la frutta	*la* **froot***-tah*	fruit
frutti di mare	**froo***-tee dee* **mah***-reh*	seafood
i funghi	*ee* **foon***-ghee*	mushrooms
i gamberi	*ee* **gam***-bair-ee*	prawns
il gelato	*eel jel-***lah***-toh*	ice cream
l'insalata	**leen***-sah-lah-tah*	salad
il latte	*eel* **laht***-teh*	milk
il lesso	*eel* **less***-oh*	boiled
il manzo	*eel* **man***-tsoh*	beef
la melanzana	*lah meh-lan-***tsah***-nah*	aubergine
la minestra	*lah mee-***ness***-trah*	soup
l'olio	*loh-lee-oh*	oil
il pane	*eel* **pah***-neh*	bread
le patate	*leh pah-***tah***-teh*	potatoes
le patatine fritte	*leh pah-tah-***teen***-eh* **free***-teh*	chips
il pepe	*eel* **peh***-peh*	pepper
la pesca	*lah* **pess***-kah*	peach
il pesce	*eel* **pesh***-eh*	fish
il pollo	*eel* **poll***-oh*	chicken
il pomodoro	*eel poh-moh-***dor***-oh*	tomato
il prosciutto	*eel pro-***shoo***-toh*	ham
cotto/crudo	**kot***-toh/***kroo***-doh*	cooked/cured
il riso	*eel* **ree***-zoh*	rice
il sale	*eel* **sah***-leh*	salt
la salsiccia	*lah sal-***see***-chah*	sausage
le seppie	*leh* **sep***-pee-eh*	cuttlefish
secco	**sek***-koh*	dry
la sogliola	*lah* **soll***-yoh-lah*	sole
gli spinaci	*lyee spee-***nah***-chee*	spinach
succo d'arancia/ di limone	**soo***-koh dah-***ran***-chah/ dee lee-***moh***-neh*	orange/lemon juice
il tè	*eel* **teh**	tea
la tisana	*lah tee-***zah***-nah*	herbal tea
il tonno	*eel* **ton***-noh*	tuna
la torta	*lah* **tor***-tah*	cake/tart
l'uovo	*loo-***oh***-voh*	egg
vino bianco	**vee***-noh bee-***ang***-koh*	white wine
vino rosso	**vee***-noh* **ross***-oh*	red wine
il vitello	*eel vee-***tell***-oh*	veal
le vongole	*leh* **von***-goh-leh*	clams
lo zucchero	*loh* **zoo***-kair-oh*	sugar
gli zucchini	*lyee dzu-***kee***-nee*	courgettes
la zuppa	*lah* **tsoo***-pah*	soup

NUMBERS

1	**uno**	**oo***-noh*
2	**due**	**doo***-eh*
3	**tre**	*treh*
4	**quattro**	**kwat***-roh*
5	**cinque**	**ching***-kweh*
6	**sei**	**say***-ee*
7	**sette**	**set***-teh*
8	**otto**	**ot***-toh*
9	**nove**	**noh***-veh*
10	**dieci**	*dee-***eh***-chee*
11	**undici**	**oon***-dee-chee*
12	**dodici**	**doh***-dee-chee*
13	**tredici**	**tray***-dee-chee*
14	**quattordici**	*kwat-***tor***-dee-chee*
15	**quindici**	**kwin***-dee-chee*
16	**sedici**	**say***-dee-chee*
17	**diciassette**	*dee-chah-***set***-teh*
18	**diciotto**	*dee-***chot***-toh*
19	**diciannove**	*dee-chah-***noh***-veh*
20	**venti**	**ven***-tee*
30	**trenta**	**tren***-tah*
40	**quaranta**	*kwah-***ran***-tah*
50	**cinquanta**	*ching-***kwan***-tah*
60	**sessanta**	*sess-***an***-tah*
70	**settanta**	*set-***tan***-tah*
80	**ottanta**	*ot-***tan***-tah*
90	**novanta**	*noh-***van***-tah*
100	**cento**	**chen***-toh*
1,000	**mille**	**mee***-leh*
2,000	**duemila**	**doo***-eh* **mee***-lah*
5,000	**cinquemila**	**ching***-kweh* **mee***-lah*
1,000,000	**un milione**	*oon meel-***yoh***-neh*

TIME

one minute	**un minuto**	*oon mee-***noo***-toh*
one hour	**un'ora**	*oon* **or***-ah*
half an hour	**mezz'ora**	*medz-***or***-ah*
a day	**un giorno**	*oon* **jor***-noh*
a week	**una settimana**	*oona set-tee-***mah***-nah*
Monday	**lunedì**	*loo-neh-***dee**
Tuesday	**martedì**	*mar-teh-***dee**
Wednesday	**mercoledì**	*mair-koh-leh-***dee**
Thursday	**giovedì**	*joh-veh-***dee**
Friday	**venerdì**	*ven-air-***dee**
Saturday	**sabato**	**sah***-bah-toh*
Sunday	**domenica**	*doh-***meh***-nee-kah*

ACKNOWLEDGMENTS

DK would like to thank the following for their contribution to the previous editions: Monica Torri, Richard Pierce, Editoria Libraria e Multimediale

The publisher would like to thank the following for their kind permission to reproduce their photographs:

(Key: a-above; b-below/bottom; c-centre; f-far; l-left; r-right; t-top)

4Corners: Gabriele Croppi 18t, 118-119

Alamy Stock Photo: AGF Srl / Lorenzo De Simone 41b, AGF Srl / Marc Chapeaux 10-11bc, AGF Srl / Vittorio Valletta 37cb, 68-69t, Album 46cr, 63cra, AlexMastro 27cl, 107tr, Alpineguide 79tl, Andia / Bnard 80br, 138-139t, Arcaid Images / Pygmalion Karatzas 26tl, 131b, Alessandro Avondo 168tl, Alan Keith Beastall 182bl, Frank Bienewald 30-31tc, Emanuele Capoferri 110t, Casimiro 71br, Mairo Cinquetti 33cb, Mirko Costantini 167cb, Classic Image 56bl, Ian Dagnall 11t, Ian G Dagnall 30b, dpa picture alliance 11br, eFesenko 79tr, 92cl, Frank Fell 165b, Adam Jn Fige 59cra, Roberto Finizio 35t, Florilegius 45tr, 45clb, Gacro74 39crb, 63tl, Godong 22br, Halpand 128b, Hemis / Mattes Renž 67cra, 80t, 114cla, Hemis / Jacques Pierre 146cr, 146-147b, 154-155tc, 156bl, Hemis / MAISANT Ludovic 62-63b, 63c, 63br, Hemis / MAISANT Ludovic / hemis.fr 88b, Hemis / Rieger Bertrand 155br, Maisant Ludovic / Hemis.fr 27t, Mattes Renž / Hemis.fr 11cr, 18bl, 22cr, 134-135, Heritage Image Partnership Ltd / Fine Art Images 140tr, IanDagnall Computing 83clb, Image Professionals GmbH / Arnt Haug 24-25ca, Image Professionals GmbH / Langlotz, Tim 40-41tc, imageBROKER / Guenter Graefenhain 72cl, imageBROKER.com GmbH & Co. KG / gourmet-vision 37cla, Independent Photo Agency Srl 42cra, 43br, 66bl, 153br, INTERFOTO / Personalities 46tl, Ivy Close Images 46crb, Brian Jannsen 105c, jn2005 / Stockimo 12-13bc, Jon Arnold Images Ltd / Hans Georg Eiben 103t, Jon Arnold Images Ltd / Ivan Vdovin 39tr, Chun Ju Wu 56cr, Joseph Manuel Kaninken 38tl, Joana Kruse 8-9b, 181b, Lanmas 47bl, Lapresse / Marcella Gastini 32bl, 42cla, Lebrecht Music & Arts 45cra, Stefano Politi Markovina 19, 86-87t, 124tl, 158-159, mauritius images GmbH / ClickAlps 40bl, Mauritius Images GmBh / Enricocacciafotografie 147tr, Naeblys 79cra, Anne-Marie Palmer 56crb, 125cl, 125b, Penta Springs Limited / Artokoloro 44t, Photoarkive 49tr, Place:Image 104cl, Luca Ponti 42cr, 145tc, Quanita 105cra, RealyEasyStar / Claudio Pagliarani 105crb, 111br, Reda & Co Srl 123cra, REDA &CO srl 42cl, 43tr, 152-153tc, Reda and Co 36-37t, Eleonora Saini 56clb, Riccardo Sala 107cb, SFM GM WORLD 35bl, Michal Sikorski 127br, SOPA Images 34tl, The Print Collector / Ann Ronan Picture Library / Heritage-Images 45tl, The Print Collector / Heritage Images 83cra, Juliane Thiere 31cla, Massimo Valicchia 49bc, Valentino Visentini 29cl, volkerpreusser 8cla, 34br, Jrgen Wackenhut 24-25tc

Armani/Silos Museum/Giorgio Armani: 115br

AWL Images: Marco Bottigelli 25tr, 64-65b, 172-173t, 177br, ClickAlps 57, 87br, 162, 168-169bc, 176t, 179br, 186-187b, Michele Falzone 6-7, 13cr, 20t, 29br, 95tl, 148-149, 150-151t, Stefano Politi Markovina 20cr, 20bl, 92t, 94clb

Bridgeman Images: Alinari / Antonio Pisanello 45bc, Giancarlo Costa 47tr, 47cb, Mondadori Portfolio / Electa 48bl, NPL - DeA Picture Library 46bc, Luisa Ricciarini 44cb

Dreamstime.com: Igor Abramovych 138br, Alenaisland 41cl, Areinwald 174tr, Kushnirov Avraham 24cla, Jan Cattaneo 85tr, Checco 49tl, Dudlajzov 106-107b, 181cl, Stefano Ember 24tl, Evgeniy Fesenko 90-91bc, 143bl, Simona Flamigni 130tl, Giuseppemasci 166-167b, Viktor Gladkov 27br, Wojciech Grabowski 31br, Ilfede 97cr, Thomas Jurkowski 82-83t, Ekaterina Kriminskaia 12t, Lestertairpolling 81br, Alessandro Mascheroni 13t, Jaroslav Moravcik 69b, Yury Morozov 58tr, Elena Odareeva 132clb, Rodrigo Oscar 8clb, Fabrizio Robba 65tr, Saiko3p 180tl, Scaliger 108-109, 188-189, Jozef Sedmak 145bl, Stanpit 185cra, Elena Veselova 36br, Alvaro German Vilela 96bl, Jolanta Wojcicka 4, Xbrchx 183t

Festival di Bellagio e del Lago di Como: 43cl

Garda Trentino: 43cr

Getty Images: AFP / Pierre-Philippe Marcou 61br, Archive Photos / Stringer 46clb, Corbis Documentary / Massimo Borchi / Atlantide Phototravel 28bl, De Agostini / DEA / A. DAGLI ORTI 91tr, De Agostini / Dea / G. Cigolini 141t, De Agostini / DEA / G. NIMATALLAH 44br, Hulton Archive / Fototeca Storica Nazionale. 48t, Hulton Archive / Handout 49bl, Hulton Fine Art Collection / Heritage Images 139cr, Hulton Fine Art Collection / Mondadori Portfolio 46-47tc, 110bl, Moment / © Marco Bottigelli 8cl, Moment / Marco Bottigelli 50-51, 175b, Photodisc / Massimo Borchi / Atlantide Phototravel 112-113bc, Popperfoto 48cb, Francesco Prandoni 33cla, 43bl, Francesco Prandoni / Redferns 32-33tc, Stone / Buena Vista Images 17t, 74-75, Velo / Pool 43tl, Westend61 2-3, 22t, 178t

Getty Images / iStock: 20crb, Apodiam 142tr, Benedek 70bl, Leila Kitlaeva 26b, Nikada 73br, photooiasson 22cl, Rangreiss 59cr, Mauro_Repossini 144-145t, Martina Rigoli 164-165t, Martin Wahlborg 16, 52-53, Silvia Zecchin 17bl, 98-99

Gruppo Culturale Artisti di via BAGUTTA APS: 42br

Shutterstock.com: Ungvari Attila 84b, Andrea Berg 185t, Paolo Bona 89t, 93b, Francesco Bonino 28-29tc, 169tr, chettarin 35cb, Claudio Divizia 114t, Nejdet Duzen 117tl, Elena.Katkova 12clb, EyesTravelling 123tr, 170-171, Danny Iacob 13br, 42bl, Istanbulfotograf 61t, Mate Karoly 140bl, Larlui64 153cla, Claudio Lepri 129t, Stefano Politi Markovina 61cra, Alex_Mastro 67t, 157tl, Alessio Orru 126-127t, Posztos 133tl, Alexandre Rotenberg 38-39b, Ozgioun Sampri 10ca, Todamo 112tl, VILTVART 129cla, Huang Zheng 10clb

Cover images:
Front and Spine: **AWL Images:** Marco Bottigelli; *Back:* **Alamy Stock Photo:** Stefano Politi Markovina tr; **AWL Images:** Marco Bottigelli b, Stefano Politi Markovina cla; **Shutterstock.com:** Ozgioun Sampri c; *Front Flap:* **Alamy Stock Photo:** Mirko Costantini cb, dpa picture alliance br, jn2005 / Stockimo cra; **AWL Images:** ClickAlps cla; **Getty Images:** Photodisc / Massimo Borchi / Atlantide Phototravel t; **Shutterstock.com:** Elena.Katkova bl

Pull Out Map:
AWL Images: Marco Bottigelli

All other images © Dorling Kindersley

Main Contributors Kiki Deere, Daniel Mosseri
Senior Editors Alison McGill, Dipika Dasgupta
Senior Designer Stuti Tiwari
Project Editors Sarah Allen, Anuroop Sanwalia
Art Editor Bandana Paul
Editors Anjasi N.N, Nandini Desiraju
Updater Solveig Steinhardt
Proofreader Stephanie Smith
Indexer Hilary Bird
Senior Picture Researcher Nishwaan Rasool
Picture Research Manager Taiyaba Khatoom
Assistant Picture Research Administrator Manpreet Kaur
Publishing Assistant Simona Velikova
Illustrators Giorgia Boli, Alberto Ipsilanti, Daniela Veluti, Nadia Viganò
Jacket Designers Jordan Lambley, Bandana Paul
Senior Cartographic Editor James Macdonald
Cartography Manager Suresh Kumar
Cartographer Subhashree Bharati, Ashif
Senior DTP Designer Tanveer Zaidi
Senior Production Editor Jason Little
Senior Production Controller Samantha Cross
Managing Editors Shikha Kulkarni, Beverly Smart, Hollie Teague
Managing Art Editors Gemma Doyle, Priyanka Thakur
Art Director Maxine Pedliham
Publishing Director Georgina Dee

First edition 2000

Published in Great Britain by Dorling Kindersley Limited, One Embassy Gardens, 8 Viaduct Gardens, London SW11 7BW, UK

The authorised representative in the EEA is Dorling Kindersley Verlag GmbH. Arnulfstr. 124, 80636 Munich, Germany

Published in the United States by DK Publishing, 1745 Broadway, 20th Floor, New York, NY 10019, USA

24 25 26 27 10 9 8 7 6 5 4 3 2 1

A CIP catalog record for this book is available from the British Library.

A catalog record for this book is available from the Library of Congress.

ISSN: 1542 1554
ISBN: 978 0 2414 6197 6

Printed and bound in China.

www.dk.com

This book was made with Forest Stewardship Council™ certified paper – one small step in DK's commitment to a sustainable future.

Learn more at **www.dk.com/uk/information/sustainability**

A NOTE FROM DK EYEWITNESS

The rate at which the world is changing is constantly keeping the DK Eyewitness team on our toes. While we've worked hard to ensure that this edition of Milan and the Lakes is accurate and up-to-date, we know that opening hours alter, standards shift, prices fluctuate, places close and new ones pop up in their stead. So, if you notice we've got something wrong or left something out, we want to hear about it. Please get in touch at travelguides@dk.com